THE YELLOW GARDENIA

THE YELLOW GARDENIA

ANTHONY MANCINI

DONALD I. FINE, INC.
NEW YORK

Library of Congress Cataloging-in-Publication Data
Mancini, Anthony.
The yellow gardenia: a novel / by Anthony Mancini.
p. cm.
ISBN 1–55611–209–2
I. Title.
PS3563.A4354Y4 1990
913′.54—dc20   89–46033
                                                    CIP

Manufactured in the United States of America

10 9 8 7 6 5 4 3 2 1

TO MY CHILDREN,
ROMY and NICHOLAS

Vivas to those who have fail'd!

—WALT WHITMAN

PART ONE

Chapter
1

MURDER ON THE MERRY-GO-ROUND

A big yellow moon floated in the windswept winter sky.

"Uh-oh," said somebody in a tone as jaundiced as the sailing satellite. "All the loonies will be prowling the streets tonight."

The quintet of news reporters at the Manhattan police shack glanced out of the smeared window and grunted over their poker hands. Connoisseurs of human depravity, experts on evildoing, they knew well how the full moon tugged the interior tides of men. It never failed, really. Whenever she turned her sunny side full on the planet the coroner had a field day. Why should this moon-kissed dog-watch be any different?

But the members of the Inside Straight Society who were now sitting in the shack didn't give a hump. Murder and mayhem were bread and butter to them. Crime reporters, after all, are creatures who scavenge on the swamp bottom for their livelihoods.

"You nail that quiff last night, Freddie?"

"Shaddup!"

"That means he didn't," said the questioner.

"Gimme two cards and blow on them first."

"Blow it out your ass."

3

So went the refined chitchat on the night of the magnetic moon on Centre Market Place in the heart of Manhattan's Little Italy as two-way radios squawked, wire machines chattered and chimed and goof-off cops snored in the background.

"Hey Rosen, gimme a coffin nail," demanded Mike Provella.

"Buy your own." For spite Hal Rosen of the AP flicked his half-smoked, butt-slavered Home Run cigarette on the littered floor that everybody used as a wastepaper basket and communal spittoon.

"Hey, Dolan," said Freddie Taschentuch, "you read about that minister who says the world is flat and that it's a sin to eat oysters 'cause they don't have no feathers?"

"You kidding?" said Rosen. "Dolan can't read."

"Eh, who said oysters got no feathers?" said Dolan.

A quart of rotgut sat on the wooden table. The bottle was half-finished but there was lots more where it came from, right across the street in a big ornate building of stone that served as Police Headquarters. The paid pipe-artist named Rosen threw in his cards and refilled his glass.

Joe Cyriax tried not to gloat as he flashed a full house and raked the pot toward his gelatinous stomach. He whistled softly and his eyebrows wagged.

"You're as lucky as Lindy," Provella said.

"It's skill," said Cyriax.

Tobacco smoke befogged the air in the dark room. Over the back alleys outside, all garlanded with hanging wash, came the caterwauling of a domestic fight. Dolan, tongue wetting his lips, dealt a fresh hand of stud.

"Anybody ever tell you look like an ostrich, Dolan?" said Taschentuch.

Dolan winked. "Only your mother when I turned her down," he said, fingernailing the cards as he dealt. "But I figured it was sour grapes."

"Hey," said Cyriax, "remember the case of the strangled ostrich?"

"Yeah," replied Rosen, nodding his head. "Some drunk, wasn't it? Wandered into a zoo in Boston and throttled the poor bird to death."

"Best story of the decade," said Cyriax, studying his hand with a serious expression.

"Nah, it ain't," said Rosen. "What about Lindbergh's flight? What a yarn that was!"

Dolan pouted. "I was there when they fried Ruthie Snyder and her boyfriend, what's his name . . ."

"Pin a medal on him," said Provella. "Gimme two cards."

Between raising and calling and bluffing and worrying they started swapping yarns about the big stories and banner headlines that they had had a piece of during the decade that roared, now in its twilight. The subject yielded a bonanza of anecdotes and inside dope—the five bluffers at the card table had formed a collective witness to most of the newsworthy and sensational events of this stormy, bloody era. They might have written a hair-raising history except that as unlettered legmen they couldn't compose a correct English sentence. They were reporters, not writers. Still, they were talented storytellers. Hand any one of them the secret diaries of the chorus-girl mistress of a United States senator or the written confession of a butcher who had ground up his beefy wife for sausages and he became a poet laureate of the oral telephone story.

So they traded yarns around the cardtable like rivals in a pissing contest.

Cyriax, a transplanted Texan, remembered covering for the *Dallas News* the murder of the Mexican revolutionary leader Pancho Villa. Rosen had vivid recollections of the funeral of Rudolph Valentino when riot police had to be called out to control the thousands of clawing, pushing, screaming dames who stormed Campbell's funeral parlor on upper Broadway. Taschentuch and Provella both had been assigned by their editors to travel to the Bay State with a horde of other newsmongers when the executioner pulled the switch on a fish peddler and factory hand, Nicola Sacco and Bartolomeo Vanzetti. Finally, scrawny Billy Dolan had very fond memories of the flagpole sitter who went splat before the impassive eyes of the wooden cigar-store Indian that stood in front of the Flatiron Building.

The raconteurs this moon-washed night also had etched in their memories all kinds of stories that might not have made worldwide headlines but loomed as landmarks in their junkyard minds. They remembered the runaway trolleys, diamond heists, kidnappings and throat slashings that they had cut their teeth on, having scrawled the gory details in sawed-off spiral notebooks and rattled them off to the cotton-brained rummies on the rewrite bank, men and women who liked to boast with Joe Liebling that they could write faster than anyone who wrote better and better than anyone who wrote faster.

For instance, Joe Cyriax still got the sweats when he visualized the Brooklyn janitor who was disemboweled by a bricklayer who caught him molesting the bricklayer's nine-year-old daughter. Dolan had seared on his memory the picture of identical twin girls who were executed together for poisoning their mother, hoping to collect an insurance policy that would have allowed them to pursue in style their lives as lesbian lovers. Taschentuch recounted the one about the federal judge whose lifeless body was discovered in a bordello, his face painted like a rampaging red Indian's, his legs clad in long black silk stockings and his mouth stuffed with a dead parrot. Rosen had a soft spot in his perverse heart for the story he covered about the arrest of the hop-smoking Riverdale housewives who told the arraignment judge that they used the dope to stimulate discussions in their weekly literary society. Provella—not to be outdone—brought up the case of the bible-thumper in the Williamsburg section of Brooklyn who one fine Sunday put angel wings on five churchgoers, firing a shotgun into the congregation after a hellfire sermon about the evils of drink. The carnage ended when the cops arrived and sent the preacher himself to meet his Maker.

"Finally won a hand," said Rosen, hugging a pot to his chest.

The radio crackled with static and the voice of a dispatcher saying, "Shooting in Central Park . . ."

The poker players didn't miss a beat.

"Raise yuh a buck," said Dolan, holding the cards to his collarbone and snorting cigar smoke. A two-bit shooting wasn't enough to get him or the others excited. This was ten years after the starch-collared phonies in Congress had passed the Volstead Act. It was also only a week after Saint Valentine's Day when seven bananas in the Bugs Moran bunch had their bodies ventilated by confederates of Scarface Al in a garage on North Clark Street in the Windy City. The reporters playing cards were not likely to elevate their blood pressures over what was probably just another tiff between suppliers of the 25,000 barrels of beer New Yorkers consumed each week.

". . . vicinity of the carrousel," continued the dispatcher.

The phrase had piqued Rosen's attention. The A.P. reporter, a creature of habit, envisioned the headline, MURDER ON THE MERRY-GO-ROUND, and he figured that this angle might give a routine shooting a sharper twist. The wire machine gave a little *ding,* indicating that more details of the shooting were coming over the police ticker. Rosen held a measly pair of jacks. He studied the inattentive expressions of his companions, signaling that nobody else seemed inclined to get off his duff, so he sighed, threw in his losing cards and pushed away from the table.

Scratching the seat of his baggy flannels, he walked over to the ticker and read the copy through his *pince-nez.* His face, a chalky, rough-carved work of nature, showed a very sour expression. Since he was out twelve smackers he was in no mood to bust up the game. But it seemed that it couldn't be helped. "Grab your hats, cousins," he said in a foghorn voice.

Earlier that night Police Officer Randolph Steiner, with a skittish look around him, had entered the park at West Seventy-second Street. Twirling the night stick, whistling softly, he tried to act natural but the tributaries of blood ran swift and warm in his strong young body. Once he was inside the relatively deserted park, his step quickened on the moonlit concrete path. The sketch of a smile appeared on his marble-smooth handsome face. He anticipated pleasure, forbidden pleasure—the best kind.

Officer Steiner relaxed and undid the top two buttons of his greatcoat. It was mild for February, a convenient circumstance for the outdoor activities he knew were awaiting him. Crossing the horse bridal path he considered the risk he was taking by leaving his beat but figured it would be worth it. Maybe she was no spring chicken but she sure had a streamlined chassis and it was common knowledge that rich dames were great lays. They didn't charge anything either. Now that he thought about it, it had seemed inevitable from the first time he tipped his cap to her as she walked her Afghan on Central Park West that it would finally come down to this. It was four months ago but it now seemed like yesterday to the apple-cheeked, muscle-bound cop. She had been swaddled in fur like a film star and had worn the sparkling, slinky dress of a movie siren. The pedigree hound strained at the leash, making her bounce along the pavement on her leopard-skin high heels like a hootchie-kootchie dancer on a runway. She returned his first greeting with a fourteen-carat smile and a wiggle before continuing on her way, tottering behind the dog. Afterward they would bump into each other fairly often and soon he started oiling her engine, giving her sweet talk. It turned out that she was hitched to some fuddy old ambulance chaser who had wattles on his neck and, Steiner figured by reading between the lines, needed starch to stiffen his ole pecker.

Well, one thing had led to another and here he was hustling over the winding paths of Central Park toward what could be called an assignation with two panting bitches, one on a leash and another wrapped in mink. "Meet me at the merry-go-round," she had written to him in a note on a matchbook cover. As good a place as any to crawl into the saddle.

She wasted no time, crushing hungry mouth against his and stroking his genitals through his winter trousers. "Let's jazz," she said.

"You bet," hands roaming.

The Afghan, tied to a carrousel pole, barked twice at the buttery moon.

"Shush, Lana," said the woman, hugging the policeman around the neck, hoisting herself up and scissoring his hips with her legs. He held her steady by grasping her rubbery buttocks.

"Where?" he asked.

She gave a shudder. "In the middle of the merry-go-round. Where there's not as much wind and it's warmer."

Soon the point of her chin was digging into his shoulder. She whimpered into his small, scallop-shaped ear, grinding against his groin.

"Oh, baby, say something sweet to me," nibbling his earlobe and reaching down to massage his fevered testicles.

"You got a juicy little box on you," he said.

She clutched his shoulder blades. "Oh, officer, give me all you got," she said, the shaft of his penis throbbing in her fist.

His throat clogged up. He pulled away, removed his coat and spread it on the ground. "Let's lie down and get comfortable."

She nodded and slid slowly down on the pinch-pleat coat, her yellow dress bunching into a bright corolla at her waist, her white kneecaps angling outward.

The night was still except for the snuffling comedy of copulation. No painted parrot could ever mime such sounds as came from the cop and the matron in the middle of the merry-go-round. Suddenly the sounds were drowned out by the brassy notes of the calliope.

"Jumping Jesus."

Somehow, it appeared, their writhing bodies had tripped the mechanism that started the carrousel. The leering faces of lipsticked horses bobbed before their eyes and the strains of "De Camptown Races" filled their ears.

He started to break the connection of flesh but she clenched his shanks with her thighs, too close to the crest to let him go. She squeezed him and held his face to the cavity of her shoulder while she stared at the sequined sky and the whirling models of horse and rooster above her.

Her senses were primed . . . she saw another indistinct and broken form on the spinning platform. It came closer and closer until finally she could see clearly the waxy, gargoyle face.

And then she screamed.

The three reporters hoofed it across the ball field. Rosen, with his knock-kneed, shambling gait, led the way. Accompanying him were Provella of the *Bugle* and Cyriax of the *Courier.* The other reporters had to stay at headquarters but they had tipped their city editors who would send other newshawks out to cover the shooting.

The scene was swarming with cops. A young one with shiny gold buttons on his coat held up two white-gloved palms as the trio of reporters approached. "Hey, where do you jokers think you're going?"

Rosen smiled and pushed his fedora back off his forehead. "Take it easy, ossifer, who's got the squeal?"

The young cop's face looked suspicious, then uncertain. "Lieutenant Mitchell is in charge."

"Now you be a good boy and tell him that Hal Rosen is here."

The officer did as he was told.

Arnie Mitchell, tall, pale, ascetic-looking, would pass for an English professor or violinist rather than a hard-bitten homicide detective. He greeted the three reporters with handshakes and the sour frown that usually emerged when he tried to smile.

"What gives, Arnie?" asked Rosen.

The detective warmed his right hand on the bowl of a pipe. He squinted. In the east he could see through the leafless trees the spire of the obelisk called Cleopatra's Needle. "Maybe you boys can tell me?"

"What's that supposed to mean?" asked Provella. Mitchell sucked on the pipe with a meditative air. He enjoyed watching these bluffers squirm with curiosity. The reporters glanced over at the merry-go-round where detectives were questioning a nervous bimbo draped in mink. Off to the side stood a uniformed young cop who also looked nervous.

"Okay, Arnie, you make a lousy sphinx," said Rosen. "Why don't you come across with the goods?" He left unsaid between them the obvious inducement: Rosen was calling in a marker from the detective for having given a boost to his last promotion with a well-timed feature story about how Mitchell had cracked a sensitive murder case involving a prominent banker's son who had slit the throat of his college roommate.

The detective jerked his head toward the merry-go-round and led the way as the trio of reporters followed him over to where the corpse lay, covered with a horse blanket. Hard-shelled as they were, the newsmen still had to brace themselves for the sight of crowbait. Who got used to it? A pair of patent-leather shoes stuck out from the blanket.

Detective Arnold Mitchell lifted the blanket from the victim's face. Teeth clamped on the stem of the pipe, he almost smiled at the frozen expression of the three news jockeys as they took it in.

"I'll be a monkey's uncle," Cyriax finally said.

The dead man's empty parody of a face was bathed in moonlight.

"Where's the closest phone?" asked Rosen.

Chapter

2

IT'S STILL BALONEY

THE ink was still wet on the pages of the newspapers that went thud on the sidewalk in front of Hamilton Terry. Turning up his coat collar, he stepped out of the door of the newsstand and with instinct sure headed straight for the stack.

The big man carried the bundle on the wide bluff of his shoulders back to the stand and set them down. Using wire cutters he untied the papers and held up headlines that his sightless eyes could not read: MURDER ON THE MERRY-GO-ROUND. REPORTER SLAIN IN CENTRAL PARK.

The story in the evening tabloid *New York Courier,* under a rewriteman's byline, read:

Homer "Scoop" Madigan, ace crime reporter for this newspaper, was found shot to death last night on the carrousel in Central Park, the apparent victim of a rubout by gangsters retaliating for his fearless exposes of their nefarious activities.

Police said that the victim, 42, had been shot point-blank in the temple with a 45-calibre automatic pistol. The body was discovered by Mrs. Blanche Lawrence, 125 Central Park West, who had been walking her Afghan dog in the area. Mrs. Lawrence's screams attracted the notice of Police Officer Randolph Steiner, who then contacted detectives of the local precinct.

Mrs. Lawrence could provide no details of the shooting, police sources added.

"My dog Lana started barking and acting funny, so I went over to investigate," the attractive blonde woman told reporters after she had regained her composure. "It was a grotesque sight."

Madigan, a prize-winning reporter and a 10–year veteran of the *Courier,* resided in Brooklyn Heights with his wife, Fanny, and two children, Timothy, 12, and Lucille, 7. His bruising and relentless reports of the activities of the dry-law hoods who infest this town had earned him the respect of law-enforcement officials and his colleagues in the news business, but made sworn enemies of the malefactors to whom his articles were a constant thorn in the side.

"This newspaper is offering a $10,000 reward for information leading to the arrest and conviction of Madigan's killer or killers.

Ham Terry, breath smoking in the cold, blew on his gnarled hands. Tall and disabled like a cassowary, he had been roosting in the green-painted newsstand on Park Row for the last twenty years, dispensing newspapers, magazines, chewing gum, cigarettes and his own acid and prescient commentary on world and local events. Blind as a bat, he was also smart as a fox.

The newsstand was situated near the southeast corner of City Hall Park, a strategic spot between the office of an ex-songwriter named Jimmy Walker and the imposing granite-and-brick facades of the literary sweat shops of the ink-stained wretches who dogged the playboy mayor's every step, never missing a chance to publish purple accounts of Beau James's lurid political and social career. It was eight A.M.—not yet the height of rush hour. Still a steady stream of office workers, bush league bureaucrats, legal beagles, judges in mufti reeking of tobacco, and tinhorn assistant commissioners of the Office of Whatnot and Thatwhich already were arriving for work. Many in passing picked up a newspaper from the blind dealer's stand and threw coins in the cigar box.

Among them was a grubby-looking citizen named John Joseph Callahan, chief obituary writer for the *Courier*.

"Morning, Mr. Callahan," said Ham, flashing yellow teeth and handing him a racing form.

Callahan had a baffled frown as he shook his head. "Tell me something, Ham—how the hell do you always know that it's me? Do I smell that bad?"

"Not bad, exactly. Just distinctive." Ham's roving pupils glinted.

"Your father must have been a bloodhound," said Callahan as he glanced at the odds sheet.

"He was a dog, all right," said the news dealer, sinking into reflection. Truth be known, Hamilton Terry's unfortunate father had been lynched in Guernsey, Texas, for quarreling with a white man over a cup of water. This melancholy circumstance contributed to the son's seeking escape in hootch. He lost his sight, in fact, by drinking poison whiskey stored in a fruit jar with a corroded zinc top, not a rare occurence since Prohibition became the law of the land. That these and other events somehow had not turned Ham's soul to vinegar was a miracle in an age of wonders.

Callahan, briefly breaking the spell of absorption in the racing form, glanced at the bundle of newspapers and caught sight of the latest headlines in the extra edition of the *Courier*. "Jesus, Mary and Joseph," he exclaimed, grabbing a copy. The cheapskate usually bought only the pony papers since he got newspapers free at the office. But this was an exception.

"Trouble?" asked Ham.

"Old Scoop Madigan's been rubbed out."

Ham's head bobbed up and down. "Now that's one for the books, ain't it, Mr. Callahan. They don't usually croak news reporters, do they?"

"You got that right," said Callahan, his eyes racing over the sentences. "They must be shitting bricks all over town."

"My oh my."

"This promises to be an interesting day at the office," predicted Callahan as he started to cross the street.

"Excuse me, Mr. Callahan . . ." hollered Ham Terry.

"Yeah?"

"You owe me a nickel."

Red-faced, Callahan dug into his cluttered pockets and paid the newsie before his greasy fedora joined the swelling tide of bowlers, homburgs, toques and toppers that swam across Park Row and up Centre Street.

He was still thinking about the story when he entered the gilded-bird cage of an elevator that would take him to the city room on the fourteenth floor of the *Courier* building, which the publisher, Major Carlos Curtin, owned outright without a mortgage.

"I guess yuh heard," said Fitch, the diminutive elevator operator who leaned out to look both ways before pulling shut the door.

"No, I read," said Callahan, rummaging again through his city-dump coat pockets for the first cheap cigar of the day. He was a card-carrying curmudgeon who specialized in brusque answers to all and sundry, scrubwomen and royalty alike. Whoever didn't like it could, in the vernacular, lump it.

Callahan's chilly response didn't faze Fitch, who had a high opinion of himself despite being short and cross-eyed. "Ain't it a kick in the pants?" Callahan couldn't take his eyes off the operator's cowlick, three straws that pointed straight up in the air. They were alone in the elevator that rose through the center of the building and provided an open view of the circular staircase connecting the floors.

"Yeah," said Callahan, striking the wooden match on his chin stubble and lighting up the smelly stogie.

Fitch glanced at the passenger. "I thought the croaker made you swear off," he said.

"I fixed that," said Callahan, blowing out billows of smoke.

"How'd yuh manage that?"

"Got me a new doctor. This one's a female."

Fitch covered his mouth. "No kidding?" "Must be fun

when she checks for hernia and orders you to cough."

"Naw. She's a bow-wow."

"Hey, they all look alike in the dark," said Fitch, jabbing Callahan in the ribs and gesturing toward the exposed legs of a secretary climbing the stairs.

Callahan was aware that Fitch used his vantage in the open elevator shaft to look up the skirts of flappers. He knew that Fitch considered this a major fringe benefit of the job. They reached the fourteenth floor.

The reception area that Callahan entered resembled as usual either a circus sideshow or the lobby of an unscrupulous casting director. The wooden chairs lining the east wall were filled by a ragtag group of publicity seekers angling for interviews with reporters or editors. Callahan took a short inventory of the group. The dame on the far end with the fancy permanent wave and the ruby pin that matched her vibrant lip rouge was probably another debutante confessing to a murder she hadn't committed. The redhead sitting next to her, squirming in an effort to appear demure and looking daggers at the debutante, might have been a stripper aspiring to break into the movie business who had swallowed the bait of a horny reporter with a line about having an uncle who was a top Hollywood director or who had bragged in the boudoir about how he was on a first-name basis with Broadway impresarios. And ten to one the milquetoast with the brush mustache who sat under the window framing a view of the Brooklyn Bridge was a bureaucrat passed up for promotion who now wanted to even the score by blowing the whistle on his boss, a corrupt official of the Water Department. Chances were that the boss was a crook all right, but the disgruntled employee did not have the goods on him and would fill an interviewer's notepad with a lot of wild rumors and half-truths. Panning for news was a grubby business, yielding more gravel than nuggets.

So Callahan turned away from the freak show and headed for the city room, hardly blinking when he nearly tripped over a trained seal held on a leash by the owner who was pestering the receptionist to allow him into the editorial department.

"Copy," ordered Callahan, settling his meaty rump into the swivel chair parked by his desk. The chair, needing oil, squeaked.

A copyboy with freckles sauntered over. "So?"

"Black coffee and two sinkers, and make it snappy."

"Ask me nice," demanded Lorenzo Casey.

"Who do you think you are, the publisher? Get me the coffee before you feel my brogan up your ass."

Casey glared at Callahan before stalking off.

Dante Viola, sitting across the desk from Callahan, clucked. "You catch more flies with honey," he said.

"I don't want flies. I want coffee."

"He's going to spit in the cup, you know that, don't you?" said the young copy clerk who served as Callahan's assistant.

Callahan started sharpening pencils. He shrugged. "Might make Pop Pietro's motor oil taste better."

Viola, who had been editing a stack of wire copy, looked up. "What puts you in such a loving mood today?" he asked the chief resident crepe-hanger.

Callahan used his tongue to slide the cigar from one side of his mouth to the other. "I don't know. It's probably because my landlady's cat died this morning." Callahan, who thought himself unloved and unloving, seemed to have a vested interest in his own apparent heartlessness.

Dante shook his head. "You're one in a million, Cal. The right man in the right job." But the young clerk knew better than to swallow this Callous Callahan act. Sure, the veteran newsman wouldn't win any popularity contests or cop any medals for acts of charity. But Dante had glimpsed under the shell. It was Callahan who went to bat for him with the city editor when Dante's probation period as an editorial clerk was up. And it was Callahan who had taken the rap for him once when Dante fell for the phone hoax about the funeral of a Long Island surgeon who was still very much alive and threatening a libel suit.

"Damn tootin'," said Callahan, patting the pile of newspapers on the desk, all bearing similar headlines about the shooting in Central Park. "Hey, maybe it was the news about Madigan that put a shine on the day for me."

Dante's usually open, cherubic features suddenly went tight and wary. He looked around the city room now filling up with workers on the morning shift. Groups of editors and reporters formed buzzing cells in the editorial wax-comb, feeding on the nectar of gossip.

"Any hot rumors?" asked Callahan.

Dante shook his head, rolling paper into the typewriter to begin rewriting telegraph wire. "All I know is they're making him out to be a martyr."

Callahan blew a heavy cloud of cigar smoke across the desk. "Whole story stinks like Friday night in Mrs. Murphy's kitchen."

Dante agreed as he squinted at the phrase he'd just composed. "How do you spell *erstwhile?*"

"F-o-r-m-e-r," replied Callahan, still a champion of plain language despite his exile to the obit desk.

Casey soon returned with the coffee and doughnuts and set them down in front of Callahan, who sized up the oily short-change artist.

"Well?" Callahan said.

"I'm keeping the four bits," announced Casey.

"Like hell you are."

"Keep your shirt on," said Casey. "I'm collecting for the Ghoul Pool." He held out a soft cap full of folded bits of paper with writing on them. "Don't you wanna be in it?"

Callahan eyed the juvenile robber baron of the city room with grudging respect. He was convinced that the kid, combining the traits of Al Capone, John D. Rockefeller and Gregory Rasputin, some day would own the newspaper. Callahan only hoped that he himself wouldn't live that long. Casey was an operator among operators. For a price—or for free, if he had a strategic reason for making you indebted to him—he could pull the strings to get you anything in town, from a piece of tail to tickets to a sold-out Broadway show. The so-called Ghoul Pool was a good example of his entrepreneurial genius: the names of a bunch of exalted personages with one foot in the grave were placed in a random lottery; the holder of the name of the first person to keel over and die would collect the sweepstakes, minus a ten-percent commission, of course, for the freckled promoter.

Like almost everybody else in the newsroom, Callahan could not resist entering the pool. He rubbed his hands together for luck before shutting his eyes tight and reaching into the cap.

He unfolded the scrap of paper: "Georges Clemenceau? Isn't he dead already?"

"You ought to know," observed Dante. "You're the house expert on death."

"Nah, Clemenceau ain't dead," said Casey. "You got a potential winner there. He's eighty-seven, eighty-eight."

Callahan's ruddy face showed an unusual big smile. "My lucky day might be one old frog's unlucky one. I get a kick out of the idea." Callahan put it in his wallet.

"The subject of dying always peps you up like a tonic, doesn't it, Cal?" Dante said.

"Sure does," Callahan admitted. He studied the burnt-umber face of his young assistant. "You're in the pool already?" Callahan asked.

"I drew George Bernard Shaw. He's pretty old but I figure he's the kind who'll live to be a hundred just for spite. Besides, I never win anything."

"Was Madigan's name in the pool?" Callahan said, straight-faced.

"No," Casey said. "You gotta be over sixty-five to qualify, you know that. Besides, he wasn't important enough."

"I'm not so sure," Callahan said, chewing the butt of the stogie.

From the other side of the city room came: "Hey, Casey!" The caller was Phil Blanchard, the head printer, who stood by the door to the composing room, where the cluttering of linotype machines could be heard.

"Gotta go," said Casey, walking away under the maze of pneumatic tubes and defunct gaslight lines that cluttered the high ceilings.

"What'd you mean by that crack, Cal?" asked Dante.

"What crack?" said Callahan, checking out a copy of the rival evening tabloid New York *Bugle*.

"About not being so sure that Madigan wasn't important enough."

Callahan hunched his shoulders, continuing to read with a slightly glazed expression. "Never trusted that gutterpup. Always thought he was up to something, you know? He was too sharp a dresser, too big a spender and he always dropped too big a bundle at the gaming tables for a sixty-buck-a-week newsmonger."

"But they say he inherited a lot of bucks when his old man died."

Callahan gave Dante a look, then turned to the sport pages to check the racetrack news. "Yeah, I've heard all that," he said, sipping coffee and biting into a doughnut.

"But you don't buy it?"

Callahan removed the cigar butt from his mouth, frowned at it, then squashed it under the sole of his shoe. "It's none of my damn business, but I keep remembering something Al Smith once said."

"What was that?"

Callahan washed down another chunk of doughnut with coffee. "Something like, 'No matter how thin you slice it . . .'" He stared into the distance, remembering. "I come from the same neighborhood as Madigan. As I recall, his old man wasn't exactly a tycoon. Matter of fact, I don't think he had a pot to piss in."

Callahan put down the newspaper, figuring it was time to start earning part of his salary. "Okay, Dago Dan," he said to his assistant. "Do we have a lead obit?"

Dante studied the copy in front of him. "I thought we might lead the page with the memorial to Lily Langtry."

"Old news," said Callahan. "Can't we do better than that?"

Dante licked the point of his pencil. "Well, Warren Harding's dog died."

Callahan scratched his stubble and lit another cigar. Executive decisions gave him a nicotine fit. "I like that one but the old man won't buy it. What else?"

Dante shuffled the pages of wire copy in his hand. "I got a juicy one from the foreign desk. The fattest man in

Europe committed suicide. He was a Hungarian butcher who was despondent because he could no longer afford the quantity of beef he needed to keep him chipper."

"How much did he weigh?"

"Tipped the scales at 560 pounds, give or take. It says he would consume two whole roasts for breakfast."

"A top candidate."

Dante continued to scan the overseas copy. "I got another one about a British machine-gun manufacturer who was killed in a hunting accident."

Callahan exhaled, a sign of satisfaction. "That's what I like about this beat," he said in a tone that was mildly enthusiastic for anybody else but rhapsodic for him. "You run across so many stories that reek of poetic justice."

"Yeah," said Dante, happy when his colleague broke out of his studied funk.

"Yeah, poetic justice," Callahan repeated. "Like Rodin freezing to death. Wasn't that something? What could be more appropriate for a sculptor?"

"Hey, I never thought of it that way."

"That's because you're not a true aficionado of the grim reaper like me. I think that most of the time people get just the kind of death they deserve."

Dante looked doubtful. "Did Madigan get the kind of death he deserved?"

"Madigan most of all." He began to focus more closely on the wire copy and making the guttural sounds deep in his throat that usually signaled the start of the mental exercise by which he decided how to make up the obituary page. He grabbed a yellow memo sheet and number-two pencil and began to dummy the layout. "Okay, we'll lead the Langtry, square off the dog in a benday box on the bottom of the page and put the fat man over here under a two-head. Let's see, does the butcher have any survivors, any mourners . . .?"

As he worked, Callahan's mind strayed to unpleasant thoughts. Who would mourn John Joseph Callahan, he wondered, despite mental oaths to keep away from this subject? Who would even care enough in a negative way to dance at his funeral or spit on his grave? The blackboard was empty.

Callahan busied himself rewriting Dante's rewrite of the Langtry lead paragraph.

Meanwhile Dante's eyes, blue-green as an alpine lake, again scanned the story of the murder on the merry-go-round. It was the kind of sensational yarn that fueled his ambition to become a top reporter for the newspaper, a goal that his fanciful and slightly mawkish nature had invested with an air of knight-errantry. The heroes of his boyhood—a chapter of life he had just concluded—had been neither the Babe Ruths nor the Louis Pasteurs of the world, but muckrakers like Lincoln Steffens and Nellie Bly, crusading columnists like Heywood Broun, and derring-do correspondents like Richard Harding Davis. Somewhere along the road the orphaned son of an illiterate Sicilian carpenter had gotten a jolt of printer's ink. Writing the instant history of news stories filled a void, connected him to the sounds of the human family. "Maybe Madigan *is* a martyr," he said.

Callahan looked up from his scribbling.

Dante grew defensive. "I mean, he did write some pretty tough stories about the bootleggers. Maybe he went too far."

"I repeat the immortal words of Alfred Emanuel Smith," Callahan said. " 'No matter how thin you slice it . . .' "

"I know," said the young man, " 'it's still baloney.' "

Chapter

3

THE EMERALD STICKPIN

IVAN Bruce sported a glossy gray-and-blond mustache that twitched like a living thing, a separate entity from its owner, as he spiked copy and grumbled. The *Courier*'s veteran city editor had a leonine head that backed up his gruff manner but masked, it was said, a soft heart. The shaggy head in question now wagged and bobbed over a celluloid collar and a sheaf of local news stories, the staff of his life. Now and then as he scrawled the pigeon tracks that passed for editing symbols over the hard copy he sighed and spat chew into a brass spittoon positioned near the rolltop desk.

Soon he put down the blue pencil for a moment and gazed through the casement windows at the tugboats furrowing under the Brooklyn Bridge, cobweb of steel and cable, that old Joe Pulitzer, the crazy son of a bitch, helped to build. Bruce idly fingered the waxed ends of his luxuriant mustache and plunged into a reverie that softened the craggy contours of his rather patrician face. He was plainly troubled.

Thirty-five years. Thirty-five years of ink-stained cuffs and pied type and extra editions and jump heads and libel suits and second-day leads and lying legmen and etaoin shrdlu and never anything like this, nosireebob. It beat all. It even beat his experiences as a beardless recruit in the fired-up legions of William Randolph Hearst, landing on the beach at Guantanamo and helping round up twenty-six petrified sailors of the Spanish navy and delivering them as P.O.W.'s of the New York *Journal,* trophies in the comic opera tinpot helmet war of 1898. No, this was the first time in his years as a news jockey that a reporter had been killed in the line of duty. It made him mad. And another thing—it, well, discombobulated him.

For he smelled a rat.

A big stinky rat.

He picked up a copy of the first edition and read for about the sixth time the publisher's editorial: "His loving colleagues on this paper editorially mourn a fearless reporter slain in the line of duty by the racketeers who feared his hard-hitting news articles exposing their corrupt practices. An attempt has been made to intimidate this great newspaper and indeed to cow the press corps in general. It shall not succeed. We vow to do all in our power to help bring the culprits to justice." Et cetera, et cetera.

Bruce held the newspaper away from his body and frowned. The biggest pile of twelve-point-type horse manure to be published in a big-time daily newspaper, tabloid or broadsheet, since Ottmar Mergenthaler of Baltimore invented the linotype machine. The *Courier,* he suspected, would fall down and go boom over this one and he loved the old gal too much to sit back and let it happen. And while he wouldn't say so out loud, he loved a commodity called the truth even more. Of course, like most newspapermen, Ivan Bruce did a convincing impersonation of a cynic. But the cynicism of journalists was usually fueled by hopelessly romantic idealism.

He flipped through the paper, browsing for angles, scavenging for errors the copy desk and proofreaders might have overlooked. He never tired of smudging his fingers on newsprint—with its bloat of drama and disaster, triumph and tribulation, ever new, ever perishable. He loved the corny phrases and sporty angles. He thrilled to the sinking

of steamships and the destruction of great cities by earth-
quake as well as to the quotidian calamities of a less epic
scale—the stranglings of shopgirls, the victories of local
chess champions, the onset of a fog in the harbor. Besides
the news of Madigan's killing, today's paper contained a
routine mix of news stories and features, photos, ads, re-
views, letters, columns and editorials. His gaze lingered on
a page-three library cut of that old snake-charmer Herbert
Hoover, his well-groomed head and smug, pudgy face
poised over a wing collar. Hoover was riding high at the
moment, having recently won his joust with "The Happy
Warrior," Al Smith, and his presidency seemed destined to
mark the beginning of a new era controlled by the new
dynasts of the industrial age. But an odor still clung to the
former Secretary of Commerce, an odor emanating from
certain ex-associates named Harding, Fall, Doheny and
Sinclair and coming from an oil field in Wyoming called
Teapot Dome.

Bruce had a talent for intuition, a quality that helped
him in the news business. Now his intuition told him that
the days of President Hoover's honeymoon with the American public were numbered.

He scanned stories on pages four and five. He smiled at
the feature about a prominent business executive who was
getting injections of monkey glands to restore his virility.
His pathetic behavior made good copy. Bruce found it hard
to put himself in the misguided gent's shoes. He figured
that he had the opposite problem: even at the advanced age
of fifty-seven, Ivan Bruce felt he needed some patent medicine to reduce his potency.

He turned to another page. Well, well, well—the society
page wrote about Jimmy Walker attending another ship-
board *bon voyage* party, probably hoping to score with a
chorine. Ah, the playboy mayor was riding high too, kayo-
ing all political opponents with a horseshoe in his glove
called Tammany Hall. You could bet your bottom buck,
Bruce thought, Jimmy Walker would get his comeuppance
someday too. Bruce had been around the smoke-filled
rooms long enough to know that eventually they all did.

Next he read Clare Parker's interview with Shipwreck Kelly, the reigning champeen of the flagpole sitters, who went from city to city risking life and limb on his tailbone at around 1,000 feet and who just broke the world record in Baltimore for such like. Bruce shook his head in admiration of the girl reporter. The dame could really write! Her prose had panache and she herself had—there was only one way to say it—balls! He mulled over the notion of volunteering to give her a raise but knew such a gesture would be almost meaningless as a way to keep her from possibly being tempted by offers from rival newspapers. As the heiress of a fabulously wealthy banking family, she was already as rich as Rockefeller. Well, almost. She was a sweet-looking dish too, he reflected. Those willowy gams and big brown eyes. He might have been tempted if such behavior didn't violate his self-imposed policy of not fraternizing with the troops. He could get chummy, but intimate—no. He would drink with them and joke with them but not sleep with them. Besides, it was just plain tacky to mix the two.

But nothing prevented him from daydreaming about her.

He tossed the newspaper back on the desk, where it immediately sank into a sea of paste pots, copy pencils and unspeakable clutter. No, he could not sit on his hands while the publisher made an ass of himself, the *Courier* lost credibility and the truth got lost in the backwash. He glanced around the city room, searching for a solution to the problem. As usual the place looked like a painting of hell by Hieronymus Bosch.

The room was filled with battered wooden desks arranged seemingly in no logical order and covered with wire baskets, old newspapers, endless mummy windings of page proofs and the flotsam of many deadlines. In the middle of the open space sat the copy desk, shaped like a horseshoe and occupied by a dozen or so chalk-faced copy readers—some pieces of work! They blew in and out of their jobs like tumbleweeds, sullen fellows, usually fairly sharp and somewhat erudite nitpickers, most of whom led guarded solitary lives (who would marry a copy reader?) in furnished rooms and residential hotels where, one tended to believe, they skewered insects on knitting needles to watch them squirm or they drooled over dirty pictures featuring underage girls. Copy readers were handed copy to read and headlines to write by a so-called slot man, representative of a phylum of life on the taxonomic scale just a notch above the haircap moss. Since there were often not enough copy readers on the rim it was common practice at deadline to hire on the spot delivery boys or salesmen who had wandered into the city room and it sometimes happened that such recruits rose to the apex of the profession.

It made Bruce shiver with unease to think that such employees formed the first line of defense against libel suits and bomb throwers and other readers angered over some real or imagined transgression of style, taste, good judgment or truth. But guardians they were against the use of banned words and expressions like *cryptic* and *erstwhile* and *not guilty* (a booby trap because of how easy it would be for the compositors inadvertently to drop the word *not,* with disastrous legal results), and against composing-room boners that made *socialists* of *socialites, rabbits* of *rabbis, brothels* of *brothers, rubbers* of *robbers,* and put *penis* in the quote, "The pen is mightier than the sword."

The copy editors also served as bluenosed censors of language deemed improper for a family newspaper. For example, they made sure that the word used was *infidelity,* not *adultery, attack,* not *rape,* and *nude,* not *naked.*

The city editor's gaze next swept over the tiers of rewritemen facing the city desk, nimble-fingered truth-benders who worked with their hats on, banging away at their Underwoods for a tidy salary of about $150 a week. For this princely sum they usually rented out in ten-hour shifts not only their bodies but also their souls, inventing quotes to suit a preconceived headline, forging letters to the editor in praise of crusading articles and extorting scoops by phone by impersonating public officials, saying things like: "This is Murphy at the Deputy Inspector's office, now where exactly was the prisoner released?" Doing the job right required the skills of an actor as well as the talents of liar and wordsmith.

Bruce saw over by the water cooler the head copy clerk, Larry Boskey, feeding bread crumbs to Benito, one of the flock of carrier pigeons the newspaper employed to bring film back from distant stories on deadline. Boskey was chatting with Stinky Roth of the circulation department whose unkempt appearance (he always wore the same grimy plaid vest and battered straw boater) and Neanderthal features belied his intelligence and the vital role he played in the newspaper's operation. By cultivating a crop of spies at the *Bugle* Roth always managed to obtain a copy of the rival paper's one-star final before it hit the stands, which enabled the *Courier* to replate the edition and avoid getting scooped. The man was worth his not inconsiderable weight in lead filings.

As he shot the breeze with the chief copy clerk Roth shucked salty roasted peanuts that he had bought from a vendor who made twice-daily rounds of the city room, tossing the shells on the already littered floorboards, and shared the peanuts with the pigeon.

Bruce's idle gaze shifted to the door leading to the composing room, where a fat printer wearing a greasy apron and a four-cornered paper hat was collecting a crisp dollar bill from a photographer for the printers' pool, a weekly lottery that could net the winner five hundred dollars. The photographer had planted his right foot on a shoeshine box and was having his cordovans buffed by the local-room bootblack. When he wasn't wasting his time in such pursuits the photographer usually joined his colleagues around town ordering starlets and socialites to "hike that skirt a little higher, sweetheart, more leg," or singeing the beards of visiting dignitaries with exploding flashguns.

Ivan Bruce concluded his visual survey of the city room at the obit desk—and an idea struck.

He pulled open the top drawer of his desk and noisily rummaged around, the biggest clatter coming from the collection of badges the city editor kept for reporters to impersonate public officials and thereby con interviews from such as the grieving widows of rubout victims or to coax, say, high school yearbook pictures from the parents of killers. In the world of journalism it was a categorical imperative that the end justified the means. Although at heart soft, and paradoxically idealistic, Bruce, like any city editor worth his galluses, never let sentiment get in the way of a good story or a Boy Scout sense of honor endanger a banner headline. Truth might count in the large scheme of things, but not in day-to-day methods. The hoard of glittering badges in his desk drawer included that of a building inspector, fire marshall, deputy coroner, county sheriff, board of elections supervisor, homicide detective, prison guard, truant officer, county clerk, even a supervisor of Mayor Jimmy Walker's newly formed Sanitation Department. Finally, under a stack of blue photos confiscated in a vice squad raid and given to the editor by a brown-nose police reporter, Ivan Bruce found the object he had been searching for.

"Copy!" His voice carried across the room.

Casey, eager to bootlick the boss, hotfooted over. "Yes, Mr. Bruce?"

The editor's eyes were veiled with disapproval. In the city room people usually addressed each other by their first names regardless of rank. "No need to call me that, Casey. A simple 'Your Majesty' will do."

"Yes, Mr. Bruce . . ." In Bruce's presence Casey's cockiness deserted him.

"Do me a favor, kid, and inform yon Mr. Callahan that I wish to palaver with him."

"Right, chief," said Casey, scootering off, anxious to shed the air of servility that the editor inspired in him. He found Callahan in a routine pose, imbibing from a hip flask.

"Hey, the old man wants to see yuh, Callahan. Toot sweet."

Dante Viola looked up from his Underwood and lifted a finely shaped eyebrow.

Callahan tried not to look surprised. He slowly wiped his

mouth with the back of his hand and narrowed his eyes at the copyboy. He rubbed his chin stubble. It had been more than two years since the obit desk had become his Elba and in all that time Bruce had not once summoned him for an audience. At this point the request did not flatter Callahan or make him hopeful, it only caused him to resent any intrusion into his dead-end routine. Well, whatever it was that Bruce wanted him for, Callahan hoped that it wouldn't interfere with plans he had made to go to Belmont Park that afternoon.

Callahan asked, "What's he want me for?"

"He didn't take me into his confidence," said Casey. "Hey, maybe he wants to give you a bonus for that dazzling lead you wrote about the death of Harding's dog."

"Fuck you," said Callahan, master of circumlocution. With exaggerated effort he rose from the chair, thinking about Ivan Bruce. While Callahan wouldn't admit to feeling affection for anybody, he respected and, yes, even admired the city editor whom he had known for about ten years since Bruce, in a reversal of the usual procedure, had been pirated away from Hearst's *Journal* to work for the *Courier*. Callahan had an inkling that Bruce had left the yellow sweatbox of William Randolph Hearst, who paid his editors handsomely, for reason of principle rather than money. Maybe it was because he agreed with Arthur James Pegler's comparison of a Hearst newspaper to "a screaming woman running down the street with her throat cut." Anyhow, Callahan admired Bruce's independence and his style, the way he combined the courtly appearance of a Virginia plantation owner with the mouth of a guttersnipe, the way he hobbled on a gimp stick (in his hands it looked more like a scepter) to get around the city room because of an injury to his left leg sustained covering the Spanish–American War, the way he loved news stories that reeked of human interest. Particularly he esteemed Bruce for his high standards of newspaper-writing. He remembered once pulling a stint on the rewrite bank, writing for the weather page, "Sunrise 5:40 A.M." A couple of minutes later, Callahan recalled, he got the copy back from Bruce with the "A.M." edited out and a scrawled note that read, "When the sun comes up at 5:40 *p.m.,* we'll splash it on page one under a four-column head." For Ivan Bruce wasting type was a mortal sin. Callahan agreed.

As Callahan tucked his shirt back into his trousers he felt Dante's sardonic eyes on him and muttered to the assistant, "Why don't you put a monkey on your shoulder and find a goddamn organ to grind, you wop bastard?"

The young man smiled broadly and began to hunt and peck at the typewriter.

Callahan hiked up his baggy trousers and with a blank expression and exaggerated nonchalance walked across the city room.

"How about a cup of Joe," said Bruce after the obit writer had settled into a swivel chair and lit a cigar.

"No thanks, Ivan. Already had me a Mexican breakfast and then some."

"Two stogies and a nip, right?"

Callahan did not reply, just sat still as a mountain mantled in clouds of blue smoke. He studied the older man's glinting green eyes for a clue to the motive behind this rare invite. He sucked on the cigar and continued to blow smoke like a financial backer of the newspaper instead of a literary undertaker. Silently, without pitching Bruce a conversational gambit, deliberately trying to make the city editor feel awkward, he waited for him to get to the point.

"Want something stronger than coffee?"

Callahan shrugged.

Without rising from the chair Bruce swiveled around and produced from the cabinet behind him two shot glasses and a bottle of whiskey. Pouring, he said, "This is real Canadian. None of that bilge straight out of the bathtub."

The color and the aroma of the whiskey stirred Callahan from his Laodicean pose. He wet his lips with his tongue and tossed the Canadian off without so much as a bottom's up or a thank you.

Bruce, on the other hand, sipped slowly. "You know, Cal," he began, "you were once a damn good reporter. Damn, damn good."

"Thanks," Callahan said, holding out the shot glass for

a refill and thinking that Bruce didn't ask him over to deliver a testimonial. Why didn't he stow the bullshit? But with the bite of good whiskey on his tongue Callahan was not disposed to hurry him. He sipped the second shot and a little smudge fire started to glow in his gut.

Bruce's expressive eyes now were liquid and shiny. "Never forget some of the beats you scored for us. You were a real ace. You could turn a nice phrase, too, back in those days. You know, you had the Irish gift of lyric blarney."

Callahan gave a slight bow. "Go away with you." *He wants something,* he reflected, then pursed his lips in a mock pout. "But why do you say 'back in those days'? You mean, I have now become a lacquered talent. A has-been? A bum?" Callahan shut his mouth and scolded himself for talking too much. Nowadays he clung to a high standard of apathy. So the snail retreated back into his shell, smoking and sipping, listening to steam hissing from the aluminum-painted radiator in the southeast corner of the room.

"Say, you did a swell piece when Snyder and Gray walked the last mile," said Bruce. "It gave me goose bumps."

Callahan stayed shut.

"And you beat the whole press corps, not to mention the bulls, when they kidnapped old man Lundy in Sheepshead Bay."

Callahan shrugged. "What can I tell yuh? I got a weakness for clams on the half shell." Speaking of clams, Callahan thought, why don't I learn to keep my trap shut?

Although he did his damnedest to appear at least a little magisterial, Bruce had too passionate a nature—particularly when it came to news breaks—to remain deadpan. In such discussions a perennial boyhood enthusiasm flared. "I sure got a kick out of the Mae West story . . ."

Ah, the Mae West story. Thinking about it struck a chord. Callahan studied the glowing ashes of the cigar. He remembered the story well. It wasn't all that long ago. It was one of his last banner headlines before falling out of favor. Mae West had appeared in a stage revue—frankly titled *Sex*—that got raided by the cops. The brassy, ballsy actress was handed a ten-day sentence for "corrupting public morals," as if the morals of Gotham in 1927 could be any more corrupt than they were already. Callahan remembered pulling strings, calling in markers and getting an exclusive interview with Mae West before the black maria took her to Welfare Island to serve out the term. It was a bang-up job of reporting, even if he said so himself. And a nifty job of writing too. If only he could pick race horses as well as he could pick words. . . .

"Yeah," Callahan said to Bruce, expelling another smokescreen, "but I could never understand how such a fat and basically plain-looking dame became a sex object. I just think she's funny."

"You wrote a terrific piece."

Callahan indulged in a little false modesty. "It wrote itself. The lady has a way with words." He flicked ashes on the pine floor.

"I thought she had a nice rump," Bruce said, "but I didn't call you over to discuss Mae West's anatomy." He popped the question: "Are you ready to go to work for me again? To come back from exile?" He smiled like a monarch bestowing forgiveness.

Callahan said, "Not really."

Bruce's cheeks burned, flummoxed by the swift negative.

Though he had nothing against Bruce, Callahan enjoyed setting him back on his heels. He talked through the cigar clamped in the vise of his teeth: "I kind of like the graveyard beat," he said. "Suits my morbid personality."

"It's also a waste of your talent."

Callahan smiled, savoring the sweetness of retribution. "You should have thought of that when you shipped me there two years ago."

"Not my doing and you know it," said Bruce.

Callahan mentally conceded the point and did not reply. He knew all the while that the city editor in banishing him had been taking orders from higher up. And he knew why. Anyway, he held no real grudge against Bruce. But there had been more than a grain of truth to the alibi that he felt at home writing obits, his fingertips doing the *danse macabre* on the typewriter keys. As a seminarian in his misspent youth he had genuflected before plaster saints. Now he worshipped at the shrine of Thanatos. Old habits were hard to break. Bah, too much thinking interfered with drinking. He polished off the Canadian.

"Come on, Cal," said Bruce. "I need you to do a job."

The direct plea hit the mark. "Okay," he said, "I'll listen. But I'm not promising anything."

Bruce tossed a copy of the first edition across the desk with the headline about Madigan's bump-off facing Callahan. "What do you think?"

Callahan shrugged.

This reaction irked Bruce. "You're not a dummy. You don't have a membership card from the printers' union. Don't be a prick. Talk to me."

"Okay," said Callahan. "It's bullshit."

"You're damn right it's bullshit."

"What else is there to say?"

"The *Bugle* knows it's bullshit too. And the *World* knows it. And the *News* knows it. And the *Journal* knows it. Even the goddamn *Post* knows it."

"How about the Tokyo *Times?*"

"Shut up and listen."

"I'm listening."

"We can't pretend that Madigan's a martyr when everybody knows it's probably not true. If we do, it won't be long before the *Courier*'s the laughingstock of this burg."

"That's not my problem."

"You work here, don't you?"

"I warm a seat and collect a pay envelope. My self-respect—if I had any—wouldn't depend on the reputation of this newspaper."

For about a half-minute Bruce said nothing, then: "What made you decide to become a newspaperman?"

Callahan rubbed his chin. "Temporary insanity."

"You want to know why I did?"

"You're an egomaniac. You loved seeing your name in print."

Bruce shook his head. "When I started out only big wheels got bylines."

"Why, then?"

"I worked as a printer's devil for a country editor outside of Macon, Georgia. I was only fourteen. Physically the man was hardly impressive. He was short, wall-eyed, spoke with a stutter. He had to ready copy through a magnifying glass. The town bankers and plantation owners would pass him on the street in their surreys and splatter him with mud. But he had a basic dignity. In his stories he never resorted to stunts or sensationalism. By hard digging and sticking to the facts he exposed cozy relationships between local politicians and franchisers, fought for parks and public transportation. He liked to quote William Cullen Bryant about how the truth, crushed to earth, would rise again. And you knew he believed it. Corny, right?"

"Right."

"Sometimes it's easy to forget why we're sitting behind these desks."

Callahan sighed. "Who said about somebody that he'd been kicked in the head by a mule when young and believed everything he read in the papers? Anyway, what's this sermon got to do with Madigan?"

"We've got to dig out the real story before our competitors do. At least we can cut our losses, salvage our pride. Besides, printing transparent tripe sticks in my craw, you know?"

"What about the publisher?" Callahan asked.

Bruce's expression iced over. "The old windbag. He won't accept reality. He wants to believe that Madigan is a martyr. He also thinks that slanting the story this way will help boost circulation. As the head of the local publishers association he's peddling this angle to the rest of them. For the time being they're humoring him, pretending to buy it, until they double-cross him."

"Yeah," said Callahan, "so? How do I fit into the picture?"

"Simple. I need a good reporter."

With his hand Callahan made a wide sweep of the city room. "Take your pick," he said.

Bruce shook his head. "You're the man I want, Cal. You're perfect for the job. You got the background, the contacts. You can't be snowed. You know the turf. You grew up with Madigan, didn't you?"

"I wouldn't go that far. But we grew up in the same neighborhood."

"Well? Will you do it?" Bruce's eyes narrowed. "I could fucking order you to do this."

"But you wouldn't."

Bruce didn't deny it. "If I can't appeal to your devotion to truth and the *Courier,* how about unlimited expenses and a bonus when the job's done?"

Callahan chewed on the cigar. "I don't need any dough," he said.

"So how come you're always dodging the loan sharks and the bill collectors?"

Callahan's voice dropped a few decibels. "Who would do the obits?"

"Viola can handle the desk," Bruce said quietly.

Callahan rubbed his cheeks with his knuckles. "I suppose the little grease baby could, with instruction from me. He's pretty smart for a dago."

"Sure," said Bruce. "Of course the obit page would sorely miss your sepulchral wit and mordant style—"

"Can the horseshit . . . where do I start?"

Bruce reached into his pants pocket and handed over an object. "You know what this is?"

Callahan examined the glittering thing, turning it over in his palm, hefting it. "Yeah, I know what it is. It's the real McCoy too."

Bruce nodded. "An emerald stickpin. And you know what it means, don't you?"

"Sure. Whoever wears one is a special pal of Jimmy the Judge. Congratulations, Ivan."

Bruce made a face. "You know it's not mine," he said.

"Where'd yuh get it, then?"

"From Joe Cyriax."

"No kidding? I didn't know he was Irish. Hey, maybe there was a mick in the woodpile."

"It didn't belong to Cyriax. He pinched it." Bruce leaned back in the chair and laced his hands behind his head.

"From who?"

"From Scoop Madigan's corpse."

"Oh," said Callahan, smoking.

Chapter

4

MOTHER SUPERIOR'S HOUSE
OF ALL CULTURES

AFTER work Callahan collected advance expenses and
walked in the guttering daylight under the cloverleaf of
the bridge toward Baker's Funeral Parlor. Located in a
brick row house on Water Street, it was a blind for the
watering hole that catered to *Courier* employees who liked
to wet their whistles with something stronger than the
near-beer that the law allowed.

Of the thirty thousand speakeasies that serviced New
Yorkers afflicted with 'thirstitis' many used ingenious covers for their illegal activities, the blinds ranging from
laundries to radio stores to convents. Callahan even had
heard of a Brooklyn synagogue whose Byzantine tile facade disguised a barroom. But the red herring employed by
Baker's tickled Callahan the most, not only because of the
inventiveness of the ruse but because it appealed to his
macabre nature.

From the ground level up the house indeed catered to
widows and heirs who counted the gold teeth in the stiff's
mouth. But behind the armored door in the basement customers imbibed their formaldehyde either straight or with
beer chasers.

Callahan rapped on the riveted door. A little round win-

dow opened in the center and old Cyclops appeared. Since
Callahan was too warty a pickle to have to give a password,
after a second or two the ponderous door creaked open.

"Top of the evening," said Callahan to the impassive
Rico, elephantine gatekeeper, Solomonic settler of disputes. In reply Rico grunted something in his native
tongue, Simian.

Callahan scanned the vaporous room. The long bar was
crowded with drinkers and all twenty-five tables were already occupied. He trod the sawdust toward some familiar
faces at the far end of the bar.

Joe Cyriax played liar's poker with Casey, the conniving
copyboy. Dante Viola was nursing a short beer and chatting with Phil Blanchard, the head printer, who wore an
habitually sleepy expression and drank what passed in the
blind pig for rye and ginger ale.

Dante greeted Callahan: "The head ghoul himself."

Callahan cupped the side of his mouth. "Not any more,"
he said, sidling up to the bar. "It's your title now. Or hadn't
you heard?"

Dante looked surprised. "What are you talking about?"
he asked, holding the glass with a ginger touch.

"You'll probably get the word tomorrow," said Callahan,
ordering a round of champagne. "Make it the real stuff,
see?" he warned the bartender. "None of that bicarb and
Rhine wine." He scanned the gallery of appreciative faces.
"Include everybody but this twerp, Casey."

The copyboy wore a superior sneer. "Hey, I don't need
you to buy drinks for me."

"You're underage anyhow," added Callahan, prompting
laughter since it was illegal for anybody to drink.

Dante took Callahan aside. "What's this about me being
head obit writer?"

Callahan put his forefinger to his lips. "Hush-hush stuff.
The old man put me on special assignment." When the
drinks came he handed the glasses around.

Cyriax held the bubbly up to his hawk nose. "You hit the
printers' pool or something?" he asked Callahan.

"What are we celebrating?" asked Blanchard, not changing his deceptively somnolent expression.

Callahan made the sign of the cross. "The entry into heaven of Warren Harding's dog." He raised his glass and intoned, *"Tantum ergo* makes your hair grow."

"Champagne's fer dames," sneered Casey.

Callahan clucked his tongue and glanced at the head printer, a man of mountainous height and bulk. "Hey, Phil, this half-pint moron is impugning your masculinity."

Blanchard blithely sipped his drink.

Dante, impatient, pulled Callahan aside again. "Will you fill me in?"

"Hold your water, kid. First I want to have a word with the Greek."

He huddled with Joe Cyriax. "How'd you do it, Joe? How'd you lift that item from Madigan's stiff?"

Cyriax's inner-tube mid-section shimmered as he laughed silently. "It was a snap. I pretended to blubber over the body of my old friend Scoop."

"And the cops fell for it?"

"Like a ton of micks." Cyriax narrowed his eyes at Callahan. "So Bruce put you on the story, eh?"

Callahan nodded.

"It figures. Welcome back to the land of the living."

"Hey, that's a hot one," said Callahan, glancing around the speak. "Here we are digging ourselves early graves in the basement of a mortuary where they stash bottle of rotgut in caskets. If this is the land of the living then Dante's Inferno is a maternity ward."

"Dante's what?" asked Cyriax, casting a puzzled look at Dante Viola.

"Never mind," said Callahan. "Have another drink."

And they all had many another drink.

The smoke in the room got as dense as fog. Cyriax went home. Casey looked around for another sucker to play liar's poker with. Blanchard drank heavily and started talking to himself in a garbled drone.

"He's cracked," observed Callahan to Dante. "Printers get that way from reading typeface upside down all the time."

Dante tugged his friend's elbow. "So what gives?"

Callahan jerked his head toward an empty booth. The young man followed him over to it. Callahan studied his companion, who had pomaded hair and wore a boutonniere, some kind of yellow flower. "Got a date later?" he asked.

"Nah," said Dante.

"Too bad. Guy your age needs it regular. Want to join me at Mother Superior's? I figure I'll be heading over there before the night's out."

"No thanks," said Dante. "What's this about me doing obits?"

Callahan briefly explained the situation to him.

"I'd give my right nut to work with you on the story," declared Dante.

"Better not go sacrificing your manhood for a yarn like this," advised Callahan. "No matter what happens you can't win with this one. It's a kill-the-messenger situation."

"Still," said Dante, "you know how I hate being a desk jockey."

"Patience, boy. Your turn will come."

Dante sipped the tepid beer. He looked forlorn. "But when?"

"You're still in knee pants."

"I grew up fast." Dante glanced up and his expression brightened as he spotted Clare Parker coming through the front door.

Callahan traced the kid's gaze. She had stopped to chat with some people at the bar. He smiled. "If it isn't our own Polly Pry," he said, "sob sister supreme."

"Ain't she something?" said Dante, taking visual inventory of the girl reporter through blue tobacco smoke. She wore a silk dress of many colors. Her arms were white, round and smooth, like stone shaped by the surf. Her titian hair was cropped short and shingled in the latest style. Dante finally caught her eye and raised his glass to her, hoping she would come over.

She nodded coolly in their direction and continued chatting by the mahogany bar, her body swaying slightly to the music. Dante's face glowed. "A dish," he said.

"Yeah," said Callahan. It was clearly so.

"And what a reporter," Dante added. "Did you read her story on the flagpole sitter? I heard she wrote a memo telling Bruce that she wants to sit on a flagpole herself and write a first-person piece about it."

"I wish she'd sit on my flagpole," said Callahan, studying the bottom of his glass.

Dante flushed.

Callahan smiled. "Relax, pal," he said. "Just pulling your leg. I never knew guineas could blush."

Dante wagged his head. "Sometimes you're not too funny, Cal."

Callahan crooked his finger at a white-coated waiter and ordered more champagne. "You'd think she was the Virgin Mary," he muttered. He unwrapped a cigar, looked at it and stuck it in his mouth. He fumbled with matches and finally managed to light it. He was making progress toward his destination—oblivion. With his prodigious capacity for booze it was a long journey.

"Why don't we invite her to join us?" Dante said.

"Take a tip from me, kid. Don't show your cards with females or you end up a doormat."

"I don't believe in playing coy. Besides, I'm not going to propose, I'm just going to offer her a drink."

"Let her buy, she's loaded."

"I wouldn't let a lady pay for my drink."

"She's a Lucy Stoner from way back."

Dante shook his head. "I just couldn't."

Callahan let it go. Presently Clare slid her trim bottom onto the bench of the booth, sitting beside Callahan and opposite Dante. The lady gave off a powerful blend of brains and sex. Her smile was friendly if reserved.

"What'll you have, Clare?" asked Dante, raising his voice above the music. The combo on the small bandstand had struck up an energetic black bottom and a few couples were dancing.

She propped her elbows on the table. "Bourbon." She

also gave off a faint odor of lavender water. Ignoring Dante, she turned to Callahan. "I hear you've been assigned to look into the Madigan mess."

"What did they do, put it on the A-wire?" said Callahan. "It was supposed to be confidential."

"The official story reeks from here to Montauk," she said, talking from one side of her mouth in a manner she affected to shed the society-deb image. "So what gives?" she added, leaning closer.

Callahan shrugged. "I'm not sure. That's what I'm paid to find out. One thing's pretty certain, though. He took a gamble and rolled boxcars. Had to take his medicine. You can fill in the blanks."

The bourbon arrived and Dante fumbled in his pockets. She waved him off. "Put it on my tab," she told the waiter and turned back to Callahan. "I'd bet there's something big behind it. Reporters don't get plugged without good reason." She drank the bourbon neat.

Callahan kept mum about the connection to Jimmy the Judge. No time for blabbermouthing. He had to play the hand close to the vest, at least for now. But the rumor pump had been primed and there was no way to stop people from gabbing and speculating. Clare's silken knee brushed his under the table and Callahan couldn't help wondering if it hadn't been intentional. He stole a glance at her sleek neck, at the shape of her full breasts under the fabric of her dress.

Clare was swirling the bourbon. "He was always putting on the ritz, that Madigan."

"Yeah," said Callahan. "Hey, I'm hungry. Anybody hungry?"

"Sure," said Dante. "Let's hop a cab over to Mulberry Street."

"What's wrong with the grub here? They serve good steak tartare."

"If you don't mind ground-up corpses," Clare put.

They decided to eat at Baker's and wait for the bulldog edition to come off the presses. Clare brought another round of drinks and told them unprintable stories about

Shipwreck Kelly, the flagpole sitter. The combo played "The Girl Friend" and Dante worked up the nerve to ask Clare to dance the Charleston with him.

Meanwhile Callahan's mind was lit with bright and seemingly unconnected images—a picture of Madigan, apple-cheeked and alive, wearing a jaunty bowler hat and checkered vest, fusing with an apparition of the pastor of Callahan's boyhood parish, as corrupt an old Pharisee as ever walked the mottled earth. What was his name again? Callahan couldn't remember, at least not in his present condition. The Madigan assignment, he reflected, might make him turn over a few rocks in his own past. He shuddered at the thought. They were cut from the same cloth in many ways. His eyes rolled at the embossed tin ceiling of the speakeasy. The sound of a bass fiddle playing jazz thumped in his head.

He pushed away the empty champagne glass, grabbed a fork and, shoved steak tartare into his mouth, with echoes of his wife of about five minutes saying how he ate like a hog at the trough. He wondered what Virginia Hess of Castleton Corners, Staten Island, was doing these days and whether she still got most of her jollies from breaking balls before lunch with a nutcracker. He had heard through the grapevine that she quit her nursing job at Seaview Hospital, having suckered another meal ticket to accompany her to the City Clerk's office. He sighed. At least it hadn't been necessary to beg the bishop for a church annulment. The marriage had cured him of a few illusions. Too bad he had had to yoke up to her to learn the truth of the sage adage: fire in the eyes, ice in the twat.

"You're pie-eyed," said Clare, interrupting the reverie as she and Dante returned to the booth.

"Success at last," said Callahan, continuing to eat the raw beef mixed with raw egg, Worcestershire sauce, onions, capers, et cetera. He didn't give two bits if she thought him a sloppy drunk. Sure, he lusted after her, but wasn't sure he liked her. Oh, he liked a lot of things about her—the cut of her jib, her style as a reporter—but he didn't quite go for the solution of the equation. Still, he could well understand why Dante mooned over her. She had style, intelligence, talent, wit and beauty, not to mention a bank-roll that would choke a rhino. So how come the formula seemed to come out wrong?

"I got passes for the fights from the sports desk," said Dante. "You two want to tag along?"

"Count me out," said Callahan. "I've got other plans." He felt soft-hearted tonight. He would bow out gracefully and give the kid a clear field.

Dante looked at Clare.

"Sure," she said after a slight pause. "Who's on the card?"

"Main event, Goldstein versus Flynn, two sluggers. Should be great." Dante's eyes glittered at her acceptance, lukewarm though it had been.

Callahan mopped his mouth with a cloth napkin, look-ing at Dante. The kid's in seventh heaven, he thought, as he mentally laid odds that she would finally make a patsy of him and hoping he was wrong. Underneath the gruff-ness he had a mushy spot for the young man. At Callahan's age he could have had a son almost as old as Dante. That is, if his crazy-quilt past had been different. But he kept his mouth shut about Clare, figuring that the kid had to learn the hard way.

A printer brought over copies of the final edition hot off the rotaries. Dante's glance was fixed on Clare's intent face as she thumbed through the tabloid, her eyes devouring the newsprint.

"How's the edition look?" Dante asked.

"Copy desk screwed up my lead," she muttered.

Newshawks were all alike, Callahan thought. Particu-larly dames with something to prove.

Dante glanced at his pocket watch. "We gotta hurry if we want to catch the semis," he said.

"Okay." She stuck the newspaper under her arm and fluffed her red hair.

They said goodbye and left. Callahan toyed with a caper on his plate, glad to be alone with his thoughts. He was focused on Dante Viola, wondering whether the kid had the balls to be a real newspaperman. He seemed to have a lot of qualifications, sure. He could write fast, breezy copy, although sometimes he got a little too fancy, but nothing that Callahan or another sharp editor couldn't cure with some strong blue-penciling. He had innate curiosity, brains, enthusiasm, charm, skepticism about most received truths, a healthy disrespect for authority, a crusading spirit (which needed bridling, Callahan thought, or it could get out of hand).

But did he have the balls?

Dante's idealism, in fact, might be the crux of the problem. Dante had once told Callahan that he'd been inspired to become a newspaperman by Heywood Broun's columns on the Sacco and Vanzetti case. Well and good, but there was too much of the Boy Scout about the kid, and it could land him in hot water.

Callahan drummed his fingers on the table. The combo played a blues tune he couldn't identify but it suited his mood. He was pretty much convinced that his surrogate son was a little too soft. He hoped he was wrong. But there was something about the kid. . . . Maybe it was just that Dante reminded him of another wobbly-legged cub he once knew, a punk from Hell's Kitchen named John Joseph Callahan.

Hey, he didn't have the balls either.

He paid the tab and headed over to Mother Superior's House of All Cultures.

Mazie Rodell lay beached on the four-poster in all her naked leviathan-like beauty. She hugged her elbows and frowned at her bedpartner's snoring. He gets it free and doesn't even take advantage of it. . . . Mazie sighed. She had the misfortune to think that she was in love with the slug.

She looked down at him again, letting her eyes travel from his mouth down to his gently heaving stomach and farther down to his phallus. It was like the Loch Ness monster—fabulously big but it hardly ever raised its head. She smiled. The only time he seemed to screw was when he wanted to time a three-minute egg.

Yielding to a rare bout of introspection, she wondered why she was nuts about him. Why didn't she, whore or no whore, tell him to take a hike? She chewed a red-enameled fingernail. The answer, she figured, was fairly simple. Not that one needed any good reason for loving a man. But she loved him for having suffered like he did in the Argonne forest, wherever that was. And she loved him for the sickness in his heart that he wore like a badge. And she loved him for the flashes of downright goodness that he showed, like the time he rushed Janie Kelly to the hospital after her appendicitis attack and then paid for the operation without asking for or getting anything in return. Mazie figured that under the mossback hull Callahan was a john with a heart of gold. He was just . . . kind of sick inside.

She lifted herself off the bed, springs creaking and mattress eddying in her wake, walked across the room and put on a flowered dressing gown. She turned on the radio, and voices came out of the magic box:

"They say Darwin's book is bunk and their grandpap was no monk."

"Absolutely, Mr. Gallagher."

"Positively, Mr. Shean."

Callahan snored.

"Looking at you, you sorry specimen, makes me think Darwin was right," she said aloud.

He stirred. "What's that you say, Mazie?"

"Nothing."

He propped himself up on his elbows and peered through drowsy eyes at her, looming over the bed, smoking a cigarette and eyeing him.

"I do something wrong?"

She stopped, lifted his limber member with her forefinger and let it flop down. "Nothing at all," she said.

He rubbed his eyes. "Mazie, you're a sex fiend."

"And you're a fairy," she said, going over to sit in the windowseat, puffing angrily on the cigarette. She stared out the window of the brick house overlooking Charlton Street, where shadows faded on the edge of dawn and a milk truck wobbled over the cobblestones. Smoky light spelled the death of night.

Groaning and clutching his kneecaps Callahan swung himself out of bed, grabbed a handkerchief from the bedstand and blew his nose. "You, my dear Mazie, remind me of a queen of old Constantinople I once read about. She sorely regretted having only three orifices to satisfy her."

She turned from the window, facing him. "What are orifices?"

"Holes, Mazie. Holes."

"Shut your own hole, Callahan."

He went over to her, nuzzled her hair and reached under the dressing gown to cup her breast. "Just kidding, dumpling," he said.

She pushed his hand away and continued to smoke.

"Be back in a few minutes, got to talk to Mother."

She glowered at him. "Don't bother coming back. I'll be asleep."

He found the proprietress in her usual place at this hour of the day, in the parlor sipping absinthe before retiring. It was an old-fashioned Victorian room, cluttered with porcelain figurines, filled with dark wood furniture, heavy draperies and overstuffed chairs. The woman was sitting on a green brocade loveseat. Hovering nearby, as always, was Caleb Forest, her black manservant and bodyguard. Her alert blue eyes sparkled at Callahan's entry, and patting the spot beside her, invited him to sit. She was a thin, rawboned woman of some sixty-five years who defied the stereotype of fleshiness and heartiness associated with her profession. Still, she suited the sobriquet of Mother Superior in every imaginable way.

"I was just enjoying a nightcap," she said, pouring the smoky liquid into a tall glass for him without asking whether he would join her. Her thin lips curled in a smile as she handed the glass to him.

They clinked glasses.

"The Lord be with you," she said.

"And with thy spirit," he replied.

Callahan had nosed out something of her personal history. Her real name was Theodora White. She was, according to a reliable source, an ex-nun who discovered the pleasures of the flesh in the arms of a novice and was evicted from the convent after being surprised in the girl's bedroom. Callahan, who had left the seminary under a similar cloud (caught in the laundry room with the daughter of the cook), sympathized with Theodora, who, he was convinced, was not a lesbian but a voluptuary whose libido had been sidetracked as a girl into religious fervor. In any case, she eventually found her true vocation, which she had been practicing now for thirty-five years with great success, becoming very rich while improving the complexions and mental health of a big segment of the male population in town. It was a happy arrangement. She also encouraged newspapermen to frequent her house and sample the wares free of charge, for she was astute enough to recognize the commercial value of free publicity and good word of mouth. She also realized a direct profit from the practice, since the reporters left plenty of cash at the bar and the gaming tables on their way up and down the stairs.

Mother Superior took advantage of her wealth and leisure to cultivate the finer things of life, becoming well-read, a conversationalist and a proficient ragtime pianist.

"I suppose you read the news about Scoop Madigan," Callahan said.

The woman made clucking sounds over the glass. "Wasn't that a shame. I liked Scoop."

Callahan grimaced. "That puts you in a very elite group."

"Oh, I know he was a bit of a showoff and a blowhard but he knew how to spin a yarn and he treated the girls well. I especially liked that about him."

Mother spoke quietly and sometimes Callahan had to lean forward to catch what she was saying. He was touched by her solicitude for her girls.

"You don't sound very surprised about how he got it," Callahan said.

"Ah," she sighed, "that's the trouble with living as long

as I have. One's capacity for surprise diminishes." She drank.

Callahan didn't want to seem too inquisitive. His voice faltered. "He, uh, came here often?"

"About once a week. He liked dark and Greek," she said with an air of someone discussing preferences in ice cream flavors. "He liked the ones with the kind of rear ends you could balance a teacup upon." She held the glass daintily and smiled. "He always behaved like a perfect gentleman."

"He spent freely?"

"He had a weakness for the roulette wheel and the dice game. He won, he lost. He was not the only one."

"Ah, but how many sixty-smacker-a-week leg men can afford the sporting life on such a scale?"

She shrugged.

"I suppose gamblers find ways," he suggested.

"You ought to know." She glanced over at Caleb, who read a telepathic message in her expression and came over to massage her shoulders. About thirty-five, he was a squat, muscular man with skin of weathered mahogany. Traces of American Indian heritage were displayed in his face, especially in the bone structure. He had worked for Mother since his boyhood, Callahan had heard, an orphan who had wandered in like a stray cat one day and stayed for twenty-five years. He rarely spoke and was devoted to his mistress. She closed her eyes and slumped languorously at his touch.

Callahan reached into his pocket and fished out a small object. "Look here, Mother," he said, holding it up.

She took it from him and examined it. Her pale face showed a shade of caution. She handed the stickpin back to him. "Interesting," she said.

"Madigan was wearing it when he got plugged."

"I see."

"He also had a fat wad on his hip. About forty-five Abe Lincolns."

"As you know, a sport is often flush, often broke."

"Sure," said Callahan.

The flat early sun came in through the window and brushed her peach-colored dressing gown. A car horn chooged outside. "I've heard tell he inherited a tidy sum from his father," she said.

"So he always said."

She gestured broadly with her right hand and her bangled wrist clattered. "Is this an idle chat or a pointed conversation?" she asked.

"As pointed as a woodpecker's pecker."

She laughed brightly. It had a girlish sound. "If you knew anything at all about the anatomy of birds you would know that the woodpecker has no pecker."

"Anatomy's your subject, Mother."

"And yours is . . . what?" She lay her forefinger against her cheek. "Death, isn't it?"

He nodded.

She paused, then said, "Tell me, why the sudden interest in the Scoop Madigan case?"

"He's dead, isn't he?"

"But his obituary has already been written."

"They did a lousy job. Besides, I've been taken off the gravedigger's beat."

"I see. You've been assigned to get the real scoop on Scoop."

"Well put."

She leaned back and appraised him. "So, they gave you back your old press card and a new lease on life."

Callahan shrugged. "I wouldn't use those words exactly."

"I knew you couldn't resist the scent of a good story for the rest of your life."

"It was the smell of expense money that really did the trick," protested Callahan.

But Mother Superior didn't buy this. She flashed a glance at Caleb Forest, who immediately stopped massaging her shoulders and stepped back. "Hooray for you," she said to Callahan. "The beetle moves."

"Beg pardon?"

"The beetle," she repeated, fitting a cigarette into an

ivory holder. In an instant the servant was at her side, lighting the cigarette. "I've mentioned this notion to you before, haven't I? No? You see, you remind me of a thanatotic beetle, an insect that plays dead to avoid the predator. You show the same morbid talent, Cal. You've gotten quite good at it."

"Practice makes perfect. What predator have I been avoiding?"

She waved him away with a glitter of rings. "Do I have to state the obvious?"

"I guess not."

Smoking languidly, she studied his rude red face with affection. "Well, I'm glad you're coming around again. How old are you, Cal?"

"Forty last month."

"Ah," she said. *"Nel mezzo del cammin di nostra vita."*

He gave her a rare smile. "Okay, I'll buy that explanation of my current mental outlook. My rebirth, if you will. Can you give me a hand out of the darksome wood?"

"Maybe. How?"

"By answering a few questions."

"Hah. Whatever, dear heart, makes you think I know the answers?"

"Come off it, Mother. You know all the answers."

She studied her painted fingernails. "You flatter me."

He waved his hand. "Like hell I do."

She rose from the love seat for the first time in the interview and paced the room, touching objects along the way. Her posture was erect, her gait graceful. The silk of her dressing gown rustled.

"All right," she said, "let's make sure everything's off the record, eh?"

"Agreed."

"I'm hungry. Will you have caviar and strawberries with me?"

"Delighted," he said.

She nodded to Caleb, who left the room, sat down again beside Callahan, raising her skirts and displaying ankles clad in silk. Her advanced age, the puckered skin around her mouth, the crepey neck had not dimmed her girlishness.

"You're a pretty homely guy, Cal. Not very courtly either. I wonder what makes women go for you."

"Who says women go for me?"

"They do."

He shrugged. "Then it's a mystery to me too."

"You must possess hidden charms," she said.

"I keep my bushel under a light."

She looked at the fedora on his head. "Why do you always keep your hat on?"

"It's a newspaper tradition."

"I'll bet it's to avoid any possible signs of civility or servility."

"Actually, it's to hide my bald spot."

"Do you wear it to bed too?"

"Only on Tuesdays."

The manservant brought caviar, berries and coffee, which he set on the marble-top table. "Thank you, Caleb," she said. He nodded and left the room.

As they ate she continued chatting. "Have you read Sigmund Freud?"

He popped a strawberry, stem and all, into his mouth. "I thought I was supposed to be asking questions."

"I'm just curious to know if you've read Freud."

"Of course not," he said, his voice flat, dry. "His books are on the Index."

"Don't tell me you're still a Catholic."

"Do I have a choice in the matter?"

"You can choose what to read." She spread caviar on a triangle of toast. "I've browsed through Freud," she continued. "He has some interesting ideas, although I don't think he likes women very much. Maybe you, Cal, appeal to women because you remind them of a distant, disapproving father."

"I like the hidden-charms theory better."

She laughed at that one. "How do you like your coffee?" holding up a porcelain pitcher shaped like a swan, the spout the bird's beak.

"Like Madigan apparently liked his women, black and sweet."

She poured, then nudged the cup toward him with the handle pointed away. "And backward," she added demurely.

After taking a sip he said, "Tell me something, Mother, now that Madigan's out of the picture, who will handle your future contracts for you?" Having taken the gamble that his hunch was correct and that she would not take offense at the question, he held his breath.

For a moment she drank silently, eyeing him with grudging respect. The gamble had paid off. "Oh, the beer and booze will find its way into my house as surely as rivers flow into the sea."

"And the slots, et cetera?"

"If they want their cut they'll send somebody around to collect."

Her words added more fuel, if any were needed, to his suspicions: Madigan was killed not because he was a hard-hitting reporter but because he was in cahoots with the racketeers. No wonder he had had such good underworld sources. A lot of questions remained. Was he just an errand boy or a major operator? Which gang was he affiliated with? Was he connected to any politicians or public figures? Most of all, who bumped him off and why? Who was Goodrich's masked tenor on the radio? All important questions.

Mother said, "I've been getting my goods from the Judge since Jack Diamond had that donnybrook with Rothstein and Schultz last year. I like doing business with Fitzgerald's outfit because they don't make a lot of commotion like most of those hoods." She sighed. "Now this happens."

Callahan came right out with it: "Who did it?"

She stiffened a little. "What makes you think I know?"

"You're smart as a whip. You live in the center of the universe. And you've got more connections than Grand Central Station. If anybody knows, you do."

"Well, I don't."

"Then you have pretty good suspicions."

"You overestimate me."

"No I don't."

Her expression softened. "Let me give you some advice."

"What?"

"Get a job in advertising."

"I'm not their type."

"Then collect your pension or something."

"What pension? I'm a newspaper reporter. Besides, a pension wouldn't cover my bar bill. I'd have to swill bay rum from the five-and-dime. You wouldn't want that, would you?"

"You're playing with fire, kiddo."

"You're probably right." He took the wrapping off a cigar and held it under his nose. "Mind if I fumigate the place?"

She shook her head.

"This assignment can help get me out of the doghouse," he said. "Much as I hate to admit it, I'm beginning to like the idea."

"Well, I'll be," she said, smiling.

"Funny thing," he said, lighting up, "but for the first time in a long time my nose itches again."

"You've gone pawky, Cal."

He shrugged. "Guess I'm a born busybody."

"An incurable newspaper reporter."

He sighed. "Right."

"Bravo for the beetle," she said.

"So?"

"Ever hear of Gaetano Pellegrino?"

"Can't say as I have."

"I'm surprised at you, Cal. You used to have your thumb on the pulse."

"I've been out of circulation for a long time."

Caleb returned with silver fingerbowl and hand towels.

"Off the record?" she repeated, dipping her fingers.

"Off the record."

"He's a young turk in the underworld—"

"I thought he was a guinea."

"You *know* what I mean. He wasn't particularly fond of Scoop. I'm afraid that's all I can say. You can take it from there."

"Thanks, Mother."

She waved him away. After a pause she added, "Watch yourself, Callahan."

"Sure."

"I mean it," she said. "I've heard strange tales of this man, Pellegrino."

"Yeah?"

"I know a lot of these gangsters. They kill without batting an eye. But it's mostly all business. Practical. Nothing personal."

"So?"

"It's different with Pellegrino. With him it's a blood sport." She dried her hands on a towel.

He found Mazie seated before the mirror of her dressing table applying a hot curling iron to her peroxide-blonde hair. She glared at his reflection.

"I thought you were going to sleep," he said, unbuttoning his shirt.

She made a moue at the smug look on his face and continued to curl her hair.

He sat on the bed and began removing his shoes. "Glad you waited for me. I'm in a good mood. We're gonna make music together." How he did go on.

She squirmed a little and the pout vanished. With a sigh and a flounce of her hair she stood up and faced him.

He was naked. "Now I'll really curl your hair," he said.

She circled the bed, eyeing his preparedness. "Promise?"

"Scout's honor. You want it in writing?"

The mattress springs groaned as she joined him on the bed.

He slipped the gown off her shoulders, revealing great breasts over waves of belly. As he waded in, he suddenly recalled his boyhood pastor's name: Father Timothy Curley.

Forgive me, Father.

Chapter

5

BEETHOVEN LOST

SOON Callahan had spent the first installment of the expense money so he figured he had to pay a visit to the city room, give Ivan Bruce a progress report and persuade Bruce to cough up some more. Was there progress to report? He wondered about it, lying flat on his back in bed and staring at the ceiling of the furnished (hah) room on Fourteenth Street where he lived by himself. Easy come, easy go, he thought. He had spent the last eight days boozing, betting and boffing—to put it in the alliterative style of the tabloid writer—but it hadn't been a total washout. He had managed to unearth a few bones to toss in Bruce's direction. He could prolong the process by rationing his nuggets of information to Bruce, like sweets to a schoolboy.

Callahan tossed on to his side, placed unshaven cheek on his joined hands and closed his eyes. He had intended to rest for five more minutes but he fell half-asleep again and the usual dream came, more vivid because of his semi-consciousness. There in the mist was the smoke of gunpowder, the reek of graphite and the scream of shells in the trench at Chateau Thierry. He saw his face again, smooth and beardless. Of course he never knew the guy's name. In his mind he called him Fritz. He saw again the innocent face, the blue eyes hollow with horror. He shot him in the Adam's apple and the eyes rolled into his head. The rifle shot now echoed in his ears eleven years later, jarring him awake.

He walked to the kitchen, stuck a dime in the gas plate and brewed coffee, cursing his conscience, if that's what it was, as if it were a nagging wife. But he discovered as usual that he couldn't bully it around, this inner voice, this vestige of another time. He was still haunted by the face of the heinie soldier who had had the bad luck to jump into the hole in the soil of France that became his grave. Callahan repeated in his mind the same old litanies: it was him or me; we were both pawns of power-hungry politicians, the old men who declared war while young men died in them; I was doing my patriotic duty. The arguments were no less true for their glibness. But they did no good.

Every morning he awoke with the boy's face engraved in his memory. It didn't fade until about his third drink.

Guilt, the Irish disease. Wasn't it guilt, after all, that had motivated him to aspire to the priesthood? What an idea: turn your collar backward and you erase guilt. He often entertained another dumb thought: that the encounter in the trench was a payback for having abandoned the priesthood. He suddenly felt thirsty.

The winds of March made men chase their hats around Foley Square as Callahan stopped at Ham Terry's newsstand to buy a tout sheet.

"How do, Mr. Cal?" said the blind newsie. "Ain't seen you for more than a week."

"I been busy," he said with a mock air of importance.

"So I heard."

Callahan frowned at the man as he gnawed a cigar butt. "Sure you don't string on the side for Winchell or Sullivan?"

"They got openings for me?"

"I'd hire you," said Callahan as he put a nickel in the newsie's cigar box and began to wade through gusts of

wind to the curbstone. Holding down his hat, he turned
and hollered, "Read any good entrails lately?"

"Beg pardon?" said Ham.

"Never mind," said Callahan.

The furnace was busted and the city room was cold as an
old maid's crack as Callahan entered, waving to Dante on
the obit desk. Most of the staff were bundled up in coats
and scarves as they scribbled on proofs or pecked away at
typewriters. Dante, in contrast, seemed comfortable in a
shawl-collared cashmere cardigan with bone buttons,
white shirt and red tie. However, he wore a concerned look
on his face.

"Where the hell you been, Cal?" he asked as Callahan
parked his pear-shaped fanny on a corner of the young
man's desk. "I don't need to tell you that Bruce is boiling."

"Good," said Callahan, shivering melodramatically.
"Maybe he'll heat up the joint." He blew cigar smoke in his
former assistant's face. "Any juicy local stories?"

"The usual. Some nut took a swan dive off the Manhattan Bridge."

"He perished, I hope."

"Nah. Just broke his right pinky."

Callahan thumbed through the paper. "Here's one about
a rancher in Arizona who was struck by lightning on his
horse. Both man and mount were electrocuted."

Dante frowned. "How did I miss that one?" He looked as
if he suddenly remembered something. "Oh, you'll like the
one about the con man in Kansas City. Seems he was con-
victed of placing banana peels on the sidewalks in front of
twenty-seven companies so's he could collect damages."

"An enterprising American," said Callahan. He leaned
forward. "Speaking of banana peels, did you get your banana peeled the other night?"

"None of your goddamn business, Cal!"

"Two to one you didn't."

"We went to the fights together," he said, avoiding Callahan's eyes. "Who said there was more to it than that?"

Callahan waved his hand. "Forget about her, Dan. Dago like you wants a woman with real apple knockers on her. Not some skinny society deb."

"I repeat, mind your own beeswax."

Cal shrugged. "Okay, Romeo." He crushed out the cigar, squinted at Dante. "What do you know about a hood named Guy Pellegrino?"

Dante just looked at Callahan.

"He's big in your neighborhood, ain't he?"

Dante nodded. "He's getting there."

"A Sicilian?"

"What else?"

Callahan was still scavenging for scraps of information to feed Bruce in the impending conference. "How old?"

"About thirty-five."

"He's a real big shot?"

"They say he's a *capo* already."

"Must have been a boy wonder."

"These jokers start young. He was already a man of respect on Mulberry Street when I was a snot-nose."

"You still a snot-nose."

"I mean, more than ten years ago."

"How come I never heard of him?"

Dante shrugged. "You've been pickled for God knows how long."

"You're a real diplomat."

"You can dish it out but you can't take it, eh?"

Callahan shuddered his shoulders at the nip in the air. "Which one of the old dons is Pellegrino connected to?"

"You mean Maranzano or Masseria?"

"Yes."

"I'm not sure. I think neither. I don't know a whole lot about him but I hear he's a new breed guy. They say he's got Jews, micks, even Norwegians in his gang. None of that Sicilian purity crap, you know?" He peered at Callahan. "Why the interest? You taking a correspondence course in gangsterism?"

"Sort of."

Dante's eyes glittered. "So you figure Pellegrino's connected with the Madigan killing?"

"Could be."

"You could use my help on this, Cal. I have contacts all
over Little Italy. And I understand what makes these people tick. Let me work on it with you."

"No chance, kid. Stick to the postmortems."

"You can do the Irish side, I'll do the Italian side. We'll
make a team. You just have to go to bat for me with the old
man. You gotta get me out of this cemetery."

The kid had a good point, Callahan reflected. But he
never liked working with partners. That was one of the
reasons his three-minute marriage busted up. He considered the proposition for another moment, then said, "Nah,
forget it."

"You're a real pal."

"You may thank me someday for keeping you out of this
mess. These goombahs can play roughly, as Madigan
found out. What kind of businesses does Pellegrino operate?"

"The usual, I guess. Booze, beer, policy, gambling, a heist
now and then. Hey, why should I tell you? Get the dope
yourself, you're so smart."

Callahan tipped his hat. "Thanks. I got plenty for now."

"Fuck you and the horse you rode in on."

"What kind of language is that for a nice Catholic boy?"

"Fuck you twice."

"See you in Baker's later?" Callahan asked as he started
to walk away.

"Not if I see you first," said Dante as he resumed typing.

Callahan found Ivan Bruce in the composing room reading lead type upside down off the page-five frame and conferring with Phil Blanchard. Bruce's pupils turned to fire-
balls as he caught sight of Callahan.

"So, you fat prick, you ran out of money, huh?"

"You got me all wrong, Ivan. I've been busting my butt
on this story." He nodded at the head printer. "How are
you, Phil?"

"Why haven't I heard a peep from you?" Bruce demanded.

"I told you, I've been busy."

"You making any progress?"

"Where can we talk?"

A copyboy rushed over and handed Bruce a pile of page proofs. "Meet me in Pop's after I put this baby to bed."

As he left the composing room Callahan congratulated himself on knowing how to handle the old man. The Lord provides, he thought, compensating us with the gift of blarney for the affliction of the bottle.

Pop Pietro ran the lunchroom, a greasy spoon tucked behind the lobby on the ground floor. Its main attraction, besides proximity to the workplace, was the row of round butts, perched on swivel stools, belonging to stenos and secretaries that greeted his eye as he entered the room. Passing the parade he found an empty booth and ordered a cup of the sludge that passed for coffee.

Pietro Carlucci gave him a curt nod from behind the cash register. Callahan considered the man pretentious and a rebuttal of the notion that all Italians were artists of the kitchen. His glutinous meatball heroes were a disgrace to the race. Heaven knew how—he even managed to screw up an order of dry toast. Callahan usually ordered nothing but coffee, making him an unpopular customer. He drank the coffee with heaps of sugar, resulting in a concoction that he believed fueled his sluggish engine and counteracted hangovers. Drinking, he studied Pietro behind the counter, with his mane of wild white hair and aristocratic profile, his air of being frozen by some quirk of fate several stations below his rightful place in life.

At least it was warm in the lunchroom, he reflected, heated by an old coal stove of cast iron that sat like a squat burgher in a corner. Callahan again appraised the pleasing array of rear ends.

"You lecherous thing," she said, having parked her own next to his on the bench.

Callahan looked obliquely at Clare Parker. He sipped coffee.

"Mind if I join you?"

He started to open his mouth.

"I know," she said, silencing him. "I already have." She took out a cigarette, tamped it on the table and stuck it in her mouth, waiting.

Drowsy-eyed, he continued to drink coffee.

When he didn't react she sighed and lit the cigarette herself. Speaking from the leeward side, she observed, "Who said chivalry was dead?"

He drank.

"So you're a connoisseur of backsides," she said, trying again. "Why do you think of mine?"

He lifted his eyebrows. "Too skinny."

"Don't knock it till you've tried it."

He laughed in spite of himself. She had moxie.

The waitress came over and Clare ordered a tuna salad sandwich and an egg cream. "Where you been this past week?"

He pretended to look offended. "Hey, it's Ivan Bruce's job to check my time sheet."

"Just curious."

"Curiosity killed the debutante."

"It's my stock in trade, Cal. Give me that." When her lunch came she asked, "What have you got against me, Cal?"

"Nothing. You're a pretty good kid." And a damn good reporter, he thought.

"For a society brat? Did it ever occur to you that there's such a thing as reverse snobbery?"

"Yeah, it's occurred to me."

"But the great John Joseph Callahan doesn't buy it in my case—"

"How did you know my middle name?"

"I know a lot about you."

Callahan felt flattered, despite not wanting to.

"So?" she said. "You haven't answered the question. Where have you been?"

"On a bender, of course."

She dismissed the answer with a wave of the hand. "You're always on a bender. Where else have you been?"

"Places."

"A master of circumlocution, yet."

"I've been to probate court."

"Enterprising. The muckraker pouring over musty records. Learn anything?"

"Take a wild guess."

She sighed, toying with a teaspoon. "Playing the clam, huh? I suppose I don't blame you. But hey, if you need any help, remember I have certain talents."

"A suggestive remark—"

She reached over the counter and touched his hand. Did he feel sparks? "I mean it," she said.

"Thanks." He stirred the dregs of his coffee. "Why does everybody want to horn in on this story?"

"Everybody?"

"Dante too."

"Oh, him."

Her tone aroused in him a surge of allegiance to the kid. "Truth is, he could be a big help to me."

"Then why don't you use him? He's a nice young man. Maybe has talent too." She ran a hand through her short red hair and smiled.

"Maybe I will," he said.

After a while Callahan looked up and saw Pietro bowing to Ivan Bruce, who had entered the lunchroom leaning on his ivory-tipped cane. The city editor's thatch of hair was disheveled and his white cuffs were smudged with ink. His eyes scanned the crowded room until they caught sight of Callahan. He waved and hobbled toward the booth.

Clare picked up her check from the table, adjusted the strap of her handbag over her shoulder and got up. Stubbing out her cigarette she said, "I'd better shimmy along. I'm sure you two have important matters to discuss in private."

Callahan didn't protest. He touched the brim of his hat. As she made her way across the room he watched her turn sideways in the crowded aisle and brush Ivan Bruce with her body. He saw her mouth move in what was probably a perfunctory greeting or apology. He also noted that her eyelashes had not fluttered coquettishly at the physical contact, that she had looked him square in the eye.

Bruce sat down and ordered a sandwich and a glass of milk. He rubbed his hands together and glanced at the door Clare had just used to exit. "She's some dish and an

A-one reporter, that kid," he said, "but I still don't think ladies should smoke."

Callahan smiled at his Edwardian attitude. Clare could bribe bootleggers, strong-arm little old ladies, lie to old bishops, browbeat aldermen, connive with ward heelers and do God knew what else to get a story, but she shouldn't smoke cigarettes.

"You look like you could use a good stiff drink," Callahan said. But he knew that Bruce was a moderate drinker (for a newspaperman) and rarely had more than a snort or two during working hours. The story made the rounds that he was promoted to city editor by a Hearst executive because he had been at that moment the only sober person in the local room.

Bruce shook his head, waiting for Callahan's report.

"Our suspicions of Madigan were right, of course," Callahan began. He held his nose to emphasize the point.

Bruce appeared unimpressed. "I'm listening," he said impatiently, on his guard for a snow job.

Callahan continued. "Naturally we expect a crime reporter to cozy up to his sources, whether they're cops or robbers. Sometimes it's hard to tell the difference. But you know all that."

"I do."

"Sure. Just because a crime reporter's buddy-buddy with a thug doesn't mean he's on the take. Hey, Jakie Smith of the *Herald-Examiner* would interview Scarface after every rubout."

"But guys like Jakie don't wear emerald stickpins. And they don't get iced."

"Right. My point exactly."

"Cut the history lesson, Cal, and get down to brass tacks."

"Hey, you asked me to work this story. Let me give my report my way."

"Okay. But not so much throat-clearing, please."

Cal laced his stubby fingers together over the table and continued. "Look, Madigan had been filing stories for years exposing the Judge's activities and they never laid a glove on him? Why not? Well, because the publicity didn't hurt business one lick. On the contrary, it probably helped. It didn't stop the flow of beer or booze. No, sir. It just satisfied the public's appetite for gory details about how the underworld operated. Jimmy the Judge must have understood that Madigan was only doing his job. Killing him would be a real bonehead move. It would upset the protection apple cart. It would raise a public outcry and force the hand of police and politicians on Fitzgerald's payroll. It would squander millions of bucks in grease money. No, Madigan was doing a service . . . he had to be in the Judge's pocket. . . ."

Bruce balled his hand into a fist. "Speculations are cheap. I want something hard for my money."

"As the john said in the joyhouse—"

"I'm going to count to ten."

"Keep your shirt on. Look, I pulled some strings and they let me examine the probate records on Madigan's inheritance."

"And?"

"Well, his old man left him a measly six hundred and twelve bucks. How do you like that?"

Bruce sat back in the booth. "That's as much as he dropped in one day at the track. . . . Okay, what else?"

"I found out that Madigan's wife holds the deed to a summer house in Far Rockaway. Now how could they afford that?"

"Maybe she has family money."

"Are you kidding? She came straight out of the potato field."

Bruce leaned forward. "So far you've given me nothing but b-copy."

"Will you sign another expense sheet?"

"Sure. Just tell me *who* killed him and *why.*"

"You want egg in your beer, don't you? Well, I'm not sure yet. But I've got a name for you: Gaetano Pellegrino."

Bruce's mustache twitched.

"You've heard of him, eh?"

"Yeah. A hood who's been making a name for himself in the South Village. A real rising star."

"Public Enemy number five or six, I'd say."

"Yeah? That big already?"

"Possibly."

"Can we nail him?"

"I need some help." Clare Parker's thoughts about Dante had prodded Callahan toward an idea. "I could use a guinea sidekick. Somebody with brains and connections."

"Who?"

"Dante Viola."

Bruce hiked eyebrows. "Come on, Cal. The kid has no experience."

"But he's smart and eager and he can read their mentality like a book. We need an Ariosto to keep tab on the Borgias."

"Can we trust him?"

"He may be green but he's dead honest."

"Okay, I'll put Pomerantz on obits for a while."

"Thanks, Ivan. Let me break the news to him, okay?"

"Sure, play Santa Claus."

Callahan reached into his coat pocket and pulled out a slip of paper that he shoved across the table. Then he took out a fountain pen and handed it to Bruce. "Mind putting your illegible scrawl on this?"

Bruce grumped but signed the expense sheet.

Callahan was already on his fourth highball at Baker's when the regulars from the day shift trooped in, a group that included Dante, Clare, Cyriax and a court reporter named Henry Dalton. They joined Callahan at the mahogany bar. "You kids are sure starting early," Callahan observed.

"Look who's talking," said Cyriax.

Clare Parker shivered. "We came over to get warm. They still haven't repaired the furnace over there."

"Hey," said Dante, "why don't we stage a wildcat strike?"

"Looks like you already have," said Callahan.

"What's your excuse?" drawled Dalton, a round man with slitty eyes.

"I'm on special assignment."

"What's so special about getting tanked?"

"My good man," said Callahan, "I'm merely oiling the engine of my journalistic genius."

"Oh, bite my ass," said Dalton, fishing a sparkler from his bag of bon mots.

While the bantering continued, Callahan pulled Dante aside for a private chat. "Say hello to your Irish benefactor," he said.

"Come again?" said Dante.

"I got yuh pulled off the obit desk to work on the Madigan case with me." He blew on his fingernails and rubbed them on his breast pocket.

"You fat slug, I could kiss you."

"You do and I'll flatten yuh."

"Thanks," said Dante. "You won't be sorry."

Callahan grunted. "You'll earn your keep."

They rejoined the group at the bar, swapping blue-ribbon leads. Clare Parker said, "What about the sportswriter who was pulled off his regular beat to cover a high school band concert? The lead was, 'The high school band played Beethoven last night. Beethoven lost.' "

Polite laughs from most everyone but Callahan. He kept glancing at Dante and hearing vague music in his head—the unwritten symphony of Dante . . . of John Joseph Callahan.

Chapter

6

LOWLIFES DRINKING
HIGHBALLS
IN A HOTSIE–TOTSIE

CALLAHAN and Dante launched their partnership with an epic night on the town. Hailing cabs and shuffling membership cards, they hit clip joints and speaks in New York from Brighton Beach to the Grand Concourse. Clare Parker, who was off from work the next day, tagged along. This pleased Dante but annoyed Cal.

"Where to next?" asked Dante after all three had tumbled into the back seat of a cab in the Bronx.

Clare, sitting between the men, said, "Paul Whiteman's playing at the *Palais D'or.*"

"Nix," said Callahan. "I make it a policy not to poison my liver in establishments whose name I can't spell. Besides, we got work to do."

Dante consulted his wristwatch. "At one forty-five A.M.?" he said.

Callahan, ignoring the protest, leaned forward and asked the cabbie, "You familiar with a hotsie-totsie on the West Side called the Pot Still?"

The driver swiveled his face to the questioner. "Now is the Divil a scoundrel?"

Callahan nodded. "Take us there."

The cabbie touched the brim of his cap and gunned the motor.

"What's the big idea?" asked Dante.

Callahan slumped in the seat and watched through the cab window the backward flight of green awnings over the entrances of new luxury apartment buildings. "I have a good reason."

Clare fished in her handbag and took out a small gold case. "Anybody want to smoke some hokus?"

"Hotcha-cha," said Callahan. But he waved the offer away. "Don't waste that stuff on me."

"No thanks," said Dante.

She extracted the reefer from the case. Dante quickly lit it for her.

They crossed the bridge to Manhattan. Callahan had lit up a cigar and the cabbie was puffing on a cigarette. The interior of the vehicle reeked with the fumes of different burning vegetables.

In the dark Clare's hand roamed over Callahan's thigh. He pushed it away. Dante, who tonight had drunk more alcohol than he was used to, dozed against the window.

As they entered the Pot Still an insouciant sax was playing the opening verse of "The Darktown Strutter's Ball." Male eyes followed Clare's hips snaking to the music as the trio made their way to a table on a platform overlooking the dance floor. The decor was cubist, chairs and tables of plastic laminate and tubular steel. Whores of every shape, size and color worked the room. The clientele consisted mainly of well-heeled lowlifes from the surrounding neighborhood, Hell's Kitchen, where Callahan and the late Homer "Scoop" Madigan were born and raised. Here and there stood a pomaded gigolo in a dinner jacket, smoking a cigarette and casing the room. Toward the rear two goons in monkey suits stood guard at the door that led to the gaming room. On the bandstand the black face of the saxophonist was spotlighted, sequined with sweat.

Clare's now hopped-up eyes scanned the surroundings. "Nice joint," she said to Callahan. "You come here often?"

"Once in a while."

A flower girl in black net stockings approached Dante. "Buy a flower for the lady?"

Dante started to reach into his pocket but Callahan handcuffed his wrist. "Save your dough. She'll clip you two bills for a paper gardenia."

They ordered whiskey, two pints of White Rock and a pitcher of water. The tab came to a stiff ten bucks.

"I got this one," said Clare, ever the sport, rooting in her bag. Dante started to protest and Callahan again restrained him. They drank for a while. When the band struck up "Can't Help Lovin' Dat Man," Dante and Clare got up to dance.

Callahan scouted the room and spotted the two men at a round table behind a droopy palm tree. Both were knocking it back pretty good and balancing cuties on their knees. He continued to sip the Irish with a meditative air.

Dante and Clare came back to the table just as Callahan was chasing away another girl peddling rag dolls at six bucks apiece. Clare leaned back in the chair, crossed her legs and ran both hands through the sides of her short hair. "You're a swell dancer," she told Dante.

"He's a wop, ain't he?" remarked Callahan.

Clare, accustomed to his delicate air, looked around the room. "Who are all these people? Gangsters?"

"Depends on your definition. You put magistrates, police brass and trial lawyers in that category, then the answer is yes."

She bought a half-pack of Camels from a cigarette girl and offered them around the table.

"I do believe the choirboy is getting stewed," said Callahan.

"Bet your ass," said Dante.

Callahan nudged Clare. "See that guy over there, the one with the busy eyebrows and the snow-white hair?"

She nodded.

"He's a deputy police commissioner. His name's Roland O'Hara."

Clare took a longer look at the subject. He wore a dark

blue suit and a bow tie, and was sitting and chatting with another man.

"He boozes here openly?"

"He owns a piece of the action."

"Who's the guy with him?" Dante asked.

"A supervisor at the Department of Health. Works in the Bureau of Venereal Disease Control." Callahan let that one speak for itself.

"He must be a busy little beaver," Clare said.

Callahan was peering at O'Hara across the room. The commissioner, he thought, was probably wearing a religious medal under his white rayon shirt. Of O'Hara's companion Callahan remarked, "His job is to make sure that the girls who work here get their regular medical treatments. In return O'Hara keeps him supplied with his preferred flavor of sugar candy."

"Which is?" asked Clare.

"Oriental boys and opium pipes."

Dante grimaced. Still protective, he apparently felt that the topic was too off-color for Clare's dainty pink ears. Of course this was ridiculous, but Dante had a wide streak of Sicilian Puritanism.

Clare stirred her drink. "How do you know all this, Cal?"

"Hey, you're not the only ace reporter in the room. Besides, I grew up with a lot of these lowlifes. As altar boys we used to take nips of sacramental wine together."

Clare smiled thinly, picturing Callahan in soutane and surplice guzzling sweet wine in the sacristy. She finished her drink and excused herself to go to the powder room.

Dante watched her leave, then turned to Callahan. "It's great to be working on this story with you, Cal. Any special . . . advice?"

"Yeah, beware of dangling participles."

"I'm serious."

"Okay, kiddo. Take it easy. Just keep asking your goombah friends about Pellegrino. Find out what he's been up to and what connection he might have had with Madigan. I got a hunch Scoop must have put a monkey wrench in some of his plans."

A working girl approached the table, a buxom tart with a flower in her hair. "Want some company, boys?" she asked, hand planted on her right hip. She had frizzy red hair and brown eyes and smelled of rose oil.

Callahan shooed her away and looked at his bleary-eyed companion. "Tempted?"

Dante shook his head.

Clare came back. The musicians were playing a ballad and she looked over at Callahan. "Dance with me, Cal?"

"Kid, I dance like a one-legged gorilla."

"S'matter," said Dante, his speech now noticeably slurred, "didn't they give you lessons in the seminary?"

"Seminary?" said Clare.

"Didn't you know?" said Dante. "John Joe Callahan hisself once 'spired to holy orders."

She looked genuinely surprised. "No kidding? What changed your mind?"

Callahan swigged whiskey. "Got struck by lightning one day on the road to Damascus, a little town just outside of Binghamton." He frowned at the dregs. "Can we change the subject?"

"My, my," said Clare, "so you weren't always the big bad cynic."

"Can it," said Callahan, getting up and tugging the edge of his coat. He looked across the room at the two men behind the potted palm entertaining the two painted ladies. "You two amuse each other. I've got a little business to attend to."

"Saving souls?" Clare asked.

"Nah. Saving asses."

"Whose?"

"Mine, for one. Excuse me," and he walked off, thinking of another ass he'd have liked to save for a cold lonely night. Walking across the room Callahan puzzled, as he had more than once, over Clare, and the way she was eroding his defenses. Why was it that sometimes possession of a certain woman's body seemed like such a small thing and then suddenly it loomed as a thing of near-obsessive importance? He felt an odd and irritating chill of loneliness.

Basil Bianco had one paw wrapped around a highball glass and the other holding the waist of a whore who sat in his lap, a brown-skinned girl with a voluptuous body. His drinking partner, Footsie O'Keefe, breathed into the ear of another girl, a skinny blonde stifling a yawn with her whitened knuckles. O'Keefe looked up at Callahan's approach.

"I'll be a son of a gun," O'Keefe said.

"Nah," said Callahan, "you're a son of a nun. And a priest, you mick bastard you."

"Them's bad words," said O'Keefe.

Bianco's bloodshot eyes managed only a wary look. He had the humorlessness of his profession. "Who's this joker?" he asked.

"An old pal from the neighborhood," said O'Keefe in the snuffling voice of an ex-pug. "He's a newspaper guy now. Right, Cal?"

Bianco perked up. Thugs like him were parched for publicity, starved for glory. "What rag does he write for?"

O'Keefe said, "The *Courier,* ain't it?"

"Since when did you learn to read?" said Callahan, filling an empty chair. He surveyed Bianco from hair-oiled head to gaitered foot. "Basil Bianco, right?"

"What's it to yuh?"

Callahan wagged his head at the two prostitutes. "Get rid of them so we can talk."

"Well, I like that!" said the blonde.

Footsie nudged her off his lap and patted her rear. "Okay, Daisy, take a hike. See you later."

Both girls left with dark looks and hip-hops of indignation.

Bianco drummed the table top. He'd keep his mouth shut and leave the blarney to the bog trotters. A heat packer had his own specialty.

"So, Callahan," said Footsie, "what's the scoop du jour?"

He smiled at his cleverness. He was waiting for Callahan to put his cards on the table. He got his nickname from the fancy footwork he once displayed in the ring.

"It's been a while," said Callahan.

"Yeah."

"I saw you get flattened by Blumenthal," Callahan reminisced with a smile.

Footsie rubbed his jaw. "I still feel that punch," he admitted.

"But I heard you wound up on your feet."

"You heard right. Wanna drink?"

Callahan considered, then shook his head.

"Okay," said Footsie. "What *do* you want?"

"A small favor."

"Why should I do you a favor?"

"For old time's sake."

Footsie looked grim. "Remember when you snitched on me to Father Trefethen?"

"Don't tell me you're holding a grudge about that."

"Hey, all's I was doing was copping a feel from a neighborhood pig. You had no call to rat on me."

Callahan winced at the mixed mammals. "I was a misguided youth trying to wave your ass from the fires of hell. Believe me, I didn't know any better."

"My ass still smarts from that paddle."

Callahan, remembering: "That priest was a tough cookie, wasn't he?"

"He was a gingersnap," said the ex-boxer. "So how's your bigshot brother doing?"

Callahan didn't like being reminded of Nick Callahan, his older brother, who sparked both disapproval and envy.

"I don't know, we don't talk much."

"You want a favor? I hear he's pretty good at giving out favors."

"I wouldn't know." He was lying. He knew what kind of favors Footsie meant, talking about his brother, the New York state senator, also the political influence peddler. The euphemism for it was patronage. Callahan's stony silence conveyed that he wanted to drop the subject.

Footsie picked up a whiskey bottle from the table and poured himself another drink. "Ah, Irish punch, makes me punch-drunk." He smiled at his wit. "All right, Callahan, get to the point. What's the beef?"

"No beef. I just wanna see the Judge. Could you set up a meet for me?"

Bianco now couldn't resist butting in. "Why would a man like Jimmy come to a sitdown with a tinhorn liar like you?"

Callahan cupped his ear. "Did I hear right? I never knew warthogs could talk."

"It's still a good question," said Footsie.

"A good question for a dumb guinea—"

Bianco lunged for Callahan, but the musclebound O'-Keefe manacled the gunsel's wrist and planted him back in the chair. "It's *still* a good question."

"Just tell him I want to discuss the late Scoop Madigan."

"As a newspaper reporter or as a guy from the old neighborhood?" Footsie asked.

"The Judge can set the ground rules. I'll go along."

"Okay," Footsie said, "I'll ask the Judge for you." A smile worked at his battered face. "But I want something back."

Callahan hesitated. "Sure," he said uneasily.

"Lemme punch yuh," said Footsie.

"You're kidding, of course."

"No, I ain't." Footsie spat on his own palm and punched it playfully.

Callahan's voice went up a register. "What the hell for?"

"For old time's sake," said Footsie, mimicking Callahan's earlier remark.

"Jesus, Footsie, those mitts are lethal weapons."

"Yeah," said Footsie, looking at his own right fist in admiration. "What's the matter? You chicken?"

"Damn right."

"Come on, just once."

Bianco sat back and smiled.

"It'll square us for the time you squealed on me."

"That's water long under the bridge," said Callahan hopefully.

"For you. Not for me."

Callahan looked around. He seriously considered the matter: it would be good to have Footsie solidly in his corner. A love tap might make bygones bygones and cement the relationship. "You wouldn't sock me with all your might, would you?"

"Nah. I don't want no homicide rap."

"Hit him where he's useless," suggested Bianco. "Like in the balls or the brain."

Callahan had to give him that one. "Okay, where?"

Footsie stroked his jaw. "In the shoulder. I'm a generous guy."

"Okay, pal, but go easy . . ."

"You bet."

Callahan steeled himself. Footsie spat on his knuckles and measured the distance across the table.

Callahan knew he was prolonging it to make his victim squirm. "Let's get it over with—"

And next he knew, Callahan felt his right knee graze the floor. The blow had come with bullwhip speed, knocking him halfway out of the chair. Heads had turned in their direction and the room buzzed. The front-door bouncer had looked up at the commotion, then resumed his insouciance after seeing that Footsie was involved.

Callahan climbed back into the chair, the punch still burning. "You still got speed, Footsie. We square?"

"I guess. Now I'd like to get my mitts on that curate Trefethen. Say, whatever happened to him?"

Callahan shrugged, touching his shoulder gingerly.

"I heard rumors about him," Footsie said.

"What kind of rumors?"

"You know. That Father Curley had to fire him because they caught him trying to do it to the altar boys."

Callahan had nothing to say about this. It was not a subject he wanted to dwell on.

Bianco roused himself. "How's your asshole, Mr. Callahan?"

Callahan got up from the chair. "Sweeter than your mouth," Mr. Bianco said as he turned and walked off, half-expecting a fist in his back.

Callahan looked pale when he rejoined Dante and Clare.

"What was *that* all about?" Clare asked, wide-eyed.

"Nothing," said Callahan, sitting down and taking two quick gulps of whiskey. "I had to do a little penance, that's all." He started to have misgivings about this reporting job. He had thought his days of doing penance were long over.

Said Dante, "Couldn't you just say a rosary or something?"

"Not this time, kid."

"Who were those guys, anyhow?" asked Dante.

"An old friend and a new enemy."

"The friend's the guy who hit you, right?" said Clare.

"Right."

"Wasn't that Footsie O'Keefe?" she added.

"The heavyweight?" said Dante.

"Heavyweight?" Clare said. "I thought he worked as a strikebreaker for Jimmy the Judge Fitzgerald."

"You're both right," said Callahan.

"A rough customer. What did he slug you for?" Clare asked.

"For old time's sake."

Clare and Dante exchanged puzzled looks.

Callahan finished the drink and announced, "Okay, I got what I came for. Let's skiddoo."

Chapter

7

PAWNSHOP FOR SOULS

CALLAHAN went home that night with a bad case of the blues that lasted two days, ignoring the sporadic raps on the door of his landlady, probably bearing phone messages. He tried not to think or dream, to keep his mind a blank, but as usual this was impossible. Whenever he dozed off his dreams were haunted.

He saw (did one actually *see* in dreams?) the ghost of Father Trefethen and the face of his brother Nick as a youth. He saw the face of the German soldier wearing the bewildered half-smile of someone on the brink of eternity. He tossed and turned and snored and snuffled in this troubled sleep.

He awoke to the sound of the cold-water tap dripping.

He looked around the sparsely furnished room lacking anything of value or beauty. He looked at a rectangular wooden table, sink, icebox, one-burner gas plate, maple dresser with five drawers and a floor lamp with a tasseled shade. The walls, painted in yellowing white, were empty except for a Sears Roebuck calendar tacked over the dresser. His coat and hat hung from nails driven straight into the wall; wooden shelves lined the foyer. He had an odd moment of reflection over his lack of property and material possessions. Forty years old and without a piss-pot. It would be one thing if he were laden with spiritual riches, but he felt bankrupt there too. Well, at least he could admit it to himself. Was that a good sign of self-pity?

He looked again at the things in the room. He owned not one thing that would bring a nickel at a pawnshop. Maybe his soul would bring a nickel. If they had pawnshops for souls. Jesus, listen to me, would you . . .

He sat up in bed, wondering what Clare Parker would have made of these surroundings had he yielded to temptation the other night. Would they have cooled her ardor or fanned it? She was a brazen one, he thought. In the taxi after they had left the Pot Still Dante fell asleep again so they dropped him off first in Greenwich Village. As soon as they were alone together Clare sat in his lap, took his head in her hands and planted a fine kiss on his mouth. Ignoring a blossoming boner, he gently pushed her off.

"Forget it, kid," he had managed, fumbling with his necktie.

Her face showed a flicker of anger, then irony. "Your loyalty is quite touching if irrelevant."

"That's not it—"

"Oh? You wanted me, Cal. I felt the evidence."

"Old Lazarus has a mind of his own."

She smiled as the taxi sped up Sixth Avenue. "You call your pecker Lazarus? Why?" But she knew the answer.

"Because it takes a miracle to raise him from the dead."

"Thanks for the compliment."

She was composed, her ego strong enough to take rejection, another advantage of the well-born, he decided.

In his bed now as the light of dawn brightened the yellowed windowshade, Callahan's shoulder still felt sore. He debated with himself over whether to try again to sleep peacefully or to give up and brew coffee. He felt some guilt over his lack of further progress in the Madigan assignment. Or was it worry that the fountain of expenses might dry up? Both. He decided to get up.

As Callahan brewed coffee strong in a drip-style pot the way his mother had taught him, his thoughts turned to the

less-than-sainted mother who bore him, his brother and
two sisters. Kay Callahan defied the stereotype of Irish–
American myth, the dry scrubwoman with ample bosom
and heart to match who took communion every morning
with a blush and her husband every night with a face of
granite. No, Kay Callahan had been wiry, bookish and ag-
nostic. And then some. She worked as a stenographer and
bookkeeper for the neighborhood dry goods merchant
while her husband was employed (in fits and starts) as a
day laborer. The kids spent a lot of time with relatives who
lived nearby, with the old man whenever he was out of
work, in the parish house on Thirty-ninth Street and on the
asphalt and concrete of Hell's Kitchen where the boys
pitched pennies and swam in the Hudson River while the
girls played hopscotch and skipped rope. Among other less
wholesome activities. It was not the age of innocence de-
picted in turn-of-the-century lithographs. It was a slum,
pure and simple. All slums bred suffering, sin and disillusion, especially the West Side of Manhattan. There the
tenements reared up among the cattle pens and slaughter-
houses spawned by the Hudson River Railroad. The Devil
cooked up some pretty foul recipes in this scullery where
children plashed in lagoons of blood flowing from the
stockyards into the gutters; where they drank alcoholic
milk from cows nourished on brewery waste. And where
the air was filled with the foul emissions of rendering
plants, lime kilns, distilleries and stables. No brimstone
could smell as rank as the oxygen inhaled by little Johnny
Callahan and the other kids of the neighborhood.

No wonder he sought refuge in the parish church, so cool
in the summer's heat.

There he at least smelled incense instead of tallow from
butchered flesh, heard Gregorian music instead of
screams in the night. Most of the other boys, including his
brother Nick, ran in street gangs with boy scout names like
the Squirrels or Wolverines. The gangs raided the boxcars
of the New York Central Railroad and fought pitched bat-
tles with the Pinkertons hired by the railway company to
guard the freight. Somehow, Callahan reflected, Nick

managed to survive the billy clubs and even sidestep the other pitfalls of his life in the shadow of the Ninth Avenue El. With financial help from his mother's employer, Nick managed to get through Fordham Law School while Callahan jousted with his conscience at Cathedral College Seminary. This facility of Nick to swivel-hip his way from larceny to law must have accounted for his ultimate success in politics, Callahan thought, tasting iron.

Old Man Baecher, his mother's boss, Callahan recalled, had been a Catholic too, a Bavarian. Even now his mind rebelled at thinking what he was thinking, but it always seemed to float to the top of his memory. The elder Callahan took a powder after the Spanish–American War and the girl who married dear old dad had to be giving some flavor of incentive to the dry goods merchant for him to take such a personal interest in the raggedy Callahan brood. The fat Dutchman was no philanthropist. Callahan often found himself wondering how chummy Baecher might have gotten with his sisters, Kat and Josie. But he drew a shroud over such notions.

Callahan poured the coffee. It was time to face his ragtime life. To cure his hangover with coffee and bullshots. To compose a lead paragraph to the day. To avoid the spike. To survive.

He had decided to go to the office and work the phones after he headed over to the Hotel Seville for a hot breakfast of corned beef hash with a fried egg on top. He counted the money on the dresser: nine dollars and fifty-two cents. As he sat down on the bed to tie his shoes a knock came at the door.

He froze in the act of looping the lace. Two loan sharks and a host of bill collectors were dogging his tail. But how could he expect to make progress in his work if he holed up like a hermit?

"Yeah?"

A masculine voice: "I'd like a word with you, Callahan." He had expected his landlady.

He didn't immediately recognize the voice. It wasn't Dante or Ivan Bruce. "Who the hell is that?"

"The big bad wolf."

It was Lieutenant Arnie Mitchell, homicide squad. Callahan finished tying his shoes and went to the door.

The tall detective sauntered in and snooped around, touching objects, opening closet doors, sniffing the air.

"Make yourself at home, you nosy bastard," said Callahan, going over to the dresser and choosing a tie.

"What a dump," said Mitchell.

"Not the Ritz, I grant you."

Mitchell sat down on the bed and lit a cigarette. "You can take the mick out of the shanty but you can't take the shanty out of the mick."

Callahan, who had no mirror, tugged at the lopsided knot of his necktie. "Look, you didn't come to offer your services as an interior decorator, did you?"

"Interior decorator, exterior decorator—there's no hope for this place."

"The door works fine."

Mitchell took a folded newspaper from the pocket of his raincoat and threw it on the bed. "Brought you a present. No charge."

"It's the bulldog of today's *Bugle.*"

"Thanks, but I never read that rag on an empty stomach."

"Wait till after breakfast and I guarantee you'll upchuck."

Callahan strolled over to the bed and picked up the newspaper, glancing at the headline: BOOTLEGGERS BUNGLE BUMPOFF ATTEMPT. Showing no emotion he read the subheads: "Police Fear Outbreak of Gangland War. Probing Possible Links to Death of News Reporter."

Callahan looked at Mitchell.

"Happened last night on West Houston," the detective said.

"Did the *Courier* get scooped?"

Mitchell nodded.

"Guess I'm in hot water. Who was the bull's-eye?"

"Some hood named Junior Riccio. Ever hear of him?"

Callahan shook his head.

"A gunsel in the employ of one Gaetano Pellegrino. Pretty name for an ugly customer."

Callahan went to the window and drew up the shade, letting sunlight flood the room. A Pellegrino henchman. It fit the picture. He put on cufflinks, waiting for Mitchell to go on.

"They cornered the chump in a phone booth in a hash house. Riddled it with submachine-gun fire and left him for dead. But he fooled 'em. Hey, some of these wops have nine lives. Anyway, he survived, with more holes than my grandpa's underwear."

"Will he make it?"

"The docs say so." Mitchell smiled. "You know these spaghetti-benders. They got this code of silence. But if we can pin some rap on him he might sing. Extortion and blackmail, that's the ticket."

"Is the *Bugle* accurate?"

"About what?"

"Police 'Probing Possible Links to Death of News Reporter'?"

"I came here to ask questions, not answer them."

"Asking questions is my job too. If I still have a job."

"Let's take turns. Maybe we'll both learn something."

"I doubt it, but where do we start?"

"With Scoop Madigan. I know you're working on the story."

"Yeah, but shooting blanks so far."

"We both know he was in with the bad guys."

"Bad guys? 'Judge not lest ye be judged.' "

"Okay. The dry-law thugs."

"Who do you mean? Grover Whalen and Jimmy Walker?"

"You know who I mean, Callahan."

"You got proof?"

Mitchell got up and paced. "Not legal proof." He turned and faced Callahan. "Let's not pussyfoot around. I'm gonna level with you and I hope you do likewise. Look, I'm not here in an official capacity."

"This is a social call?"

"Off the record?"

Callahan nodded.

"Promise me?" Mitchell insisted, his trust frayed by many years of dealing with deceitful newspapermen.

Callahan piously held up his right hand. "What's the beef?"

Mitchell looked down at his big hands. "The Volstead Act! You know, Callahan, we live in a crazy country."

"Stop the presses."

"Also corrupt. Everybody's on the take. Everybody. Goddammit, even the Statue of Liberty's got her hand out."

"Look again," said Callahan, who had a reporter's eye for detail. "She's carrying a torch and a book."

"I'll bet the book's a grease sheet. I tell you, everybody's corrupt."

"Except you, right, Arnie?"

"So far," he said.

"You been tempted?"

"Who hasn't?" The cop noted the bottle of hootch on the bedside table. "You're under arrest," he said.

"Want a snort?"

Mitchell nodded.

Callahan poured a dollop into a handy tumbler and gave it to Mitchell, who held the amber liquid up to the slanting sunlight. "There it is, Cal, the root of all our trouble. For each drink we take somewhere a soul is lost. Bottoms up." He drained the glass. "Maybe I'm the one who's crazy."

"You're not crazy," said Callahan, envying the detective's ability to wrestle with his conscience. Callahan wondered if he hadn't already left the arena.

"You know," continued Mitchell, "I used to be proud to represent the *law*. Proud, no other word for it. But now? Now we have a goddamn law called Prohibition that everybody thumbs his nose at and that makes us the laughingstock of the whole world. Like somebody said, the law is an ass, an idiot." He held out the glass for a refill. "What does that make me?"

Callahan poured. He had been impressed by Mitchell's speech. How about that . . . a cop who read Dickens.

Mitchell stared at the whiskey glass. "I've been getting pressure, Cal. Pressure from the brass downtown."

"What kind of pressure?"

"To whitewash the Madigan case."

"Where's it coming from? *Who's* it coming from?"

"I'm not sure. My guess is Roland O'Hara."

"Deputy Commish, eh?" said Callahan. "That's pretty high up but no surprise."

Mitchell's eyes blazed at Callahan. "Are they all crooks? From Walker to Hoover?"

"Most likely. At least could be."

"Well, it gets my Irish up, I tell you. I especially don't like it when they put the screws to me."

"Hey, Arnie. You've been out of kindergarten a long time."

"Okay. What can you tell me?"

Callahan told him what he knew, from the emerald stickpin to the probate records to the rumored involvement of Pellegrino in Madigan's death. Mitchell listened quietly, then abruptly said, "I'd better get back to the squad."

"I guess you've put two and two."

"Madigan worked for Jimmy the Judge. He did something to piss off Pellegrino. It may mean war between the micks and the wops."

"Could be," said Callahan.

"Riccio probably rubbed out Madigan, and yesterday's hit was the payback."

"Sounds right."

Mitchell snapped down the brim of his hat. "Thanks for not much."

"You're never satisfied," said Callahan.

"We still don't know *why* they knocked off Madigan."

"Hey, the question is, what happens next? Killing Madigan has probably got Pellegrino in dutch with the higher-ups. It was a bonehead move, impulsive, bad for business. It was probably done without a sign-off from the Sicilian patriarchs, who think they still run the show. Bumping off a reporter makes bad publicity. The pols have to do something to save face. They got to find a sacrificial lamb. I wouldn't want to be in Pellegrino's spats."

"You're right there. Killing Madigan pleases nobody."

"Especially not the Vanities and Follies ladies he was screwing."

"Then maybe the goombahs tried to hit Riccio," said Mitchell.

"Maybe." Callahan polished off a drink. "Hey, don't leave without giving me something for my editor."

Mitchell filled Callahan in. The report contained little that was new other than a few details of Madigan's finances. The deceased police reporter had over $200,000 stashed in various bank accounts; he speculated in the stock market in partnership with a person still unknown to investigators, most likely an outwardly respectable businessman, maybe even a politician.

"They operated a bucket shop on the West Side," Mitchell said. "There's a lot of profit in shady stock deal nowadays. He was also mixed up in policy, bookmaking, bootlegging, maybe even some opium traffic."

Callahan shook his head. "And he still had time to file exclusive stories, play the ponies and hump chorus girls. The flame burned brightly."

Mitchell wore a hangdog look. "And I can't even make the mortgage payments on my house in Brooklyn."

"That's because there's a Greek named Diogenes carrying a lantern in the daylight looking for you."

At this remark the gloomy look on Mitchell's furrowed face seemed to deepen. He said nothing. How could he?

"Well," said Callahan, "what are you going to do now? About the pressure from downtown?"

Mitchell hunched his shoulders. "I'll probably cave in."

The reporter had finished dressing, and standing near the window, squared the fedora on his head.

"What are *you* going to do?" asked Mitchell.

Callahan considered the question. He was already an unsuccessful idealist. He wondered if he had any chance of becoming a successful louse.

"I'm going to have hash and eggs for breakfast," replied Callahan.

Chapter

8

AVOID CLICHES LIKE THE PLAGUE

AFTER breakfast Callahan treated himself to a haircut and shave at the hotel barbershop. Expecting a tongue-lashing from Ivan Bruce, he procrastinated and pampered himself like a condemned man. He decided to get a manicure too, mostly so he could peer down Ginny's cleavage as she buffed his nails.

Thus distracted, he thought about the conversation with Mitchell. He felt sorry for the homicide dick floating, as the soutaned jebbies would say, between Scylla and Charybdis. Oh, it was tough to be an honest cop in this town nowadays. Callahan wondered if things might have been different had Al Smith beaten Hoover. Probably not. Just another champion of repeal, sure, but one who owed a debt to the Tammany Tiger and all that that implied. He figured Mitchell would bow to the inevitable and Diogenes would keep swinging that lantern around.

Callahan rehearsed what he would say to Bruce. He would propose scoring a beat on the competition by running a double-truck thumbsucker on Madigan's links to the underworld. Make a clean breast and head 'em off at the pass. This strategy would minimize the embarrassment, cut the losses the paper was bound to suffer when the real story of Scoop's death inevitably got out. If he combined the results of his own legwork with the stuff Mitchell had just given him off the record he would have enough facts and details to write the story in an authoritative way. Then they could claim publishing the truth without fear or favor. Besides, it was the right thing to do, and this consideration still carried weight with the ex-seminarian despite his denials. The question was, how much weight? He stared at the valley between Ginny's breasts, surrendered himself to Michelangelo the barber's soft hands.

Suddenly he felt pain.

"Ouch." His hand went to his cheek, where blood flowed.

"Oh, *Dio mio,* Mr. Callahan," said Michelangelo, "I beg your forgiveness."

Callahan stanched the blood with his fingertips. It was pretty clear to him that the barber's eyes also had been on the manicurist's bosoms.

"Forget it, Mike. We're all human." Including Bruce.

He took the subway to work, getting off at Park Row.

"How come you're looking so chipper, Mr. Callahan?" asked Ham Terry.

"How the hell do you know how I look?"

"You denying it?"

"No, but how do you see without headlamps?"

"The Lord atones for sending affliction, sir. He gave me antennae like an insect." Ham's wayward pupils went up and down for emphasis.

"I don't see any bug's ears on you."

"They're there all the same," said Ham. "Everybody's blind to something."

"*That's* the God's honest truth." Callahan grabbed a newspaper and dug deep into his pants pocket. "I owe you a nickel for this newspaper."

"But you get the *Courier* for nothing," Ham said, looking puzzled.

"This is a copy of the *Bugle,*" Callahan said, relieved that

Ham didn't know everything. "I get that free too. But, say, I'm a big spender."

The newsie looked troubled. "You pay five cents," Ham said, "some pay blood for that paper."

"What do you mean?"

"The goon squads. You know, they don't let me carry too many *Bugle*s. They put the muscle on me. What can I do? I'm just trying to make a living."

"Goon squads?"

"I thought you knew about them muscle boys. They ride with the *Courier* trucks. Ride shotgun, I hear tell. Some even heft Thompsons."

Callahan felt embarrassed. He supposed he would have known about this if he hadn't been exiled to the obit desk. Still, he blamed himself, a so-called news reporter imitating an ostrich. Ham had put it right . . . everybody's blind to something.

"Who provides the muscle?"

Ham removed his soft cap and worried it in hands textured like tree bark. "They say the Judge do, Mr. Callahan. You heard of him?"

"You bet I have."

"You remember the newsboy and delivery-man strike threatened couple years ago? They say the Judge, he fixed that up for your Major Curtin too. It seems those two have a regular understanding." Wind blew in off the East River, ruffling pages in the newspaper stacks. "Rain on the way," Ham predicted. "Of course the other boys ain't got clean hands neither. I hear tell they jump on trolleys to snatch *Courier*s right outta the readers' hands. Bold as brass."

Callahan wondered if the poisoned hootch had not robbed Ham of his sanity as well as his sight. He knew that the circulation war was no school picnic, but it was hard to believe that the publishers, even his publisher, would hire mobsters to do their dirty work. Or was it? He gave Ham five cents and went to the office.

He appeared before Ivan Bruce with a small adhesive strip covering the wound the barber had inflicted. It might prompt sympathy. To Callahan's surprise the boss seemed only mildly annoyed at his delinquency, as if he were dealing with an incorrigible schoolboy rather than a forty-year-old rumpot with a breezy writing style and tarnished concepts of truth and objectivity. Callahan noticed a copy of the first edition of the *Bugle* on the desk near Bruce's collection of pipes, but the editor was not waving it around like a red flag as Callahan had expected. Callahan took the opportunity to propose printing the long backgrounder on Madigan's double life.

Bruce fondled his walrus mustache. "Okay, Cal, we'll give it a go. But first we have to get the approval of upstairs."

Callahan sucked on a stogie, picturing Major Carlos Curtin, publisher and owner of the *Courier,* a man he considered not only despotic but a bit of a crackerbox. Still, he believed Curtin was smart enough to grasp the wisdom of the strategy once he had the facts. He doubted that playing pattycake with the Judge would cloud his judgment as a newsman.

"Think he'll go along?" he asked Bruce.

"I learned a long time ago never to predict his reaction to anything."

"I believe he has no choice," Callahan said, and glanced around the city room. With time before the next edition had to go to press, the elves in the green eyeshades were fairly relaxed. Lorenzo Casey sat at the copyboy station, frowning because he was stuck with the menial job of "making books," folding copy paper with carbons for the rewritemen. Printers in denim clothes and paper hats loafed around reading Tijuana bibles or playing gin rummy. Circulation boss Stinky Roth, battered straw boater sitting at a rakish angle, was standing by the water cooler scrutinizing a tout sheet with Murray Rockwell, sports reporter. Roth might be fat and sloppy, Callahan reflected, but he was a force to be reckoned with. He showed much deviousness and ingenuity inventing strategies in the circulation war with the *Bugle.* One ploy was legendary—a few months ago he had sent a copyboy who used to work for the *Bugle* to the rival paper's composing room with a bogus story about a streetcar-conductor's strike. The story was handed directly to the copy cutter and passed on routinely to the linotypist. Thirty thousand copies rolled off the presses and reached the street before the prank was discovered. Two *Bugle* execs were fired. Callahan admired Roth's creative flair.

Bruce's voice broke into his thoughts. "Meanwhile, Cal, you're going to sweat for your paycheck."

"What?"

"While we're waiting for the Major to okay the story I'm putting you on general assignment. You're to report to me every morning for a story."

Callahan's cheeks burned.

"Okay," he said. "I'll phone you up every day."

"You mean from Mother Superior's, the speak or the track, right? No, you report to this desk by nine A.M. In the flesh. I want to make certain I can smell your breath without keeling over. I want you fit for duty."

"You spent too much time with the Rough Riders."

"Can it." Bruce opened the desk drawer containing day-book clippings and assignment memorandums. He riffled through them, pulling one out. "You can start with this," he said, passing the memo across the desk.

Callahan scanned the assignment. A tearjerker about an immigrant girl from Limerick who, sailing up New York harbor on the S.S. *Hebrides,* got excited at the sight of the Statue of Liberty, waved her arms and dropped her purse with $85 and her passport into the drink, rendering her a penniless nonperson.

Callahan tossed back the memo. "Not my meat and potatoes. Give it to some sob sister."

"You'll take the assignments I give you and like them."

"It's been a long time, I forgot how to write features."

"Hey, just follow the advice I've overheard you giving Dante."

"What's that?"

"Avoid cliches like the plague."

Very funny. But he took the assignment, and many more from Bruce's grab bag over the next few days. And it came as a mild surprise to the veteran reporter that being on general assignment again and having to stay relatively sober acted as a tonic. He felt ten years younger. The routines returned like the words of the litanies of his Catholic childhood. He rediscovered the pleasures, the stimulations of earning one's pay envelope as a professional witness to the big city's small dramas. He liked how the script and the cast of characters changed from day to day; he especially liked the professional requirement of detachment from what he wrote about. Caring was somebody else's burden. A relief.

So he slogged around the city, covering a real Mulligan stew of stories. He went to the YWCA meeting in Manhattan where Governor Roosevelt's wife Eleanor commented on the new president's support of Prohibition. In his story Callahan quoted the wife of the Wet governor: "A woman of my acquaintance remarked that while she never had lived up to the Prohibition law, she almost believed Mr. Hoover could get her to do it."

Scribbling the quote in his notebook, Callahan had muttered, "I'll drink to that."

He was sent to a meeting of local Stalinists outraged that Communist expatriate Leon Trotsky had penned an exclusive story for the New York *Times* describing the underhand methods Stalin had used to seize power and boot Trotsky out of the Soviet Union as an exile in Constantinople.

"Trotsky is hooked up with capitalism," screamed a local leader of the Worker's Party.

Callahan yawned as he put the absurd quote in his lead paragraph.

He reported on the hung jury in the Manhattan slander trial of Sir Joseph Duveen, first Baron Duveen of Millbank, English art dealer accused by a New York dowager of falsely branding her heirloom Leonardo a bad copy.

"The right eye is dead," the haughty British connoisseur had said of the portrait of *The Blacksmith's Daughter.*

Meanwhile Callahan's attention was riveted by the flesh-and-blood face and shapely legs of the court stenographer, a bona fide work of art if he ever saw one.

He wrote brisk, colorful copy and never missed a deadline. He tried to avoid cliches like the plague and reminded himself that prepositions were parts of speech he should never end a sentence with.

More than two weeks passed without word from Major Curtin on the Madigan double-life story. Callahan was getting suspicious. One morning he asked Bruce about the publisher's foot-dragging.

"You know the Major. He won't be rushed. Besides, I believe he's been having domestic troubles lately."

Yeah, Callahan thought. Like convincing his daughter Lily to stop treating her pussy like lunch meat at the Piggly Wiggly. Callahan knew first-hand about Lily Curtin.

"Don't blame me if we miss the boat," Callahan said, washing his hands of the matter. His patron saint of the moment was Pontius Pilate.

Bruce peered at Callahan. "You've been working pretty hard lately," he said. "Take a day off. Get laid and get loaded."

"You got the order reversed. But you don't have to ask me twice." Callahan wondered about the generosity, but you didn't look a gift horse in . . .

He was out the front door in a shot.

Mother Superior had a liberal policy toward the girls who behaved themselves, so it wasn't hard for Callahan to persuade her to give Mazie the day off. He took her to a matinee of Douglas Fairbanks in a talking picture, *The Iron Mask.* Mazie, in a ruffled spring dress and high-heeled shoes, was rhapsodic at the unexpected pleasure of having a date with her favorite john. In the darkness of the movie theater she stroked Callahan's genitals as she listened to the celluloid swashbuckler's tinny voice.

"Gee, Cal," she said, caressing, "doesn't he have a swell face and figure."

"Breathtaking."

"I adore the talkies."

"Yeah," he croaked, his throat clogging.

Mazie squeezed him with gratitude; he stifled a howl.

After the movie they hopped into a taxi. "Let's have lunch in some high-hat establishment," she suggested.

"Let's go to Baker's where I can put it on the tab," said Callahan. "I'm running a little low on funds."

"No," insisted Mazie, who felt liberated, a prisoner on parole, "let's go to the Waldorf-Astoria. *My* treat." She instructed the driver and settled into the seat. She was decked out in a straw picture hat over blonde banana curls. Her mouth was a circle of shiny rouge.

Callahan gave her a funny look as the taxi sped away from the curb. "Two questions: who's the sugar daddy and does Mother know you're skimming?"

Mazie gazed out the cab window at the sun-drenched streets and sidewalks. "Mother always *gives* us a cut. I've been saving my pennies—"

"I repeat, who's the sugar daddy?"

She turned to him. "Hey. You can't expect a girl in my line of work to be all true-blue." She flounced the banana curls.

"I'm just curious." And jealous?

She looked out the window again. "I suppose curiosity is an occupational disease with you." She stole a glance at him. "You're a little jealous," she added hopefully.

No comment.

They lunched in Peacock Alley, where Mazie consumed mountainous portions of cold chicken mousse, egg and anchovy sandwiches, fried oysters, followed by veal cutlets with mushrooms and potatoes, stuffed turnips and green salad. To top it off she had baked coconut custard and black coffee that she sipped with pinky held aloft.

Callahan, who had ordered roast beef, nursed a glass of near-beer, marvelling at the epicurean display.

"So," Mazie said when her mouth was at rest, "you still curious?"

"About what?"

"My so-called sugar daddy." She seemed pleased with herself. It was not often that whores got to play Desdemona.

Callahan did not believe he was jealous. He felt affection for Mazie, maybe one could even call it love. But it was, he thought, more the love reserved for a sister, unadulterated by possessiveness though curiously mixed with carnality. Was it unnatural lust? Maybe that increased its power.

But he was curious, and said so.

She cupped her rosy mouth to cover a smile. "He's very handsome. He reminds me of an older Charles Farrell. *Very* handsome."

"Unlike me."

"As a matter of fact he looks something like you."

"Really?"

He glanced over at the head waiter, who hovered nearby. He was a pompous fellow with gray sidewhiskers and dressed to the nines like a diplomat at an embassy ball. The patented sneer was clearly designed to make Callahan and Mazie feel about as welcome as John L. Lewis at a mine-owners convention. Well, thought Callahan, he could go hump himself. He knew that Mazie carried a wad of greenbacks big enough to choke a dromedary. Money talked to these jokers, with all their fancy airs.

"And a little older than you," Mazie added about her mystery benefactor.

"Yes?" Callahan popped a dinner mint into his mouth.

Mazie's round mouth parted slightly. A speck of crust from the baked custard clung to her lower lip. "You'd be real surprised to know who he is, Cal. Real surprised."

"Let me guess—Charlie Chaplin?"

"No, Cal."

"You enjoy torturing me, don't you," he said, clutching his heart.

"I'll tell you this much. He's a pretty big politician." She paused for melodrama. "And . . . you and he had the same mamma."

Callahan was, as they say, struck dumb. He was surprised to hear that his brother, the busy lawmaker . . . and broker . . . still had enough hours left to prong his favorite tart.

"You have lousy taste," he finally said.

She looked surprised, and wounded. They sat in silence for about two minutes, hearing the drone of other diners' voices.

"Let's clear out of this dump," he said coldly.

He dropped her off on Charlton Street in front of Mother's townhouse. She got out of the taxi and waited for him to join her. The wind ruffled the skirt of her spring dress. She gave him a black look as it dawned on her that he wasn't about to top off the occasion in the expected way.

"I got indigestion," he said.

She leaned into the window of the cab. "If there's a God in heaven, it'll be nothing less trivial than ptomaine poisoning."

"You say such sweet things."

She turned and fumed into the big brick house.

The next day, Tuesday, March 26, a rumble was heard on Wall Street. Bruce assigned Callahan to take his throbbing head a few blocks south of Park Row and cover the commotion on the stock exchange, where the word *crash* was being uttered for the first time in Herbert Hoover's reign. That day the stripe-vested guys had taken a tidy $25 million out of the market. In a deluge of selling, money opened at twelve percent, a three-point rise from the previous day, and it soon rose to twenty percent. Small-time investors turned tail. Trouble in paradise?

Callahan returned to the office and discussed possible story angles with Bruce.

"I think I'll say there's trouble ahead. The Republicans with their easy-money policies are screwing up the works. There's too much credit and installment buying. Too many amateurs and tinhorn gamblers in the market. The piper's going to call in his marker. Yeah, that's what I'll write."

"Look, don't go out on a limb," said Bruce. "After all, you don't know beans about the stock exchange."

"Then why did you assign me to the story? Hey, I know plenty about tinhorn gamblers. I'm one myself."

"You interviewed experts. What do your sources say?"

Callahan leaned back in the chair, lacing his fingers together behind his head. "Come off it, Ivan. You know it depends on who you talk to. There's the gloom-and-doom types and the rose-colored-glasses types, take your pick. I'll say one thing: there's a lot of talk about uneven distribution of good times and how farmers and unskilled workers are getting the short end. I also heard grumbling about how the Coolidge-Hoover tariff and war-debt policies are eroding foreign markets." He took the ragged cigar out of his mouth. "But I'll level with you. Most of them say we'll pull out of this thing tomorrow."

"Then why don't you write that?"

Callahan shrugged, unconvinced.

"You want to panic people?"

"I just want to write the truth."

Bruce shook his thickly thatched head. Callahan envied the older man's abundant hair. "The truth? Sure, Callahan. Now just as soon as you snatch that pretty butterfly in your net, you hand it over and we'll take a picture of it. We'll run it on page one. Meanwhile you'll cop the Nobel Prize, a chair at Princeton and a lifetime box at Minsky's."

Callahan muttered and fiddled with the keys of a typewriter.

"Truth?" Bruce was wound up. "When it walks through that door and bites you on the ass, you give me a holler, eh?" Bruce's face was ruddy as he closed his mouth and leaned back in the chair.

Callahan flexed his fingers over the keys, stared at the blank sheet of copy paper. He had no good answer to Bruce, which bothered him. To hell with it . . . fish wrapping, old news.

"So what's your stuff?" Bruce asked.

"Only my fingers can answer."

"Sounds reasonable," said the city editor before hobbling

off on his ivory-handled cane. Suddenly he turned. "Don't forget."

"What?"

"Avoid cliches like the plague."

Callahan nodded and started to type.

Chapter

9

NEVER END A SENTENCE
WITH A PROPOSITION

THE bell attached to the front door of Cervantes Rare Bird Emporium jangled as Callahan entered, greeted by the jeers, hoots and squawks of exotic birds. Don't take it personally, he told himself.

He nodded to the clerk behind the counter, an olive-skinned man who peered through dark glasses at the newcomer and returned to reading the newspaper. Callahan covered familiar territory, heading straight for a side door that opened onto a flight of stairs. As he descended, the cacophony receded, and at the landing he rapped on another door.

Now he heard the drone of not-so-rare birds—horse players. He sank into a flowered sofa, ordered a drink from a leggy waitress and looked about. The sporting crowd. High-hatters with time to kill and money to burn. They sipped cocktails and dripped with insouciance. The women wore sparklers on wrist and neck that would dazzle a flock of snow owls. The men squinted at racing forms, well-fed mystics studying cabalistic scrawls. Hoods and swells, pony-addicts all.

Callahan also studied the tout sheet. He preferred going in person to the track but frequented Cervantes' in Greenwich Village when he had time to kill during working hours. That morning Bruce had assigned him to track down a tip concerning allegations of graft in the County Clerk's office. Callahan had made a date with the stool pigeon for late afternoon. Meanwhile, he had a couple of hunches to play.

He had arrived between the second and third race at Belmont and had a little time before having to place his bet at the bird cage. There had been a morning shower so he searched for wet-track performers. At first glance he liked Red Hot Mamma in the third but her record in the slop was weak. His second choice, Eskimo Pie, was a late scratch so he settled on Cat's Pajamas, a newcomer with good breeding who had set a snazzy pace in a recent key race and, like a lot of fillies he could name, preferred it long and wet. As he licked the tip of the pencil before marking his selections he felt a tap on his back and looked up at the lopsided face of Footsie O'Keefe.

Bingo.

"How's the shoulder?"

"Better. Have a seat."

Footsie rubbed his mashed-in nose and sat down. "Want a hot tip?"

"Sure."

"Meet me in the men's room," followed by a bray of laughter.

"You're a real card, Footsie. You ought to be on the stage. I hear there's one leaving in a half hour."

"You're a card yourself, Cal. I like you."

"I'm overwhelmed." He got up from the couch. "Would you excuse me a minute while I kiss my dough goodbye?"

Footsie shrugged. "I ain't the type to get in the way of romance."

Oh, God.

When Callahan returned from placing the bets he asked where Footsie's pal Bianco was. The place was part of Jimmy the Judge's empire.

Footsie motioned toward the nearby chair, where beetle-browed Bianco was sizing up Callahan. His shirtsleeves were rolled up, and Callahan noted a tattoo on his arm of a heart etched with the words, "Sorry Mom." *Sorry, world,* would have been more appropriate, Callahan thought.

"What's a wop doing working for a Hibernian corporation?" Callahan asked, straight-faced.

"We're modern. We allow one or two in the outfit to do the dirty work. Basil's a pretty good egg when you get to know him."

"I like my eggs scrambled." Getting in the swing of things.

"Wouldn't try it if I was you. He's pretty tough. I once seen him crack a guy's coconut in the crook of his elbow." He made a cracking sound. "Just like that."

The results of the third race were announced. Callahan's horse finished out of the money. He made confetti of the betting slip and floated the bits into the ashtray.

"You're a hard-luck guy," Footsie observed.

"There are six more races."

"One thing about you—you never squawk. Not like a lot of hamburgers I know."

"Thanks, I guess."

"Scoop never squawked either. You two birds of a feather."

Callahan never thought of himself and Madigan as kindred souls. "What do you mean by that?"

"Both sportin' men from the West Side. Both news monkeys. You had a lot in common."

"Somehow I don't much like the idea."

Footsie shrugged. He had a detached philosophical nature, useful whenever he had to pulverize an opponent in the ring. His father had been a butcher. Growing up in a meat locker put callouses on your heart. "I put in a good word for you," Footsie said.

"Come again?"

"With the Judge. He says he'll give you a meet."

"When and where?"

"Friday, eight P.M. Pinky's Clam Bar in Hoboken. You can take the ferry or swim."

"I'll take the ferry." Footsie had no doubt sunk more than a few in the waters.

"We used to swim in that muck when we was kids. Remember?"

"We did a lot of dumb stupid things back then."

"Not you so much," said Footsie. "You was kind of a holy Mary."

"Hey," said Callahan in mock offense. "Holy Moses, not Mary. Anyway, the only thing holy about me was my underwear. Mostly, I was just scared."

"Of what?"

"Burning in hell, mostly."

"Don't tell me you really believed in that malarkey."

"I still do."

"So why ain't you scared no more?"

"I've been there already."

The punching-bag face looked puzzled, then lit up with understanding. "Hell's Kitchen, right?"

"I've been in all the rooms," Callahan said, waxing too philosophical for his own comfort. Come off it, Callahan . . .

After Footsie left Callahan returned to following his picks. By the time the last horse in the ninth race had crossed the finish line his mood had improved greatly. His horse paid fifty-to-one. He collected his winnings and on the way out gave a raspberry to the taunting parrots. Now at least he wouldn't have to dodge his landlady.

On the street he bought a two-cent snowball from a pushcart peddler and sucked the fruit-flavored ice with schoolboy relish. He took the streetcar down to Bowling Green, where the pigeon from the County Clerk's office had arranged to meet him in front of the statue of Abraham de Peyster, a colonial major. Standing on the spot where Peter Minuit bought Manhattan Island from the local-yokel redskins for twenty-four bucks, Callahan read the New York *Times* and waited more than an hour. The stoolie never showed. It happened.

He went uptown to the office and riffled through phone messages. Nothing from Herbert Hoover, Henry Stimson or the Aga Khan. A whiff of her spicy odor came first, then her breath in his ear.

"What kind of hair oil you use?" asked Clare.

He looked at her.

"Whale blubber."

"It's sexy," she said.

He shook his head. "What does a classy dame like you see in a chump like me?"

She hunched her slender shoulders. "Freud might say I have a father fixation. Except you're nothing like my father."

"If I were your father I'd take you over my knee."

"What a swell idea," she said.

The lady was on a single track, it seemed.

"I wanted to invite you to a soiree Saturday at the family shack in Glen Cove."

"I keep telling you to speak English."

"A party, as if you didn't know. I tried telephoning you at the number listed with the city desk but I reached some old bat with a hard case of the mumbles or some sort of speech impediment."

"My landlady. What's the occasion?"

"April Fool's Day."

"Naturally you thought of me."

"Will you come?"

"I'll think on it."

"Oh, such noblesse oblige!" She took a notebook from her handbag, scribbled something, tore the sheet from the pad and handed it to him. "If you decide to come just give this address to the hack driver. Excuse me, I have a story to cover."

Still playing tough guy: "What, some society dame bruise her pinky at a tea party?"

"As a matter of fact, sweetie, I'm going for a ride in a zeppelin. Care to come along?"

She didn't wait for a no.

Friday Callahan took the ferry across the North River to scenic Hoboken for his meeting with Jimmy the Judge Fitzgerald. The fresh air was like a tonic, and the escape from the honks, toots, squeals, whines of the city traffic provided a bit of serenity. Over Clams Casino he rehearsed what he would say to the beer baron and wondered if Jimmy would remember him from the old neighborhood. He certainly had a vivid memory of Jimmy Fitz, who even then had been marked as a born leader of the outlaw gutterpups who raided boxcars, dodged truant officers, knocked off stores and snatched handbags. It was in 1910, Callahan recalled, that Jimmy lost his left eye to a billyclub in a pitched battle with the mercenaries hired by the New York Central Railroad to stop the freebooting of their freight cars. The result had give him a look of pure menace, which he needed like Lindy needed publicity. A great hulk of a man, they called him 'the Judge' not because of any gift of Solomonic wisdom but because his word was law in internecine gang disputes and he could enforce it. At bottom Callahan felt no more qualms about interviewing and breaking bread with him than he would, say, grilling a captain of industry or an elected official. And he also knew that, unlike those presumed worthies, Jimmy the Judge would pick up the tab for the fine meal that awaited him.

The gargoyle-faced bootlegger was picking his teeth after the meal when he told Callahan, "I wouldn't wipe my ass with your newspaper."

"Me neither, Mr. Fitz," said Callahan, digging into the peach parfait. "I prefer the New York *Graphic* for that purpose."

Footsie O'Keefe, sitting beside the Judge, gave a nervous laugh. "I told yuh he was a jokester, Jimmy."

At first the Judge did not look amused. He beaconed the reporter with his surviving eye, then chuckled. "I remember you now," the Judge said.

"You do?"

"Yeah, you was the snot-nose altar boy, the one who was always kissing some priest's heinie. The first one in line when they were handing out haloes."

"That was me to a tee," said Callahan, dabbing his lips. "Delicious peach parfait."

"What happened? How come you ain't a bishop or something instead of a two-bit news monkey in a cheap suit?"

"I fell from grace," Callahan said with a satisfied smile.

"You mean you discovered tail."

"I deem that a very astute observation," said Callahan.

"You bet your ass," said the Judge.

He handed Callahan a cigar and stuck another into his own mouth. Footsie instantly leaned in with a lighter. "Of course, I ain't never known a bishop who didn't have some quail on the side," continued the Judge expansively. "Except for them who was sweet potatoes and they broke their vows double." He exhaled clouds of smoke. "These here are Jamaican," he said, indicating the cigar.

"Wonderful smoke," said Callahan, puffing with genuine pleasure.

"I like your style," the Judge said, beaming him again with his good eye. A waiter came over and put a bottle of cognac on the table. "I like your style too."

"Me? I got style whores complain about."

The Judge smiled and offered Callahan a glass of cognac. "Myself," the bootlegger added, "you may have noticed I never touch no hootch."

"Your self-control is both admirable and remarkable," said Callahan, taking his glass.

"Okay," said the Judge. "We ate and drank. Now what do you want to see me about?"

"I want to interview you."

"About what?"

"An ex-person named Scoop Madigan."

"A scumbag."

"Can I quote you?"

"Sure, if you wanna sleep with the fishies."

"Okay, off the record. Why was he a scumbag?"

"Why? He was born that way. He was an arrogant bastard and he had no morals." Fitzgerald puffed. "But he was a useful scumbag."

"He worked for you?"

"In the long run everybody works for himself," replied the Judge. "Let's say he handled a few contracts for me on a regular basis."

"He freelanced too?"

"We like to give our boys a long leash. Providing they played by the rules, keep everything on the up-and-up."

Fortified by cognac and a little success, Callahan continued with the direct approach. "What was he rubbed out for?"

"Now if I did hard time in the seminary like you I would call that question impertinent."

"I merely ask. You don't have to answer."

"You fucking right I don't have to answer." The Judge cyclopsed the cigar he held in his fingers. "How much time did you end up doing?"

"Three years." Callahan understood he meant in the seminary.

"That's a felony sentence. You at least get out of doing them as a doughboy?"

"No. They shipped my ass to France."

Fitzgerald shook his head. "Double jeopardy. You wasn't too bright."

"I was always first on line for haloes, not for brains."

"I dunno. I think you're smart enough to play dumb." He sipped soda water. "Let's say Madigan overplayed his cards. That explain it?"

"Where does Guy Pellegrino fit in?"

"He fits in a fucking pine box pretty damn soon. If we don't get him the Mustache Petes will. He put out a contract on a newsboy without a sign-off."

As they talked Footsie kept scanning the place. Naturally the trio occupied a table backed up to the wall and facing the front door. Bianco sat by himself at a table fifteen paces away. Standard security measures.

Callahan leaned back and unbuttoned his vest. "If you weren't very fond of Madigan how come you gave him a present?"

"What present?"

"The stickpin."

"How do you know I give him one? Ah hell, who cares? Put it this way . . . does a general have to love every soldier he kisses on both cheeks? It wasn't no good-conduct medal."

"What was it for?"

"Services rendered."

Callahan realized that was probably all he would get out of him, but he took one last fling. "So what pies did he have his fingers in? Gambling? Policy? Hootch? Broads? Junk?"

The Judge shook his outsized head. "Hey . . . that's inside dope."

"I hear he ran a bucket shop."

"No kiddin'," said the Judge.

"Union activities."

The Judge hunched his shoulders.

Callahan gnawed on his lower lip. He figured the interview was closed. He hadn't learned too much that he didn't already know.

"Who's your favorite cowboy?" Callahan asked, out of the blue.

The Judge looked baffled. "Tom Mix. Why?"

"Because I was dying for a straight answer."

Footsie took over. "Don't be a wiseass."

The Judge put a restraining hand on the pug's arm. "Never mind, Foots," then turned to Callahan. "Now I got a couple of questions for you."

"Shoot," Callahan said, immediately regretting the choice of word.

"How much they pay you over at that rag you write for?"

"Fifty a week."

"That don't buy graham crackers."

Callahan's silence conceded the point.

"Hey," the Judge went on, "Madigan may have been a bozo, but having a news reporter in the organization was good for business. It gave us a cover for a lot of things. He had great contacts with the bulls and pols and the prosecutors. He made a nice go-between when we needed one. He had plenty of sources of information—inside dope that businessmen like me find useful, you know? Early stock prices. Race results. He got the info for our handbooks before you could say Jack Robinson. This kind of stuff comes in handy."

"I see what you mean."

"So I got a proposition for you. Why not take his place?"

Callahan's first impulse was to laugh the offer off. Then he got to thinking about fifty bucks a week from a leg-it hood like publisher Curtin. An argument could be made . . .

"Thanks, Mr. Fitz, but no thanks."

The Judge leaned across the pine table. "Think it over, don't brodie this one, Callahan." He pointed to his own head. "You're good in the gray-matter department. We could use you. I'd put you on the books at six yards a year."

Twelve times what he was making now.

"And you'll be in some high-class company. We got three district attorneys, a passel of judges and politicians, top cops and feds. If they don't turn down our dough, why should you? You wanna be a slum brat all your life?"

"Maybe I don't want to end up like Madigan."

Fitzgerald sniffed the aromatic stogie. "Better you end up in the poorhouse with a phony gold watch? Or in a drunk tank counting bugs that aren't there? A man has to take risks, Callahan. At least you go out in style."

"That's one way of looking at it," Callahan said.

The Judge, energy sapped by the oration, leaned back and smoked, then said: "Take a month or two to think about it. No big hurry."

And in parting the Judge made this sage comment: "Don't be a meatball all your life."

Walking home from the ferry Callahan actually felt pretty chipper. In an odd way the Judge's offer—though he wasn't seriously considering it—made him feel valued, like a major player in the game. His recent windfall from the ponies didn't hurt his mood either. He felt happy to be alive, a little sappy in the spring air. On the stroll across Fourteenth Street he winked at homely women every chance he got.

The last homely woman he met he did not wink at. She was his landlady, Mrs. Magdelene Brannock, who glowered at him from the stone stoop of the tenement house. Rent was five days overdue.

"Who is this vision of beauty in a cotton wrap?" he called out. "Why, as I live and breathe, it's Mrs. Brannock. And here I was thinking that Clara Bow had paid a visit to our humble precincts."

The tall, frizzy-haired widow looked daggers at her delinquent tenant, rubbing her hands up and down her apron, steeled to tongue-lash him. She was, it occurred to him, beautiful in her hideousness, a cobra poised to strike.

And how quickly the venom vanished when he produced the billfold from his pocket and began to peel off banknotes. "There's a little matter of the rent, isn't there?" he said with an angelic smile. "It seems to have slipped my mind. Ah, you know how we ink-stained wretches are, so absentminded when it comes to quotidian matters and homespun details. Quite understandable, of course, when you consider that our attention is riveted on the need to record history-in-the-making—matters like the forming of the League of Nations, the collapse of empires, the election of presidents, the assassination of archdukes, the hurling of no-hitters, the slaying of streetwalkers, the price of tea in China. You understand."

As she counted the bills with a wet thumb and gleaming eye, Callahan cleared his throat. "I have seen fit to include—you'll notice—a modest advance on next week's exactment as well. I hope, dear lady, that this meets with your approval."

"You bet your chowder ass it does. And stow the blarney."

"You're a woman of great astuteness. Not to mention your unparalleled ship-sinking beauty."

"And you're full of shit."

"Your words prove my point," he said, removing his fedora and bowing low.

"Spifficated already, eh? You ought tah be ashamed."

"I *beg* your pardon, but I am stinkingly sober. I hope, however, to rectify the condition." He waved the remaining bills before putting the wad in his pocket.

"Nigger-rich," she said scornfully.

"No, mick-rich," he corrected.

Mrs. Brannock reached into her apron pocket. "I've a message for yuh."

He stopped on his way up the concrete steps and she handed him a powder-blue envelope. "It was delivered this morning by some flunky in a driver's uniform."

Callahan glanced at the return address. It was from New York State Senator Nicholas T. Callahan. His airy mood deflated like a pricked balloon.

Chapter

10

APRIL FOOL'S DAY

CALLAHAN felt like a dunce as he sat the next evening on a hard pew in the nave of Saint Agatha's Roman Catholic Church on West Forty-first Street, the terrazzo of which he last trod more than fifteen years earlier when he escorted a certain Irish virgin up the center aisle to the strains of the wedding march. He got a bellyache just thinking about it. He yearned for a cigar as his doubter's heart pitter-pattered in rebellion at being here. Every sound echoed with a past disillusion and every sight evoked a troubling memory. But his reporter's curiosity had led him to accept his brother Nick's invitation to meet him at the church amid the symbols of his former faith. He had not, after all, laid eyes on Nicholas Timothy Callahan in some six years.

On the side aisle an old priest was hearing confession and the murmur of *mea culpa*s burned in Callahan's ears. He wondered how *he* could have endured hearing the guilty secrets of anonymous penitents had he not aborted his vocation to the priesthood. Still, he supposed being a reporter entailed much of the same thing, shouldering the sins of the world. Except that priests swore a vow of secrecy while reporters swore one of disclosure, and priests forgave while newspapermen usually condemned. He

112

glanced around at the portrayals in sculpture, painting, mosaic and stained glass of the crucifixion, thorn-crowning, scourging, stigmata, beheading: God is love, he mused. He was especially moved by the image in stained glass of the church's patroness, Saint Agatha, the virgin martyr shown according to tradition, holding her severed breasts on a plate. He remembered the irreverent kick the altar boys got out of gazing at this one. He also recalled the story the nuns told about her: she was a first-century Sicilian maiden who had her breasts cut off for spurning the advances of the Roman consul. So Saint Agatha was named the patroness of bell ringers, wet nurses and jewelers and served as a talisman against volcanic eruptions. Damn if it didn't work, too. Callahan could not recall a volcano ever erupting in Hell's Kitchen.

Callahan shifted in the pew. Being in church made him ponder. He had, face it, failed as a priest and as a husband, and he wasn't *exactly* a huge success as a newspaperman. Was he looking at three strikes . . . ?

He glanced at his pocket watch. The big shot was fifteen minutes late. He'd give him five more minutes before he took a hike. Waiting, he speculated about Nick's motives for arranging the reunion. Brotherly love seemed out. His mother's elder son didn't get his juices from that source. Unless he's changed, Callahan thought. He also ruled out nostalgia, art appreciation, religious fervor or any incentive that required a heart fueled by blood. Which left Nick Callahan's enduring driveshaft—greed.

The clack of tapped soles on tile. He didn't need to turn his head to know it was Nick.

The state senator slipped into the pew beside him and stuck out a manicured hand. Callahan, unlike a politician, gripped it lightly.

"You look good," Nick said.

"You don't have to lie. I'm not a registered Republican and I never vote anyhow."

Nick chuckled. "Okay, Johnny boy. You look fat and seedy and you've lost a lot of hair."

"That's better. Remember, you're in church."

He appraised his older brother. The hair was abundant, slate-gray and thick; the eyes were large and twinkly; the face tanned and still ruggedly handsome. He was dressed well, of course, in a beige double-breasted suit, canary-yellow tie and white silk shirt. The thumb, forefinger and middle finger of the left hand held a brown fedora at the indentations in the crown.

"Where'd you get the tan?" Callahan asked.

"Monte Carlo. I just got back from vacation."

"At taxpayer's expense?"

"No."

"Horseshit."

Nick tut-tutted. "Remember, we're in church," he said.

"Since when do you find the interior of a church so sacred? Save the sanctimony for your campaign speeches."

"Come on, Johnny. I came to make friends."

"Why?"

"We have the same blood in our veins."

Callahan studied his brother's expression. Maybe he was on the level. Maybe he had changed. "So," he said in a more friendly tone, "what'd you do in Monte Carlo?"

"I drank and gambled legally."

"That must've taken the fun out of it. What kind of action?"

"Baccarat, chemin de fer, roulette, slots. And you should have seen the women."

"Did the wife go?"

Nick nodded.

"Tough luck. Sounds like the kind of place for me. Get off this treadmill."

"I understand. I got this place picked out in La Condamine, a house sitting smack on a cliff overlooking a beach and the blue Mediterranean. I made a down payment on the place before I left."

"I didn't realize state senators made so much dough."

Nick made the sign of the cross. "I been playing the stock market and getting some lucky breaks."

"Bully for you." Callahan looked around. "Why did we have to meet here?"

"It's quiet and convenient. And I have a special friend lives right down the block."

Callahan thought about Mazie and felt a flare of anger. "Let's go somewhere that we can talk in a normal tone of voice, okay? A speak."

"I'd better not."

"Oh, I forgot. You have to keep up appearances . . . Like the time you voted against Al Smith's resolution to modify the Volstead Act. And against the bill to repeal the New York enforcement law. Meanwhile you and your Republican cronies were swilling Irish in Oyster Bay like there was no tomorrow."

"There *is* no tomorrow, Johnny. And there's no yesterday either. There's only the here and now. Besides, my constituents happened to oppose those measures."

"What constituents, Nick? Big Bill Dwyer? Dutch Schultz? Arnie Rothstein? Sure, they favor Prohibition. It's the cow with twelve tits."

"Don't bust my stones, Johnny boy."

"I need a drink."

"It's illegal."

"Since when did that stop you or me from indulging our weaknesses? Mine is hootch. You have two—chasing gash and making cash. Hey, I'm a poet."

"You could have been, if you'd stayed away from the bottle."

"Yeah, and you could have been the Pope if our old man was a wop."

Nick clucked his tongue. "Maybe you were right about going someplace else. Come with me back to Oyster Bay. I'll take you out in my sailboat."

"Boats nauseate me.

"And I have the same effect, right?"

"I didn't say that."

"It wasn't always that way, was it, Johnny? We used to have a lot of laughs together. Even the last time. Remember?"

Callahan remembered. It was in Madison Square Garden the night Gene Tunney took Harry Greb's light-heavyweight belt away from him. They hollered themselves hoarse rooting for the fellow bogtrotter to avenge his earlier defeat. He remembered that the bout went the full fifteen rounds with Tunney pummeling the Pittsburgh pug's body to a pulp while Greb butted like a nanny goat throughout the match. They got their money's worth that night, squinting through the blue smoke at the fighters.

"We were friends once," Nick was saying.

"Yeah."

"We had pretty good times."

"We weren't the Rover Boys."

"Even the Rover Boys work on Wall Street now."

Callahan gave Nick a look. "What's the pitch?"

"Come work for me."

Callahan was reminded of the Judge's offer. Must be Corrupt Callahan Month.

"Doing what?" he asked.

"As my press agent."

"Politicians have press agents now?"

"Sure. Good press is important, you of all people should know that. Free publicity helps win elections and that adds decimal points to the bank balance. I'll pay you one hundred a week."

"That's all you think my integrity is worth?"

"It's a lot of cabbage. What does the paper pay you?"

"Half that much."

"Well?"

"What's the gimmick?"

"No gimmick. I want us to be close again."

Callahan could almost accept this explanation, but in the end didn't buy it. "You sure it has nothing to do with Scoop Madigan's death?"

Nick looked puzzled. Callahan wondered if he was shamming.

"Let's go for a walk," Nick suggested.

They strolled along Ninth Avenue where the El blotted out the sun. They passed fruit stands and Italian food stores. They turned east on Forty-second Street and stopped in front of an amusement arcade. "What say we go in and see the freaks and the hootchy-kootchy dancers?" Nick said.

"In my line of work I see plenty of freaks, it's a regular sideshow."

Nick smiled. "Remember that house of joy we visited that featured a girl with two vaginas?"

"Yeah, she was a freak and a hootchy dancer all in one."

"Which pussy did you like better?"

"It's like comparing the Lincoln and the Holland tunnels."

Nick liked that one.

They walked without talking through Times Square and the theater district, jostled by pedestrians. After a while they reached Beekman Hill overlooking Turtle Bay. Nick gestured from this high ground at the sprawling city. "There's a lot of jack to be made out there. You could live like a prince."

"Yah, but I'd know better. Once a punk always a punk."

"Am I a punk?"

"I'm speaking for myself."

"But I know what you're thinking. And you're no punk, at worst you're a piker."

"Meaning?"

"You break the law but in petty ways. You swill belly-rot in every blind pig from here to Buffalo. You patronize bookies and whores. You just haven't got the spine to sin in a big way."

"I break dumb laws like everybody else in this cockeyed country. But I draw the line somewhere because I believe the line is real, not because I haven't got spine. Maybe I corrupt myself, but I try not to do it to others. And I don't corrupt our institutions—"

Nick shook his head. "You could never cut the mustard as a priest."

Callahan ignored that. His engine was in high gear "I'd draw the line—just for an instance—at using my exalted position to get government contracts for manufacturers of alcohol for so-called medicinal purposes when I knew they were fronts for bootleggers."

"You can't prove I did that."

"*And* I definitely draw the line at taking blow jobs from gentlemen of the cloth."

Nick blanched. "Hey, we were *poor,* remember? He gave me two bucks. That was a considerable payday back then. Especially for a kid in our neighborhood. Trefethen was giving and I wasn't the only kid taking."

"May the Lord Mammon be with you and with thy spirit."

Nick squinted at Callahan. "Get everything off your chest?"

Callahan pushed the fedora back on the crown of his head and scratched his receding hairline. "I dunno."

"Wise up, Johnny. You're not going to live forever. Will you at least consider my proposition?"

"Maybe."

Nick peered down the quiet street, and seeing an approaching cab, stuck out his hand. The Yellow Cab glided to a stop. With one hand on the door handle and a brown-and-white shoe on the running board, Nick turned and said, "I'd like to see you once in a while."

Callahan nodded in a noncommittal way and sketched a wave goodbye. Then, in a reflective mood, he strolled the streets of east midtown, an odd melange of slum tenements and fashionable townhouses. A doorman standing under the awning of the newly constructed Beekman Tower Hotel appraised Callahan, who tried to imagine what it would be like to have plenty of dough and creature comforts.

Was his brother right? Was he sentenced to a life of being a piker? For the first time in memory he envied Nick's lack of conscience, his elegant amorality. Where was that pawnshop for souls?

Later that evening Callahan boarded the Long Island Railroad with a ticket for Glen Cove. He didn't want to spring for the price of a cab as Clare had suggested. He had decided on the spur of the moment to go to the party, at least see how the other half lived. As the train chugged through Queens and headed for the North Shore he smoked a cigar and read the *Saturday Evening Post*. He had gone home and changed into his best spring duds, a blue blazer shiny from long use, white ducks with ragged cuffs, a striped tie and blue shirt. On his head sat a newly blocked gray homburg. It was a pretty spiffy outfit for Callahan.

Getting off the train at Glen Cove station he could see the red sun plummeting down over Sands Point, a tongue of fire that reminded him of pictures of the Holy Spirit. He hailed a taxi to take him the short distance to the Parker mansion.

It sat at the end of a big green lawn that rolled down to the lathered rim of Hempstead Harbor and Long Island Sound. The house had baronial proportions, adorned with bay-windowed porches and gingerbread molding, striped canvas awnings and a balustraded captain's walk. It had a tower here and a turret there and rambled endlessly with extensions and architectural afterthoughts, a greenhouse, servants' quarters, garages and stables. It was flanked by two gigantic yews and surrounded by sculpted hedges, ivy and gooseberry plants. The gardeners had already begun spring planting of petunias, morning glories, asters, snapdragons and roses. They had broken their backs, Callahan could see, to make sure that spring came early for the Parker ménage. Callahan saw a tennis court a few yards east of the main house and he was fairly certain that a swimming pool lay behind the hedges in the rear.

The driver left him off at the main gate, which was adorned with a wrought iron *P.* He walked up a meandering driveway that was already filled with motorcars, sleek roadsters and stately sedans trimmed with polished wood and brass fixtures that sparkled in the dusk. He could see the glow of chauffeurs' cigarettes, blinking like fireflies with each puff. The tall arched windows of the mansion spilled pools of electric light onto the lawn. Through the immense door he heard a babble inside, sudden gales of forced laughter, the parrotry of greetings and chitchat.

Callahan pressed a button and chimes sounded. The

door swung open. A snooty manservant ushered him indoors and took his hat.

Callahan thought he had a hard shell, but he felt awkward when he saw the glittering array of guests in the ballroom, and suddenly understood why the butler had treated him like a panhandler. All the other male guests not only sported tans derived from sailing to Buzzards Bay, contrasting with Callahan's speakeasy pallor, and not only had physiques toughened by daily sets of tennis or squash, contrasting with Callahan's pot-bellied amorphism, but they all wore formal attire. He was tempted to turn around and go home when he heard his name called out.

"Hey, it's swell to see you," said Dante, clasping his hand and patting him on the beefy shoulder. The young man's bright eyes canvased the surroundings. As usual he was impeccably dressed in black dinner coat with peaked satin lapels, black bow tie over wing collar, white carnation in the buttonhole. His thick hair sparkled with brilliantine under the chandeliers.

"Isn't this a dandy house?" Dante said. "Come on, they have real champagne over here."

Callahan needed no coaxing to head for the trough. He quickly swilled a glass of nose-tickler, and after wolfing down a couple of canapes said to Dante, "I didn't know you'd been invited."

"Ditto. But I'm glad to see you."

Callahan surveyed Dante again. He concluded that unlike himself the kid's dashing good looks suited the surroundings. He searched the room. "Seen our hostess about?"

Dante's face turned sappy. "You bet, and does she look smart!" He jerked his head toward French doors that led to a terrace. Clare stood amid a cluster of guests, holding court and flourishing a cigarette in a long holder.

"Why don't we go over and say hello?"

"Not yet," said Callahan, devouring beluga, then a rollmop.

"When's the last time you had a square meal?"

"I opened a can of pork and beans this afternoon." From

a passing tray he speared a shrimp and a sliver of Parma ham wrapped around green melon.

Dante, hands on hips, marvelled at the gourmandizing. "You're sucking up food like a vacuum cleaner."

Callahan's mouth was too full for him to voice a snappy riposte. Besides, the kid was right. Then he spotted someone among the guests who made him forget food for a moment. "Well, well, well," Callahan said in a metallic tone, "I see where old Spit-and-Polish is mingling with the troops."

Dante turned to glance at the squat figure of Major Carlos Curtin, publisher of the *Courier*. "I wouldn't call it that," Dante said. "He's a fellow club member and business associate of Clare's old man. That's him standing next to the Major."

Callahan trained his eyes on Angus Parker, chairman of the National Water Resources and Paper Company, member of the New York Stock Exchange, director of two banks, member in good standing of the Nassau County Country Club and the Metropolitan Club, elder of the Presbyterian church, former polo champion and—for about ten years—a contented widower. Tall and regal-looking, he was clean-shaven and almost bald. He looked to be in his late sixties, though his jawline was still firm and his gaze still sharp.

In contrast Major Curtin, mainly because of his short stature and round face, looked faintly ridiculous with his bantam strut and the three tiers of ribboned medals on the breast of his white dress-uniform coat.

Nonetheless, a nimbus of power surrounded both men.

Callahan had a sudden insight: "I get it now," he said. "Angus Parker's company must supply his daughter's employer with the paper that her farfetched yarns are printed on."

Dante wouldn't brook even oblique criticism of her. "Cut it out, Cal. Her stories are the straight dope."

"Did I say they weren't? But the old man has the paper's newsprint contract, right?"

"How the hell do I know?"

"I'd bet my last quarter on it."

"You'd bet on anything."

Callahan's mind sailed into byways of speculation. He knew that the power trusts had been gobbling up shares of newspaper stock across the country. And he was dimly aware of a Senate investigation exploring the relationship between newspapers and power trusts that were lobbying against federal intervention in the water resource industry. He remembered something Nick had said earlier that day about how there was plenty of jack to be made in New York in this boom era. The byword was get rich quick. Hey, he thought, the nabobs of the news biz were not immune to the easy-money infection, were they? They knew as well as the next joker with the gold chain on his vest that consolidation and monopoly were the wave of the future. It was enough to make a cynic out of an angel. And he was no angel.

Watching the tall man and the short man chat in low tones at a distance, Callahan pictured them in togas in the Roman forum—and wondered whether the newspaper publisher ever would authorize an editorial critical of the power executive's efforts to prevent government meddling in his affairs. Of course there was ample historical precedent for publishers (witness Pulitzer and Hearst, for examples) to betray their class in print. But maybe those days were gone forever.

"As I live and breathe," said a throaty female voice coming from behind him.

Callahan did an elephantine pirouette and faced the owner of the ripe contralto, Lily Curtin, otherwise known as the boss' daughter. He gave her the once-over. Her hotcakes had maybe lost a little yeast, but she was still a sizzling dish. He noticed her breasts jostling for room at the top of her party dress. A blue eye was curtained by a loop of hair the color of cotton candy. Her expression was, of course, mildly ironic.

He sketched a bow. Two could play at this irony game. "Miss Curtin," he said.

"That's *Mrs.* Ferrand, or hadn't you heard?"

"I beg your pardon, I forgot for a moment."

She gestured to the tall man standing beside her. "I'd like you to meet my husband Max. Max, this is Johnny Callahan. He writes for the *Courier.* Or *scribbles,* as he likes to say."

Callahan gripped the man's slightly moist hand and took a quick inventory. Handsome, in an oily continental way. No horns visible on the broad forehead.

"Pleased to meet you, Mr. Callahan. What sort of things do you write?"

"Lies, mostly."

Lily gave forth a tinny, counterfeit laugh, and Callahan suddenly remembered how much he disliked the woman. Basically. But just standing there, she gave him a boner.

He introduced Dante, and Lily's eyes lit up and her voice turned to treacle at the sight of this hunk of Roman statuary.

"Dante Viola," she echoed. "What a perfectly charming euphonic name. It sounds so poetic, like a musical instrument."

No doubt she would like to play his piccolo, Callahan thought.

She held out her hand and, nearly helpless, Dante stooped to kiss it.

"And what do *you* do, Mr. Viola?" she asked, leaning forward to convey avid interest and provide a glimpse of the land of milk and honey.

He managed, "I write for the *Courier,* too."

"Do you?" she said. "I don't remember seeing your by-line."

"I don't have a byline, ma'am. I write for the obituary page."

She winced at the word *ma'am.* She was, after all, only two or three years older than he was. She said, "Let's say you don't have a byline *yet.* You look like a boy with a bright future."

"Thank you," he said.

Lily placed the heel of her hand on the swell of her sequined hip and turned to Callahan. "Last I heard *you* were writing obits, Cal."

"I got tired of covering the lighter side of life." He decided not to make even a veiled reference to her role in his exile to the obit desk. He made a mental note, though, to warn Dante never to dally with the boss' daughter if he wanted to advance at the *Courier.*

Max Ferrand gently touched his wife's elbow. "Shall we, Lily? There are so many people we should be saying hello to."

As Ferrand steered her off, Callahan watched her silk rudder waving while they melted into the crowd.

Dante gave a long, low whistle.

"She's poison, kid," said Callahan.

Dante peered at him inquiringly. "By the way, Cal, what gives with the Madigan story? I've been nosing around but I don't have anything solid yet."

Callahan nodded in Major Curtin's direction. "Better ask the commanding officer," he said. "I gave him a memo on a takeout we could do but he's been sucking his thumb over it for a very long time."

"What's he waiting for?"

"Like I said, ask him," Callahan repeated, knowing that Dante wouldn't. "But I'm still plugging away. You should do the same."

"Okay," said Dante, and the two of them strolled around the room until they ran into Clare, who looked askance at Callahan's outfit.

"Having a good time?" she inquired.

"Swimming," said Callahan, lifting a fluted glass from the tray that bobbed through the sea of guests. "Who *are* all these dames and dandies?"

"Oh, friends," she said, primping her rusty hair. She wore an aquamarine sheath, chiffoned at the neck and hemline, breast garnished with a white orchid.

"You have a swell house," said Dante.

"We just opened it today for the season."

The hunting season, thought Callahan, but Dante, the kid from Mott Street, looked puzzled.

"It's the summer place," she explained. "Daddy also has a townhouse on Gramercy Park."

Dante was clearly impressed. Too much so, Callahan

thought. But he supposed Dante would have to learn the hard way, like the rest of mortal mankind.

The dance band struck up "Oh, Lady Be Good," and Dante asked Clare to fox-trot.

Callahan found a chair next to a potted palm and settled in to sip champagne and watch the world go by. He hiked up his frayed trouser cuffs, exposing his garters, and let the giggle water lay siege to his senses. He could think of worse ways to spend an evening than scoffing free champagne and caviar in a Long Island mansion. So, he wondered, why was he itching to blow the place? Why did he feel like a fish in a birdbath? He watched Major Curtin stand on his tiptoes to whisper something into Angus Parker's pendulous ear.

Soon Dante and Clare returned, breathless, her cheeks tinged with color. "Oh, lady be *bad,*" she said, hallooing across the room for another glass of champagne and provoking a glare of disapproval from her father. She was unfazed, hellbent on revelry. She polished off the wine and said to Callahan, "I saw you chatting with Lily Curtin earlier. So you're old friends . . ."

Callahan wore a blank look. "She's the boss' daughter. I knew her back when. I talk to her."

"I see."

Callahan looked at her. "You're surprised she gave the time of day to a guy from my side of the tracks?"

"Not at all. As the band played "They Didn't Believe Me" Clare said, "Dance with me, Cal."

"I dance like a ruptured dodo. I'd step on your tootsies from here to the Bronx."

She took his hand. "It's a slow number."

"Go ahead, sport," said Dante magnanimously.

Cornered, Callahan gave in. Holding her in his arms was not unpleasant, he discovered as he shuffled around the marble floor, his fingertips getting heat from the swell of her hips. At the end of the second tune he announced, "Okay, my dance card's used up."

"You're weakening, Cal," she said, then turned and left him standing there in the middle of the dance floor.

As he jostled his way to the hors d'oeuvres table he mulled over her remark, and by the time he had swallowed his third oyster he had come to the conclusion that she was right.

The night ripened. The jazz band started cooking, the revels grew livelier. Outside on the terrace he could see brightly colored oriental paper lanterns sway in the breeze. He too swayed on his feet, tipsy. Did he sense himself retreating from his rough code of never screwing a friend's girl and never taking grease money? An insidious voice whispered to his psyche something to the effect that frying in hell included no time off for good behavior, whether one was a piker or a polecat. Might as well sin in style, he told himself, though still not at ease with the notion.

Many older guests had retired from the scene while the young, the randy and the crooked raised the party's tempo. Callahan was pretty well soused but he declined an invitation by Clare and Dante to join an impromptu swimming party in the pool organized despite the chill in the early spring air. He stumbled over to the French doors overlooking the pool to get a gander at Clare in bathing costume, a clinging deep blue jersey that revealed the streamlined curves of her body. She had long muscular legs and, to his surprise, large breasts. He watched her dive into the pool, knifing the water with hardly a ripple. He sighed, deciding it was time to call it a night.

He got his homburg back from the snobbish butler, who looked down his snout at this weaving newspaperman. Callahan crooked a finger at the man, who bent his head and cocked an ear with his hand.

"Your fly's open," Callahan whispered.

The servant's startled hands shielded his groin.

"April Fool," said Callahan, who burped and made his exit.

"Kill the Madigan story," Ivan Bruce said on Monday.

"What?"

"Spike it." He gave Callahan a wintry smile. "And take a three-week paid vacation."

Callahan removed the fedora and scratched his pate. They were sitting in Pop Pietro's munching ptomaine sandwiches. "I thought Saturday was April Fool's Day. Who says we got to kill it?"

Bruce raised his eyeballs skyward. No words were necessary.

"No explanation?"

Bruce wagged his shaggy head.

"Off the record?" said Callahan, probing.

Bruce lowered the half-eaten liverwurst sandwich from his mouth. "The Major says the story's stale."

"Goddammit, Ivan, so's the bread you're eating. You buy this explanation?"

"I don't," conceded Bruce, "but he's the boss." He pushed away his plate and lit a pipe.

"I'll be a monkey's godfather," said Callahan.

Bruce shrugged. "At least you're off obits."

"This stinks," said Callahan, all the way to high heaven."

Bruce had the decency to look embarrassed.

"What if somebody turns up with information on the Madigan killing and claims the reward? That'll blow us out of the water."

"The publisher figures he'll cross that bridge when and if he comes to it. Readers have short memories, Cal."

Cal visualized Major Curtin at the party the other night, a supercilious, medal-bedecked johnny pump, and was surprised at the depth of his own anger. He supposed that Mother Superior's character analysis had been on the mark: under it all he was a dyed-in-the-wool reporter, a bull terrier with a story. Why was it so hard to let go? Once upon a time he would have fried orphans for a paid vacation. Now he was angry, confused and deeply disappointed.

Callahan began the vacation that very afternoon, listening to the radio in his room. He heard singers like Bing Crosby, Kate Smith and Elsie Janis and tried to sink into

a schmaltzy mood, blotting out thoughts of headlines and
deadlines and his frustrated lust for the big story. That's
what he got for caring again, he told himself. April Fool on
you, John Joseph Callahan.

As the days passed the *Courier*'s competitors, scenting
blood, fired a few salvos in the circulation war, printing
tales based mostly on rumors and quoting unnamed
sources about Scoop Madigan's outlawry. The *Mirror* ran
a think piece portraying the slain crime reporter as having
been the man to grease whenever a shady promoter
needed clearance to launch an illegal enterprise, from dog
races to one-armed bandits. The *American* gave splashy
headlines to a rumor that a police raid on an East Side
speak had provoked Madigan to beef to a corrupt precinct
captain that he had given the joint thumbs up to operate.
The *Bugle* blared the loudest in a series of articles detail-
ing Madigan's links to the Irish mob and to a certain "high
police official" whom Madigan sicked on illegal enter-
prises that refused to pay tribute. The report sparked con-
jecture about Jimmy Walker's hand-picked Police Commissioner Grover Whalen, a popular guy who reputedly
ran an independent department that didn't shrink from
harassing the Mayor's gambling pals. Whalen was known
to be soft on speakeasies but who wasn't? Most, including
Callahan, discounted the whispers about him. Callahan
figured the articles referred to Roland O'Hara, but he supposed it wouldn't have knocked him off his chair to know
that Whalen was on the take too. Anything seemed possible in this rogues gallery of a city, a burgh that ran on palm
oil.
   Anyhow, the rival rags were making noise while the
Courier played dumb. Callahan reasoned that the paper's
silence only confirmed Madigan's guilt, tarnished its
image as a truth-seeking crusading tabloid and lost the
Courier impulse sales at the newsstands and on street corners where hawking headlines was an effective selling
technique. Aping the sphinx made little journalistic sense,

not to mention ethics of the deal. So why did he give a damn if nobody else did?

By the time he went back to work he had damn near persuaded himself that he didn't care anymore either. Passing Hamilton Terry's newsstand he was reminded of what the blind man had told him not long ago about the publisher's hookup with Jimmy the Judge, and on this windswept corner in late April it all seemed to become clear to Callahan. Why, he wondered, had he been so dim-witted? One hand washed the other. Curtin had to put the Madigan yarn on the spike and treat Fitzgerald with kid gloves. Callahan knew, of course, that no newspaper could survive without publishing stories about gangsters. But the stories could go only so far, not cross a certain line. Honest coverage of the Madigan case, it seemed, would for some reason cross that line. Maybe it was a simple case of Fitzgerald calling in markers from the Major. But what were the markers?

He walked unhappily toward the newspaper office and his fifty clams a week. Raindrops added to his mood. As he crossed the street Callahan hitched up his coat collar and a jumble of images flashed in his mind, including Nick Callahan, Father Trefethen, Jimmy the Judge's ugly face, Clare Parker's cherry-tipped breasts in the bathing suit, the hand of the young German soldier clutching a religious medal—

It all happened with blazing speed. His ears were deafened by the warning blast of a horn. In a split second he saw the grinning mouth of the taxi's steel grille bearing down on him. He tried to dodge it but was sideswiped as the driver jammed on the brakes.

Callahan lay near the curbstone, his side and hip radiant with pain. A crowd had gathered to gawk as the hack driver got out of the cab and ran over to him. Of course his words were defensive rather than concerned.

"Hey, are you screwy or what? Why don't you watch where you're going?" With upturned palms he appealed to the bystanders. "He walked right in front of my damn cab."

Callahan struggled to his feet, dusted himself off and felt his sore hip.

"You okay?" the cabbie finally asked.

"I'll live," he said, picking up his hat and dusting it off. He walked in a dazed state toward the office.

Reaching the east side of Park Row he leaned against a lamppost to collect himself. A brush with death was supposed to make one's life pass before one's eyes. It also caused some people to mend their ways, slow down and smell the flowers, draw closer to God.

Callahan's confrontation with mortality drove home that his passing from the scene would not make an ounce of difference to anybody he could think of. Maybe Dante would shed a tear and Clare would feel a twinge of regret. Mazie? She was a business lady. A few ripples in an ocean of indifference.

He looked up at the drizzly sky, at the gilded dome of the old Pulitzer Building and the russet brick Tribune Building with its imposing clock tower. He felt the ghosts of newspapermen past—William Cullen Bryant, Charles Anderson Dana, James Gordon Bennett—mocking him. What had John Joseph Callahan in common with these legendary journalists? All his life he had been making vows and breaking them, first to Mother Church, then to an unsuitable mate, finally to the profane gods of journalism. What remote progenitors had bequeathed him this frayed conscience? What use had it been to *them* in the torch-lit caves of Stone Age Eire? . . .

He felt himself drifting toward a decision. All right, he would accept Jimmy the Judge's offer to work both sides of the street. Of course, he told himself, he would only pretend to be another reporter on the make and on the take . . . his real purpose would be to nose out material for the crime scoop of the century, when the climate of corruption finally cleared. He would be playing a very dangerous game, and to play it persuasively, he reasoned, he would have to tell absolutely no one of his decision—not Bruce, not Dante, no one. If Madigan had lived a lie as a reporter, Callahan would live a lie as a crook. Of course, he would have to accept the Judge's money, otherwise the charade would be less than convincing. . . .

Callahan held tight to this offering to conscience as he pushed through the brass revolving door that led to the lobby of the Courier Building. And as he crossed the moral Rubicon freighted like Caesar's jackass with his fair share of the human propensity for self-deception, he even believed it.

PART TWO

Chapter
11

THE YELLOW GARDENIA

DANTE Viola walked into the flower shop on Baxter Street to choose a boutonniere. It was a sunny Saturday in early June and he wore a straw boater with a band that matched the burgundy-and-white-striped blazer that made him look more like a boulevardier on the French Riviera than a denizen of the skewbald streets of the Italian ghetto. He placed a forefinger to his delicately carved lips, considering the choice with great care: red rose, white carnation or yellow gardenia? He decided that the gardenia would look best with his outfit.

"Could I have the yellow flower, please?" he asked the shopkeeper, Mrs. Angelina Califate.

The woman's expression seemed to indicate that she approved the choice. "Ah, *la gardenia!* The yellow one is rare—they are usually white." She added admiringly, "A rare flower for a rare boy." She removed the flower from the showcase and, perspiration dewing her upper lip, wired a sprig of fern to it. Pinning the fragrant flower to his buttonhole she said, "Be careful now. The gardenia, she bruise easy."

Dante looked down at the waxy petals.

She stepped back to admire him. "You looka joost like

135

Rudy Valentino," she concluded, hands placed emphatically on her well-padded hips.

He handed her a dime. "I sure hope not, Mrs. Califate. I'll bet he's looking pretty rotten now."

She wagged a stubby finger. "I mean when he was alive." A shadow of grief passed over her face, dimming its usual sunniness. Gray hairs sprouted from her prickly-pear chin. She crossed herself with solemnity. "Even in the coffin he looka like an angel. I never forget that day."

"What day?"

"The funeral on Broad-a-way. I bring him the gardenia too. And rose and lily and jasmine, every flower God put on the earth. I try to kiss his face but they put glass over the casket. It rain that day, I remember even though it's three year ago. I hit a pickpock' with my umbrell'—show that son-a-mine-bitch!" Her misty eyes studied Dante. "Why you no go Hollywood? You be another Valentino."

"Oh no, Mrs. Califate. I'm a newspaperman."

"Bah," she said. "You rather be a snoop than a star?"

"It's what I love to do."

She peered at him, studying him like an exotic hothouse plant. Mrs. Califate was known in the neighborhood as a gifted woman, a *strega* of sorts, skilled in the herbalist arts, to whom the transplanted villagers of Little Italy came for potions and formulas to abet their quests for fertility, revenge, love and death. Solutions derived from the earth itself.

She touched her head and said, "You craze," over the sound of the bell that jangled as he moved the door on the way out of the store.

Walking north toward Hester Street, Dante, smiling to himself, thought that maybe he was crazy to want to be a low-paid scribbler. Hands stuck into his trouser pockets, he strolled past a living frieze of four old men, wattled condors with fierce eyes, sitting on bentwood chairs turned backward or leaning on gnarled walking sticks. He passed a fishmonger, fruit peddler and kids playing potsy on the fractured sidewalk. What a morning, he thought. A coin from the mint.

Sticking his thumb under his lapel, he bent down to inhale the gardenia's sweet fragrance. A horse-drawn delivery truck rattled over the cobblestones. Reaching the curb Dante hopped over a puddle deposited by a light spring rain that morning, careful not to muddy the cuffs of his white flannels. Soon he reached the cafe on Grand Street, where he had an appointment with Patsy Secundo.

He was early. He sat down at a sidewalk table in the shade, ordered coffee and lit a Home Run, reviewing the events that had led to this meeting. Callahan had informed him that for mysterious reasons the Madigan investigation had been spiked. But Dante was reluctant to give up his cherished newfound role as muckraking reporter, hoping to find a way to persuade Bruce to keep the story alive. Meanwhile Patsy had sent word that he wanted to talk to Dante, who figured that the young hood was acting as an ambassador from the boss. It was an opportunity Dante didn't want to pass up.

Patsy and Dante had attended grade school together. They had never been close buddies and they hadn't seen each other for many years except in passing. Still, it was a connection. The engine of diplomacy in the neighborhood was fueled by connections, lineages of blood or race, village or school, social club or penal institution. One had to have some sort of pedigree to conduct business in Little Italy.

Though he was a thoroughbred Sicilian, Dante's credentials were a little frayed. He read poetry and novels rather than the racing form, and he worked with words and paper rather than bricks and mortar. He glanced inside the cafe, where the waiter was arranging items on a rattan tray under a framed portrait of Benito Mussolini.

The waiter brought the espresso in a small crockery cup decorated with the Italian tricolor. A newsboy appeared and Dante bought a copy of the *Times* taken from a canvas bag slung over the boy's shoulder.

Sipping coffee, he heard the brass winds of a dirge floating down the street, a funeral in progress at the corner church.

"Whenever you see the hearse go by / You never think you're going to die." The ditty was recited by Patsy Secundo, a red-haired hood with the face of a rodent. He had arrived unnoticed by Dante. "Hey, Danny, what's the good word?" The slender young thug looked around skittishly as he sat down. "I like funerals," he said. "Don't you?"

"Sure, Patsy."

Patsy peered at Dante across the table. "How come you always dress like a fairy?" He himself was dressed conservatively in a plain white shirt, navy jacket and gray slacks.

Dante smiled. Patsy was not physically imposing but an aura of menace, a sense of cruelty came from the unpleasant chinless face with small pulled-back ears and pointy nose. Dante remembered that Patsy in his boyhood liked to drown stray cats in rain barrels and carve initials with his penknife in other kids' forearms. Such qualities made him, at only twenty-one years of age, an important member of the Pellegrino gang, where brutality and brains marked the novice for a future leadership role, and brutality alone earned a good spot in the rank and file. Dante was pretty certain that Patsy packed a Roscoe, so his reply to the sartorial question was tempered. "Sorry you don't like my threads."

The waiter came over. "Want a coffee or Coke or something?" Dante offered.

"Nah," said Patsy, getting up, "let's take a walk. I got work to do."

Dante signaled for the waiter, paid the tab and accompanied Patsy as he made the rounds of the neighborhood, collecting the take from the small bookmakers the gang had organized among candy stores and pushcart peddlers who took bets in return for a weekly salary of $100 to $150 a week depending on volume. The gang took the rest of the profits from the storekeepers and peddlers. The mob took the financial risks and paid the overhead, including graft, telephone bills and the fee for laying off part of the risk with a large central bank. Profits usually were high, and part of Patsy's (and Roscoe's) job was to make sure that the moms and pops in their employ didn't hold out. Which he did by checking the books. Patsy was good with numbers. One skim equalled one broken arm. Two skims equalled two broken arms. Three skims equalled a kiss from Roscoe and two cement overshoes. Basic arithmetic, just like your multiplication tables.

"Do you usually take newspaper reporters on your rounds?" Dante got up the nerve to ask.

"You won't write nothing about this," said Patsy, wetting his thumb and counting a roll of bills that a tailor on Prince Street had just handed him.

"How can you be sure?"

Patsy put the money in a briefcase and made a note in a pad. "You're Sicilian, ain't yuh?"

"I'm also a journalist."

"Yeah, but you wanna be a breathing journalist, don't you? You don't want somebody else writing your obituary."

Dante was about to remind him that it wasn't considered wise to bump off newspaper reporters, but then he remembered Madigan. Anyhow, he was not after some small-potatoes story about neighborhood bookies.

As they left the tailor shop and walked toward Elizabeth Street Patsy spoke in a melodic tone, an incongruously ironic rock-a-bye-baby voice. "Okay, Danny boy, why you going all around the neighborhood asking questions about the big guy?"

"Why was Junior Riccio ventilated?"

"I asked a question."

"Why was Madigan rubbed out?"

Patsy looked hard at his ex-schoolmate. "I don't like you, Viola. Never did."

"That's neither here nor there."

"That's neither here nor there," Patsy mimicked in a falsetto.

"I'm only doing my job."

"Fuck your job."

Dante stopped in his tracks. An old woman nearby scattered bread crumbs before strutting pigeons. A young girl, crossing the street against the wind, tugged at the hem of her short skirt. "I guess the interview is over," Dante said.

"You're lucky."

"Yeah?"

"You're lucky your old man and Pellegrino's old man came from the same whistlestop in Sicily."

"Campofelice?" said Dante. "Did they really?"

"Yeah. For some reason those things are important to the big guy. He's a sentimentalist. So he told me to lay off unless your balls get bigger. But you gotta lay off too or, hick town or no hick town, Sicilian brotherhood or no Sicilian brotherhood, your ass will be *carne maginato.*"

Dante recalled enough Italian to translate—"chopped meat."

"Get it, Danny boy?" And Patsy spat on Dante's lapel.

"What's *that* for?" yelled Dante, surprised and disgusted.

"I'm watering your flower."

Dante's feet were frozen to the sidewalk. He clenched and unclenched his hands.

"See yuh in the funny papers," Patsy said, walking off toward the Bowery.

The encounter depressed Dante for many days. Days of pecking out obits, dummying pages and mooning by the water cooler over Clare Parker. Actually he was bewitched by her competence as much as by her beauty.

He had wanted to tell Cal about Patsy's threat, but he couldn't get him to sit still and listen. Cal's behavior unnerved Dante. He was baffled by Cal's reaction to any mention of the Madigan case lately, by how he seemed to dodge the subject like a punching bag. While Dante wrote obits Cal did general assignment work, gravitating more and more to his old speciality, crime reporting, slowly but surely filling the void in the staff caused by Madigan's death. At times it made Dante stop and think.

But he refused to credit his darkest suspicions.

He remembered Callahan's treatment of him when he first came to work on the obit desk. At first Dante was scared of the crusty veteran with his blasphemous mouth and exacting standards for writing plain English. But as he got to know him better he grew fond of the bay-windowed booze hound. Callahan always treated him square, writing captions for him once when he was slowed down by a head cold, pleading his case with Ivan Bruce for a five-dollar merit raise. He became Dante's adopted Irish father, or maybe older brother.

Dante's actual father, Giorgio Viola, carpenter and mason of Campofelice, had perished when his son was only ten, buried alive in the rubble of limestone and timber of a cave-in during the construction of the IRT subway on Fourteenth Street. Dante's mother followed her husband to the East Broadway cemetery three years later, crushed by more metaphoric though equally deadly walls—overwork, deprivation, a broken heart. Dante had faced the void early in life; it toughened some kids, others it made brittle. Intimacy with the coquette called Death sometimes enhanced her terrible allure, or so said Callahan.

Dante, his brother and sister were farmed out to grudging relatives, and whatever family life he could lay claim to soon dissolved. He had heard nothing of them in many years. His sister, he learned, had gotten married and moved back to Sicily. His brother Anthony, last he heard, had emigrated to Argentina.

After he graduated from Regis High School, Dante quit the household of sour Zia Laura and struck out on his own, seventeen years old, head filled with the songs of Virgil, Ovid and Homer, heart pumping with ambition to write and stamp his signet on the world. He got a job hawking the *Courier* on street corners, pestered editors and executives until they made him a copyboy and later promoted him to editorial clerk. And soon he found himself posted to a grizzled obit writer named John Joseph Callahan.

Callahan became family, newspapering his life.

For a while Dante took Patsy's threat to heart and laid off the Madigan investigation. Instead of snooping around the neighborhood asking questions that could get him boiled

in oil by that sentimentalist Gaetano Pellegrino, he filled
his spare time with innocent diversions . . . saw a talking
picture called *Saturday's Children,* with Corinne Griffith,
whose voice grated on his ears; attended a play by Molière
at the Manhattan Civic Repertory for only $1.50; read
Dodsworth, the new Sinclair Lewis novel.

On Sunday he visited the Metropolitan Museum of Art
on Fifth Avenue, and they ran into each other while exploring the tomb of an Egyptian pharaoh.

"Don't I know you?" she asked, primping spun-candy
ringlets.

He peered at her in the charcoal light. "Miss Curtin?"

"Mrs. Ferrand," she corrected him. "Of course, I remember now. You're the boy who writes obituaries for my father," she said, offering her hand. "How fitting that I
should meet you again in a tomb." Her mouth formed a
crimson oval of amusement. Her fingers felt warm and
satiny, lingering in his a moment longer than necessary.
"So nice to see you again," she said.

Color tinted his clean-shaven, bay-rum-splashed cheeks.
"You're an art lover?"

"Oh yes," she said, scorching him from head to foot with
her look-see. "And I've just decided to collect Italian art."

Dante's heart began to pound.

They continued the conversation at a *konditorei* on Third
Avenue and Eighty-sixth Street, where they had coffee and
cloyingly sweet cake under a photograph of von Hinden-
berg. Lily wore a slouch hat that shaded the hungry look
in her eyes. Outside a subway train thundered over the
tracks of the Third Avenue El. Her small talk was spiced
with double meanings, her appetite for pastry ravenous.
The half-moons of her breasts crested the top of the sleeve-
less summer dress. Confectioners' sugar from the Frank-
furt Crown she was devouring powdered her full lower lip.

Dante, in the same outfit he had worn the day of his
meeting with Patsy Secundo, wore another yellow gardenia on his lapel. She reached across to touch it. "What a

sweet-smelling flower. I do love sweet things."

He wished it were Clare Parker making this play. But Lily Ferrand's overtures seemed to be working, her finger lingering on the flower sent a tiny current direct to his groin. Perhaps he'd been a fool to carry a torch for Clare.

Lily carried on, a nymph without artifice. Among other things, she revealed that her apartment was located a few blocks away on Park Avenue and that her husband, a trader in grain and petroleum, was off on a business trip to Rouen. An engraved invitation.

He hesitated, nibbling on a wedge of Black Forest cherry torte. Not for long, though.

A half hour later he found himself savoring a comparable triangle of Lily, while her fabled sweet-tooth was occupied with what she perceived as his candy cane. She was saucy and uninhibited; he was affectionate, energetic and eager to please after a long drought.

As they rested she cupped his scrotum and said, "Once in a shop on a side street in Taormina I saw these postcard pictures of boys that they sell to homosexual tourists. You remind me of the models in the photos—little Greek fauns."

He gave her a quick offended look.

She slightly squeezed his testicles. "I'm not impugning your masculinity, dear boy," she assured him. "Far from it."

He stirred and lengthened at the pressure and she quickly rolled on top of him and straddled his hips. . . .

As he dressed to leave he felt a sense of awe at having bedded down a married woman but at the same time guilt resonated out of his Catholic boyhood. Mother Church was like a clinging wife who treated her prodigal husband with an exasperating mixture of disapproval and forgiveness. Stray as he might, she knew he'd come back in the end. He felt unreasonably guilty at having betrayed Clare Parker, or at least the marble ideal of her he had fashioned in his mind. And he was afraid of the possible consequences of an affair with the boss' daughter, especially when she was married. Echoes of Callahan's warning on the subject mixed with his masculine vanity over the bedding of such a wealthy and desirable woman (overlooking that she had been the aggressor).

He was still trying to untangle his feelings as she helped him into the sleeve of his blazer and handed him the straw hat. Her lip rouge was smeared, giving an impish look to her pale, pretty face. Her eyes were drowsy.

Saying goodbye she gave him a long kiss, pressing her body close to his, crushing the fragile gardenia in his buttonhole.

Chapter

12

RIDING THROUGH A SEWER IN A GLASS–BOTTOM BOAT

THE stars hung unseen over Hamilton Terry's wooden newsstand on Park Row as he arrived for work, cane tapping on the pavement. From his pocket he produced a chain of keys and, after feeling the surface of the ledge, fitted one key in the big brass lock that secured the plywood door. He stepped inside, leaned the walking stick against the milk crate that he used as a seat and prepared for the day's business. He arranged magazines, cleared space for the bulldogs and put small change in the cigar box.

His built-in scanners picked up the faint fading night breezes that heralded a hot day. From somewhere, too, he picked up the scent of apocalypse.

In his eagle-eyed imagination he saw buzzards circling over the Jazz Age. He heard saxophones jeering about hard times ahead. Everything had a boiling point. In the visible world pigeons flapped and glided over City Hall Park, and subway-train wheels zlithered the tracks down below.

Delivery trucks pulled up to the newsstand and soon it bristled with the headlines of the day. An array of papers were lined up under the Drink Coca-Cola sign: the *World, Herald, Tribune, News, Mirror, Journal, American,*

Graphic, Bugle and *Courier.* The pages mingled myth and
fact, handled the trivial and the momentous with the same
air of portentousness, in stories about the Goodrich radio
show's masked tenor and the papal concordat; in ads tout-
ing runproof hosiery and halitosis-fighting mouthwash; in
accounts of soaring stock prices and plans by the Pennsyl-
vania Railroad to start forty-eight-hour coast-to-coast rail-
and-air travel.

Ham Terry, blind to the inflated words on paper, placed
a heavy iron weight on each bundle and waited for the
customers. The start of a long hot summer, the sun began
to beat down on the figure of Justice surmounting the cu-
pola of City Hall. Justice was at hand, all right. The day of
reckoning was around the corner. He felt it in his bones.

Further uptown in Mazie Rodell's bed John Joseph Callahan let rip a musical one.

"Ah," she said, rolling over, "essence of Callahan. You
should bottle it."

Callahan snored.

"What do yuh know," she marveled, "he even farts in his
sleep."

The leaves of the elm outside her window were newly
green.

Callahan propped himself up on his elbows, frowned at
his paunch and growled, "What time is it?"

She glanced out the window. "Just daybreak. Go back to
sleep."

"I can't. I've got insomnia."

"Conscience bothering you?"

"I got no conscience."

She frowned, sensing now an undertow of truth in the
remark.

Callahan looked preoccupied as he scooped his belong-
ings off the dresser top—loose change, nail file, handkerchief, rabbit-foot key chain, increasingly useless pocket
comb, stack of speakeasy membership cards. He shoved it
all into his baggy pockets as Mazie's eyes scorched his

back. He planned to go home, grab some sleep in his own
pestilential room, if Ivan Bruce would leave him in peace.

Soon he was tiptoeing past his landlady's door. But his
shoes squeaked. Her bulk invaded the corridor.

"Your boss called," she announced.

"So early?"

She vanished inside her apartment, not volunteering to
let him use the phone, so he went around the corner to the
United Cigars store payphone.

"You up with the fucking roosters?"

"There was a rubout," Bruce told him.

"Who."

"Frankie Marlow."

"The Broadway gambler, Rothstein's pal."

"Right."

"Serves him right. I'm going back to sleep."

"Like hell you are. Get your ass in here, *crime* reporter."

Callahan frowned into the mouthpiece. "Ah, let the public see it on the Movietone news."

"I'll give you half an hour. Unless you want a pink slip."

"Not my color."

At the office, Callahan made a few phone calls. Marlow,
partner of Big Bill Duffy and Larry Fay in a few speaks,
had been taken for a ride. None of Callahan's contacts
could or would tell him why. He uncovered a negative
fact—that Marlow's assassination had no connection to the
feud between factions of the old Sicilian Mustache Petes,
sometimes known as the Castelammarese War. The rubout of a booze czar like Marlow had nothing to do with
regional rivalries planted on foreign soil or medieval matters of blood and honor. It was a true-blue American killing, an imperative of economic rivalries. Callahan decided
to use this angle in his story—murder and mayhem in the
grand spirit of American capitalism. He could prop it up
with enough reliable sources to provide Bruce with a col-

umn and a half. He might have tapped the Judge for inside dope, but his instincts told him to save this marker for a more important occasion, when and if their association had a longer history.

Callahan batted out the yarn in two hours and then handed the hard copy to Ivan Bruce. Bruce read with a frown of concentration, brandishing a copy pencil, toying with the waxed end of his mustache.

"Not bad. Printable." He looked at Callahan. "But it's more a column than a news story."

Callahan shoved the pearl gray fedora back off his brow. "I'm bushed," he said. "Can I go back to sleep now?"

Bruce peered at him. "That a new hat?"

"Yeah."

"Nice."

"Thanks."

"Don't get lost. I may need you."

Callahan looked wounded. "Do I ever get lost? Look, you know where to reach me."

But Callahan did not go to sleep. He ran into Clare Parker in the elevator, whence one thing led to another. They ended up in a booth at Baker's downing boilermakers.

Clare sipped from the shot glass and looked Callahan up and down. "You're looking pretty spiffy lately," she observed.

"Think so?" Callahan touched the knot of the silk tie, blue with white anchors. "Thought I'd turn over a new leaf. I'm angling for a job at *Vanity Fair,* see? Or maybe *The New Yorker.*"

Clare laughed and shifted position on the studded leather upholstery. "That'll be the day." A pause. "Some spinster aunt die and leave you a bundle?"

"Nah. Why do you ask?"

"New duds cost money."

"I'm unlucky in love," he said, hinting he'd hit some kind of jackpot.

She seemed to buy that. She reached across the table to cover her hand with his, a lily pad on a toad. "It's your choice," she said.

"What?"
"Being unlucky in love."
Again Callahan felt his resistance crumbling.

As Dante bought the yellow gardenia from Mrs. Califate, Callahan went about the business of business with Jimmy the Judge. At first he wasn't asked to do much. He channeled early race wire results to horse parlors around town. He passed along tips from the City Hall and Albany bureaus about bills or committee activities that might affect the price of beer and booze. Most of such info could have come from operatives at Tammany and other precincts of the molochs. But Callahan was required to demonstrate his fealty. He pictured himself one day besieged by pols seeking judgeships, badgered by cops wanting promotions, having to take rakeoffs on works projects, skimming from the sale of hospital alcohol to rum-runners, pushing into partnerships in bail bond outfits. A pretty picture. Well, it would be worth it. How else did you get the big story, he rationalized again and again, except by being there.

Was he ready for such a headlong plunge into the fire? And without getting burned?

He was going out on assignment, this one from the Judge. He had a date at Nigger Mike's in Chinatown with a cop who wore a braid on his hat and whose stink no amount of bay rum could camouflage—Roland O'Hara.

In the cab heading downtown he thought about Dante. The kid still touched a chord in him. He supposed one might label it parental. He knew by now he would never have a son and he disowned his spiritual offspring, but it troubled him. He felt an odd sense of loss. As the taxi passed the Lyric Theater on Third Avenue where a Chaplin picture, Tom Mix shoot-em-up, a Pathé newsreel and a short were featured, he tried to put it out of his mind, but didn't have much luck.

The tenements of East Houston Street, festooned with flapping laundry, passed by. After a few blocks Callahan ordered the driver to drop him off on Division Street in front of the Gambetta snuff shop, where he wanted to buy a fistful of stogies. He left the store lighting up a Havana Imperiale, patted his hip pocket to make sure the envelope was still there.

He speculated about why the Judge had tabbed him for this. The offered explanation—that it would appear normal for a deputy police commissioner to hobnob with a reporter rather than a hoodlum—rang false. After all, the meeting was to take place in an illegal watering hole. Callahan figured he knew the real reason: Fitzgerald wanted to entangle him more tightly in the web, testing his loyalty by having him perform a few overt acts. The Judge was no fool. Callahan knew it was a dangerous game he was playing.

O'Hara, tomato face looking even redder under the mane of pure white hair, was downing gin bucks. He gave Callahan a hearty greeting of bonhomie as his washed-out blue eyes said welcome to the ranks. They chit-chatted about Knute Rockne's winning streak and Johnny Weissmuller's retirement from swimming competition. Finally Callahan took out the envelope and handed it to O'Hara, who took the graft and slipped it into his pocket. "Had dinner?" he asked Callahan pleasantly.

"No thanks, I have a date."

Callahan, of course, was lying. He did not want to spend any more time than he had to with the likes of O'Hara. He clung to his secret professional motives, yet also was honest enough with himself to feel like shit.

Jimmy Walker, ex-song writer, had a way with words. He defined a reformer as "a guy riding through a sewer in a glass-bottom boat." But Callahan figured the description fit himself and his activities to a T nowadays. The glass-bottom boat was his double life—even if one was in the service of the other, or so he saw it—as a crime reporter moonlighting as a gangster. The sewer was New York City and environs at a time when the legendary alligators were among its more benign denizens.

Once at a meeting in a chop suey palace the Judge, looking even more than usually like a gila monster, asked Callahan why he wasn't wearing the emerald stickpin he had given him.

Callahan could think of lots of arguments against wearing it but rationality in such heavily symbolic matters was not among Jimmy's strong points.

Callahan put the stickpin on. The Judge managed a facial contortion, a rictus that was his version of a smile.

Another time, in the back room of a gambling casino near Jamaica Bay, Footsie pressed upon Callahan a belly gun with a pearl handle.

Horrified, Callahan tried to give it back. "I'd only shoot my own foot off," he said. Visions of barbed wire in France sparked in his head. But Footsie forced him to take the gun. It landed in his dresser drawer, under the onion skins of an aborted novel.

On the credit—or was it debit?—side the money rolled in. A consolation prize for a damaged conscience? Although he blew a lot of it at the crap tables, it was something new not to have to duck creditors on every corner. He was even considering saying goodbye to the flea trap he lived in but nixed the idea. After all, he reminded himself, he wasn't doing this to live the life of Riley, was he? His object was to get the goods on the bad guys. The line between illusion and reality was getting blurred enough without making it worse by curling up in the lap of luxury.

One night the guided tour included a three-day detour to Cape May and points of interest in between. The side trip (which sent Bruce into conniption fits when Callahan went AWOL) included a for-real trip in a boat, though not glass-bottom, motoring beyond the three-mile limit to rendezvous with a freighter out of Port Glasgow carrying a shipment of liquid gold that would net a half-million when cut and sold.

Callahan had received the order to accompany the divine Footsie to the booze drop as he came out of a Ziegfeld show featuring Clayton, Jackson and Durante. Callahan was still humming "Who Will Be With You When I'm Far Away (Far Away Out in Far Rockaway)" when Footsie took him to Leon and Eddie's to buy him a drink and break the news about the job. The tone of the request brooked no protest. In a few minutes Callahan found himself in the rear seat of a cream-colored Minerva Landaulet burrowing through the Holland Tunnel. Footsie finally volunteered a few words of explanation.

"We need you to taste the stuff, make sure it ain't been cooked from rotten potatoes. And we need you to flash the old press card if we meet up with the feds."

Horseshit, Callahan told himself. The Judge figured he was just rubbing his nose in it. Don't blow it, he told himself, as he sank into the black leather and smoked a Manila, wind from the open car window cooling his face.

Footsie said, "Better shut the window."

"It's hot tonight."

"The glass is bulletproof."

My hide isn't, thought Callahan, shutting the window and gazing at the oak-paneled dashboard loaded with gauges and needles.

When they reached the coast it was night and an invigorating breeze wafted off the ocean. Callahan got out of the car and quickly lit another cigar, inhaling the salt air, listening to the serenading surf.

"Squash the stogie," said Footsie.

"It's a fifty-cent panatella—"

"The coast is crawling with feds."

Callahan heeled the cigar into the sandy ground. God, he detested Footsie.

"Say a rosary, bright boy, that you get back to New York with no lead in your butt."

Basil Bianco, chauffeur for the outing, had parked the car in a sheltered inlet of Delaware Bay. Basil stayed in the car while Footsie wagged at Callahan to follow down a path through scrub pine and dunes. Distant stars provided the only light. In a few minutes they reached a grove of tall trees under which were parked four large trucks bearing signs that read *Philadelphia House Paints*. Footsie told

Callahan to wait by the side of the road while he conferred with the drivers and bruisers in soft caps who, Callahan assumed, rode shotgun.

Returning, Footsie said, "Everything's copacetic. Come on."

They walked a few yards to a dilapidated pier and waited, water sloshing on the wooden posts. No other sound until the putt-putt of an Evinrude outboard reached their ears. At the rudder was an old salt with the gray face of weathered driftwood. He bit down on an unlit pipe and said nothing. Callahan and Footsie scrambled into the dinghy.

They sailed to the middle of the bay, where they transferred to a large launch, *Sabrina,* brandishing a light machine gun in her bow. Callahan, already holding his stomach, tottered below decks to lie down.

Lights extinguished and motor muffled, the launch plowed out to open sea. In the hold Callahan groaned. It all reminded him of when he was a doughboy on the gut-wrenching voyage to Calais.

Somehow the vessel managed to avoid running into any Coast Guard cutters as it made its way to the Scottish freighter seven miles off the Jersey Coast. Here on the Stygian ocean they were temporarily safe from the searchlights and guns of the dry-law enforcers. Callahan, his instincts as a reporter aroused, went topside to watch the operation.

The launch was tied up to the small freighter. Her decks swarmed with a crew with holsters at their hips and tommyguns slung over their shoulders, signaling some distrust of the moral rectitude of their clients . . . pirating booze from suppliers was no rare event.

Footsie, who had gone aboard the freighter to powwow with the skipper and, Callahan assumed, lade the sailors' pockets with U. S. currency, soon returned with a big smile and a small brown paper bundle under his arm. He ordered the crew to start loading.

Two hours later 1,300 cases of uncut high-quality Scotch whiskey were stashed under the *Sabrina*'s tarps. A crescent moon raced above the scudding clouds.

Footsie said they were on schedule in their race against daylight. Callahan looked at his watch. It was one-thirty A.M. At about three they would start loading the trucks. At six the convoy would roll into the warehouse outside Philly, beating the dawn. With luck.

Everything went smoothly. State motorcycle cops would pass the phony paint trucks with salutes of recognition. Transporting booze was a federal rap and a federal headache. Out of range of the revenue fleet, the bootleggers could breathe more easily. Of course they could not let down their guard entirely, the United States Attorney's Office still had its Izzie Einsteins prowling the back roads of America.

Ten minutes before dawn the sleek Belgian-made Minerva pulled up to the warehouse in Clifton Heights, trailed by the trucks. Callahan, puffing on a cigar, wondered when he was supposed to put the hootch to the palate test. The dangerous assignment had some delicious perks. He knew, of course, this had just been a way to get him deeper into a hole where if he should stool on the Judge he would incriminate himself. But judges could make mistakes too. . . .

A couple who rode shotgun now scrambled down to unbolt the exterior doors and the vehicles passed into an enormous garage where a crew of five more armed men waited. What at first appeared as a solid wall at the north end of the garage opened up to reveal a gigantic freight elevator that, Footsie explained, would carry the loaded ten-ton trucks down to a sub-basement where the contraband would be stored. Callahan had to marvel at the scope of the Judge's operation. He knew that, besides this and other warehouses, the gang had a cutting plant where Scotch was mixed with pure grain alcohol made in distilleries licensed to produce legal liquor for hospitals and other uses. The gang also controlled a printing plant making phony labels and revenue stamps and a factory to manufacture bottles just like the Scottish ones. The operation could turn one bottle of whiskey into three or four with little loss of quality to any but the most educated palate. Most speak patrons were too pickled to tell the difference between fine whiskey and camel's piss anyhow, and the hybrid stuff packed a powerful wallop.

"We made it," said Footsie.

"Yah," said Callahan, "no feds on land or sea."

"I wasn't worried about agents. I was worried about hijackers. They don't haul you before a nice proper judge." He mocked a throat-slash with his forefinger.

"We ready to head back to New York?" Callahan asked.

"Pretty soon."

"My city editor, he'll be—"

"Hey, let's have a taste of the real stuff," Footsie suggested, and they went over to the car and grabbed a bottle he had removed from the cargo. "None of that circus water you're used to swilling," he added, breaking the seal.

"Excellent idea," said Callahan.

Basil was told to fetch three glasses.

They tossed down the whiskey neat. "How's the shoulder?" Footsie asked.

"Fine."

"You're lucky it wasn't your nuts."

"I know."

Footsie poured again and raised his glass. "Here's to the fucking Volstead Act."

"I'll drink to that," piped up Basil.

Representative Andrew Joseph Volstead, Callahan thought, patron saint of the bootleggers. He drank.

Footsie smacked his chops. "Sit tight for a few minutes. Gotta make a phone call."

It was noon by the time the sedan emerged from the tunnel and rolled into Manhattan. They had stopped for breakfast at a roadside joint in New Jersey, but even three cups of coffee hadn't prevented Callahan from nodding off on the ride. Now Footsie jabbed an elbow in his ribs.

"Home sweet home," he announced. "Rise and shine, Callahan. We're in New York."

Footsie had a copy of the racing form in his lap. A fly buzzed the bulletproof window glass. "The Judge has another little job for you," he said.

Callahan sighed, and inwardly wondered if he could take it. "What now?" he asked.

Footsie reached down and picked up the brown package Callahan had seen him take off the freighter. He handed it to Callahan. "A drop," he said.

Callahan hefted the bundle, shook it next to his gnarled ear. "What is it?"

"Sweet dreams."

"Jimmy deals in—?"

"He's expanding his business. Al Smith lost the election, sure. Thanks to rum-runners saying rosaries against him. But the Judge says Prohibition ain't gonna last forever."

". . . What kind of stuff is this?"

"A brick of raw opium. The skipper picked it up in Athens just before sailing here. Hey, the Chinese live on this stuff. It's good for you."

"Why can't *you* deliver it?" And knowing the answer as he asked. Another test. But he needed to protest to be credible. . . .

"The Judge has his reasons," Footsie said.

Damn right he did.

As the car turned sharply on Fourteenth Street, Callahan bumped against Footsie's rock-solid body. Driving east they passed the Corinthian facade of the Civic Repertory Theater, and Callahan idly studied the carved face of a woman (Minerva?) over the arch of the door. "What's the deal?" he asked.

"It's all arranged," twanged Footsie through his bent septum. "You go to the Confucius Republican Club on Doyers Street tomorrow night at ten sharp. You tell them at the door you're delivering the shipment of black tea and you wanna see the head man. They'll take it from there."

"The Chinks really smoke this?"

"Sure. They even give it to their kids to keep them quiet. The yellow bastards got no morals."

The sedan stopped in front of Callahan's apartment

building near Union Square, across from the S. Klein department store ("Serving the Best Dressed Women"). Callahan, package under his arm, got out the rear door and saluted Footsie.

The punchy trigger man showed his sparkling bridgework. Rubber squealed on the cobblestones.

"Hell," said Callahan to himself, the package searing his armpit. "Damn it to hell." A helluva price to pay. What would be next? He studied the statue of Lafayette in the park before turning and tramping up to his room, where he quickly fell into a deep sleep.

The next day he was reluctant to go to the city room and face Ivan Bruce, so he did a very mature thing: he went to the racetrack instead. After all, he reflected, why face the music when you can write your own tunes . . . and besides, you're really working for Bruce even if he doesn't know it. Such rationalizations still provided some necessary comfort. But for how long . . . ?

He returned to Manhattan with a wad of winnings and got ready for his excursion to Chinatown. On the door to his apartment had been tacked several notes from his landlady, which he tore up without reading. How does one dress, he pondered, to get stabbed in the back by a pigtailed hophead? Or shanghaied by a crew of Manchus? He decided on the same rumpled seersucker he was wearing. Seersucker for a sucker. Before the dresser mirror he planted on his head at a jaunty angle a battered straw boater.

He took the streetcar downtown through the Lower East Side. The people, fleeing the infernal tenements, filled the fire escapes and streets where kids squealed in the open hydrants and boys and girls necked on stoops. Some couples cakewalked on the sidewalk. The streetcar rolled over the cobblestoned Bowery, past a candy-striped barber pole in front of a tonsorial school, past the Fulton Hotel, past the Blossom Restaurant featuring oxtail stew and Vienna roast beans, past a strictly Kosher chicken market with trussed-up birds hanging on meat hooks in the display window.

At Chatham Square Callahan hopped off the streetcar, crossed the thoroughfare and found the narrow winding alley the city planners called Doyers Street. He saw old men trotting along, wearing wispy goatees, skullcaps and what looked like black silk pajamas. Squat tenements were plastered with posters in Chinese calligraphy of black and red. The bystanders treated Callahan as if he were invisible.

He found the Confucius Republican Club in the basement of a four-story brick house. The moon-faced man who answered the door peered at him suspiciously, but he nodded and stood aside after Callahan repeated what Footsie had told him to say.

He followed the duck-footed guide into one big room on the landing, a room filled with teacups, water pipes and cardboard boxes.

Four men in silk mandarin coats were playing mahjong. In unison they looked up at his entrance, regarded him with eyes glittering with mistrust, then resumed the game. As Callahan walked past an old Cannon Ball stove toward another door in the rear, he pictured the head man to whom he was about to deliver the package. He would be a bronze Mongol, with the belly of Buddha and a jagged kris under his belt. Better still it would not be a man at all but a raven-haired mixed breed with violet lips and a slit up her silk kimono reaching her hip.

The person he met in the back room sitting behind a large steel desk fulfilled neither vision. It was his brother, Nick Callahan.

"Park it, pal," said the silver-haired state senator who was Callahan's next-of-kin, motioning to a chair.

"I'll be a cross-eyed coolie," the younger brother said.

Nick Callahan wagged a finger. "Better watch your syntax around here."

Callahan sat on the wooden swivel chair. "So. You peddle junk to chinks." An unintended pun. He removed his fedora and mopped his forehead.

"They're loyal constituents, these people, salt of the earth."

"How low can you sink?"

"Come off it. You refuse to be my press agent but you agree to be the Judge's errand boy. I can't figure you out."

Callahan grimaced, tasting crawfish. He wanted to push Nick off his high horse with a protest that he wasn't really a turncoat but a snoop on the trail of a big story.

"So welcome to the club, brother. It's about time you wised up."

Callahan dangled his arms between his knees, looking like he just swallowed castor oil. He avoided looking directly at his brother's smug expression. He took out a panatella. "You hooked on this stuff yourself?"

Nick waved the idea away. "Not on your life. I've tried it, though."

Callahan lit the cigar, blew out the match. "Did you have a mystical experience, a deep insight into the nature of reality?"

"Yah. I saw a skywriter saying Fiorella LaGuardia was really Al Capone in disguise. No kidding, though. What it mostly does is make you not give a hoot. It puts things in perspective. You're a speck in the universe. The great tragedy of your existence is reduced to flyshit."

"Doesn't booze do that?"

"The opposite. Booze inflates a man's sense of his own importance. Makes us all think we're King Lear or something. Or Oedipus with fucking bleeding eyeballs."

So much for a college education, Callahan thought. He looked around the room. Romanticized portraits of Warren Harding, Calvin Coolidge, Herbert Hoover and Chiang Kai-Shek glowered down from the blistered walls. In a display case behind Nick's desk stood a matchstick reproduction of a Chinese memorial gateway. Piles of newspaper and campaign literature were stacked about.

Nick wigwagged his fingers. "Give it here."

Callahan had almost forgotten the package. He handed it over. Without bothering to open or inspect it, Nick put the contraband in a briefcase that sat on the floor next to his feet, buckled it securely and grinned. "Thanks," he said. "And don't snitch to the League of Nations."

Callahan chewed the cigar. "Looks like you got a lot of irons in the fire, Nick."

"Pays to diversify."

"Were you . . . in cahoots with Madigan too?"

"You asking as reporter, brother or fellow capitalist?"

"As a born busybody."

"I work with anybody who has fat in the fryer."

"Including Pellegrino?"

"Ever known me to discriminate against wops?"

"Roll out the pork barrel, right?"

"Right." Nick narrowed his eyes. "Look here, I never pretended to aspire to sainthood. You know that. Not counting campaign speeches, of course, which everybody knows are bullshit, I have always laid it straight on the line. At least I'm honest about my dishonesty, which is more than I can say for most people. I may try to pull wool over the voters' eyes but I don't try to kid myself."

Callahan blew out a cloud of smoke. "What kind of business did you conduct with Scoop?"

"Looking for pointers?"

"Maybe."

"Among other ventures we ran a bucket shop together."

"Shady stock deals?"

"A redundancy if I ever heard one."

"How's it work?"

"Like everything else in commerce, dear Brother, the engine is fueled by a combustible mixture of greed and ignorance." Nick seemed to revel in his own knavishness, as some sort of emblem of superiority. "We tell the suckers we're buying a certain stock at margin and that the certificates are in the hands of a bank. Meanwhile we sell the stocks at a slight profit, pocket the difference and go on charging the client interest. A pigeon here, a pigeon there. It adds up."

"I'm not sure I get it."

"Neither do the clients. Gives us the upper hand."

Callahan flicked ashes onto the floorboards. "What happened between Scoop and Pellegrino?"

Nick playacted washing his hands. "I stayed clear of that one. I'm like Switzerland. I try to keep neutral in time of war. A healthy foreign policy."

"It's not always possible, though, is it?"

"I work hard at it."

Callahan almost envied the simplicity of his brother's code of behavior. "How's the wife?" he finally asked, moving from foreign to domestic affairs.

"Peg's fine."

"Kids?"

"I don't run into them much. Gwen's at Vassar, majoring in petting, I think. Dominick plays the ukelele and cracks up roadsters for a living. You know, Flaming Youth and all that. They usually pass fingernail inspection."

"Maybe I'd like to see them sometime," Callahan proposed tentatively.

"Come over to the house. I'll try to arrange it through their social secretaries."

Callahan threw down the half-smoked cigar and stepped on it. "Sure was different when we were growing up."

"Not *when* so much as *where.*"

"Yeah."

"Oyster Bay is paradise compared to the freight yards." Nick looked rueful. "Though I think my kids could use a billy club across the head once in a while." He looked up sharply at his brother. "When are you gonna climb out of the slums, Johnny boy?"

"Me? I'd be a fish out of water."

"That kind of thinking is what keeps you down. The sky's the limit, that's my motto."

Nick flashed a puckish smile, and in that instant Callahan thought he glimpsed the secret of his brother's roguish charm. It was based on pure physical magnetism, with nothing much at all behind it. In spite of the silver in his center-parted hair, the man radiated boyishness, the illusion that he was as green as a shoot of new grass. It all came from the way he looked. The twinkling eyes of a sprite, the dimpled smile of a cherub camouflaging the heart of a snake.

"What about the lives you wreck along the way?" Callahan asked.

Nick stared at his brother. "Guys like you and me didn't start out life with any aces in the deck, right? Only jokers."

"And that gives us a license to lie, steal, cheat and kill?"

"I don't need a license. I'm not hunting or fishing. I'm getting the most out of life while I'm here. Trouble with you, you still think in terms of the Ten Commandments. Right and wrong, sin and retribution. Hey—when it's all over you won't know what hit you."

"Meaning?"

"Meaning the Man Upstairs, if He exists, is running a bucket shop, John Joseph Callahan. He's taking you for a ride."

"You're a bad guy, Nick. Rotten through and through."

"I know."

Callahan probed more. "You in league with O'Hara too?"

"He owns a piece of the Wall Street operation. That's just a fraction of the business he conducts around town. You know how a sailor has a girl in every port? That copper has a bagman on every street."

"And Whalen?"

"I shot my mouth off enough for one day. Remember, you're still a reporter." Callahan had been trying to do just that.

"Aren't you afraid of getting caught?"

"Who's gonna squeal on me, the Democrats? Who's gonna prosecute me? Everybody in town's got his hand in the cookie jar."

"Things could change. And soon."

Nick shrugged. "You take your chances."

"Prohibition won't last forever."

"I agree. That's why I'm into sweet dreams, one-armed bandits, stocks. The market boom is here to stay."

Callahan wondered. He recalled the old days in Hell's

Kitchen when Nick was always conniving how to steal from a shopkeeper or remove freight from a boxcar with the same enthusiasm other boys applied to making Halloween costumes.

Nick asked, "The Judge treating you right?"

". . . Fine."

"How much?"

"More than I ever expected to make in my life." True.

"How much?" Nick repeated.

"Six yards a week."

"Candy corn," Nick said. "You should get that much for this one errand—"

"It's enough for me." Maybe too much . . .

"You got a bargain-basement soul."

"Maybe."

"Not me, Johnny boy. Always priced myself high. While the other kids were pinching pennies from the collection plate I ran patent medicines based on cocaine for Petracci at five bucks a day—big money then. Yeah. To buy my soul you gotta make a trip to the mint."

Listening to this odd boast, Callahan wore an icy smile. He reflected on Nick's roguish sense of humor, how he wore the emblems of corruption like a bright row of medals on his chest. Callahan touched his tie; he wasn't wearing the emerald stickpin.

Callahan got up. "I'll be leaving."

"Johnny?"

"Yeah?"

"I'm glad we had this heart-to-heart."

Is that what he called it? "Sure."

"Wait a second." Nick reached into the breast pocket of his silk jacket and placed a wad of bills in Callahan's hand, then closed his brother's fingers over it.

"Take it. Butter for your bread."

Frowning, he flipped through the bills, a cyclorama of Alexander Hamiltons. "That's a pretty big smear," Callahan said.

"It's a grand. You take risks, you earned it."

In more ways than one. Callahan was tempted to hand the money back, but that would look suspicious. After all, this was his brother. . . .

He pocketed the money and went out to get pissed.

As he walked through the cobbled streets of Chinatown he had to wonder whether he had what it took to finger his own brother if and when he finally blew the whistle on these activities. He also wondered whether he would live to feel guilty about it.

Chapter
13

DANTE'S INFERNO

AFTER the encounter with Lily the faun grew horns. Night after night he tossed and turned on a bed of fire in his Bleecker Street apartment. The taste of sex after a long abstinence had roused hunger for more. It was hard to say no whenever Lily telephoned to suggest that he visit her. But he steeled himself to make excuses. Seeing her meant playing with fire, he had decided. Of course spurning her also carried risks. Hell hath no fury, after all . . . The infernal images kept springing up like effigies in a spook house.

Dante got up from bed and went to the newspaper office, consoling himself by writing of death.

Occasionally the shape of a secretary's behind stoked his libido. Or a memory of Lily's lovemaking surfaced to distract him. But he managed to plow his way through the day's work without giving in to temptation and phoning her up.

Thinking about the Madigan case helped distract him from desiring Lily. The rubout of Frank Marlow kept the rumor mills grinding, and the tabloids tooted statements and efforts by reformers to expunge crime, graft and vice while readers clucked their tongues, swilled their hootch and yawned.

The Madigan killing ebbed from the public memory. But Dante couldn't forget. And wouldn't forget. Even though Callahan had told him about the publisher calling off the investigation (for some mysterious reason), Dante felt personally affronted by the Madigan killing. To him it was not just another rubout but a blot on the escutcheon of big-city journalism, the adopted shield of this passionate avatar of Sicilian bravoes. It was a matter he sometimes believed he could die for.

As he typed a caption for the overset Dante noticed that Clare Parker had come into the city room to file a feature story, a feeling of depression swept over him, an indigo longing. He saw her stop to flirt with Callahan, and he suddenly grasped the irrational truth of her attraction to the veteran reporter. He had been obtuse. Now another fire licked at him. But he had no proprietary rights, so how could he be jealous? Nevertheless the emotion gripped him and it was very painful.

As he watched Clare and Cal, Dante thought how easy they were with one another. He waited until they had left the office together before wrapping up his own work and calling it a day. He pointedly avoided Baker's speakeasy, where he supposed they had gone. He bought a bag of peanuts from a street vendor and sat on a bench in City Hall Park, feeding pigeons and collecting his thoughts and feelings. As the birds warbled around his feet, the tinder-box of memory sparked with images from readings in high school. He saw the minotaur's coiling tail and heard the cry of cranes. He saw the infernal pit into which libertines were hurled. The Jesuits, he reflected, did a thorough job of indoctrination, enlisting great poets and thinkers. Reason might repudiate the teachings, but the symbols clung, they clung like barnacles. There were good and bad among the Jesuits, of course. Dante never forgot a kind old jebbie's reminder that he bore the name of a great classical poet. Which had a major impact on his decision to become a writer. His Jesuit mentors also had given him the tools to educate himself, to learn without having gone to college . . .

He dumped the contents of the peanut bag on the ground for the pigeons and headed uptown. He stopped at Ham's newsstand for a copy of Bernarr MacFadden's *Graphic,* a tawdry tabloid if there ever was one. Dante was addicted to Walter Winchell's Broadway gossip column. He took a trolley home to his Greenwich Village walkup, kicked off his two-tone oxfords and read of love nests and divorce trials and an axe murder staged photographically in a so-called composograph. Soon he was engrossed in Winchell's snappy style and piquant morsels of gossip.

One item made him sit up and take extra notice:

What rising star in the underworld firmament that goes under the nefarious name of "The Black Hand" has taken up residence in a penthouse of the swank Barbizon Plaza, giving him an eagle's view of the city he hopes to subjugate? Tsk, tsk, hoteliers. I guess you don't give a hoot how soiled the greenbacks are as long as they fatten your profit line. Oh yes, the public enemy in question sports the moniker "Big Guy."

A.K.A. Gaetano Pellegrino, Dante concluded.

The telephone rang.

"Put your feedbag and your glad rags on, dear boy, I'm taking you out for a night on the town."

He winced at the sound of Lily's voice. "Sorry, but I'm bushed."

She ignored him. "I've got it all planned. First we grab a juicy steak at Peter Luger's. Then dancing at the Dernier Cri. Finally breakfast at the Brass Rail. Or maybe we'll skip the last stop and have meat pie at your place." Giggling, she added, "My kennel's out, I'm afraid. The big bad wolf is back from France."

"I'll take a raincheck," he said. "I had a real rough day at the office."

Silence at the other end. Finally she replied in a clipped tone, "My Daimler will pick you up in an hour." She hung up.

He frowned at the phone and replaced it in the cradle. The implied threat in her voice still echoed. The unspoken message had been clear: Daddy pays your salary. Do you want him to continue to do so?

He sighed and went over to the wardrobe to air out the camphor odor from his soup-and-fish.

The steak was delicious and a rare treat. On the salary Daddy paid him Dante couldn't afford T-bone very often. Bowing to the inevitable he ate with gusto and anticipated the carnal pleasures to come.

She, on the other hand, hardly touched her chateaubriand. She obviously was pouting over having had to imply blackmail to get him to see her. Sawing away at the steak he had to admit that she looked pretty juicy in the strapless black dinner dress. Her mouth, scarlet and sulky, looked inviting. Egotism aside, he admired the singlemindedness of her pursuit of him and the candor of her sexual appetite. If she weren't hitched he might consider her in a more serious light, maybe even convince himself to fall for her or at least use her as a distraction from his infatuation with Clare. Pouring catsup on french fries he said, "You look pretty swell tonight."

Her mask of pique loosened. "Thanks. That goes double for you, lover boy."

"I'm sorry I hesitated about going out with you tonight. I've been working pretty hard lately and I have to be at the office early."

"Take tomorrow off, I'll square it with the boss."

"No. I don't want special favors."

"Don't be silly, Dante. Take whatever edge you can get. That's my philosophy. You're wasting your talents on obituaries anyhow. I'll see what I can do about getting you a spot on the reporting staff. What beat would you like to cover?"

Get thee behind me, Satan, he thought. "No thanks," he said.

"What gives with you? Why be a sap?"

"I know it sounds corny, but I want to make it on my own merits."

She rolled her eyes. "Oh brother!" That's what you're doing, pumpkin. I got a gander at your merits."

That sounded like condescension. "No, thanks," he repeated. He added a boast, stretching the truth a little: "I'm not only writing obits, you know. I'm working on an undercover story."

"Really? Tell me all about it." She propped her elbows on the table, laced her fingers together and leaned her chin on them.

"It's kind of hush-hush."

"All the more intriguing."

"Well, I can tell you this much: it has to do with Scoop Madigan."

Her face grew thoughtful, wary. "Oh. The reporter who was mixed up with gangsters."

"Was it that obvious?" Dante asked.

"What's the big deal about a reporter being in league with the rum-runners? Don't you know everybody's in bed with those bastards?"

"It's different when it comes to newspaper reporters," Dante said heatedly.

"You really think so? And how about publishers?"

"How about them?"

"My father's no better than a gangster, under the spit and polish. Neither are his competitors."

"That's a lot of hokum," he said, a defensive note in his voice, but he also began wondering about how the Madigan story got put on the shelf.

"You think they're all John Peter Zengers? Grow up. They are not, dear boy, a collection of altruistic crusaders and muckrakers whose only interest is publishing the truth without fear of favor. They are, first and foremost, businessmen. They own pulp forests and rail lines and paper mills and real estate. They make shady deals with trade unions and political parties. They play the same cutthroat game as everybody else."

"Maybe so," said Dante. "But what about Pulitzer's exposés of the Panama Canal scandal? And look at Hearst. His editorials brought down the criminal trusts. He supported the striking miners in the anthracite coal fields. Let's give credit where it's due."

"They took on those causes because it sold newspapers and brought them profits and power, pure and simple."

Dante wore a reflective frown.

She softened and reached across to caress his hand. "But we don't have to solve the world's problems tonight, honey. My horseless chariot awaits. We'll dance, drink champagne, play roulette and make glorious love."

"Aren't you afraid we'll be seen together by somebody who will report back to your husband?"

"Pooh," she said, rising as a waiter held the back of her chair. "He has his own fish to fry."

He shook his head and got up. "Okay. But, remember, I have to be home fairly early—"

"Fat chance," she said, winking. "We're gonna shimmy all night, in both the vertical and horizontal positions." The draft from an electric fan made her dinner dress flutter around her plump dimpled knees.

Dante was hardly fit for work the next day but he managed to stagger in. He did his editorial tasks by rote. While he usually tried to give even two-heads a touch of polish or a twist of originality, today he resorted to serviceable cliches. His body was sore from the exertions of dancing, drinking and lovemaking. And he was troubled. He kept thinking about the conversation with Lily in the steakhouse and the confrontation with Patsy Secundo, and wondered what he would do next. Tired in body and mind, he made a decision.

At the end of the workday he got up the nerve to ask Ivan Bruce for a private conference. The city editor, amused, said okay.

"What's up, kid?" Bruce lit his pipe.

"Why have we dropped the Madigan story?"

Bruce smiled, but his words were provocative. "None of your business, pipsqueak."

"I have a right to know."

Bruce conceded the point with a shrug. "Orders from upstairs."

"Okay. Can I still work the story? Informally, I mean. See what I can come up with?"

"I need you on the obit desk."

"I'll investigate on my own time, okay? Nights and weekends. I'll just ask for a small amount of expenses."

Bruce took the pipe from his mouth. It was clear from his expression that he admired Dante's moxie. Maybe, he thought, the kid had what it took. He considered what his old country editor in Macon, Georgia, might have done in his shoes. He also reflected that Dante had another quality that had been gathering dust in Bruce's own bosom—professional ethics. "Okay," he said. "It's a free country."

Dante rose from the swivel chair. "Thanks," he said sincerely.

Bruce put his feet up on the desk, a look of concern etched into his rugged face. "And, son . . . ?"

"Yes?"

"Keep me posted. Keep it under wraps. I'll do what I can for you."

"Thanks again."

Dante went to bed that night bone-tired but in an improved mood. It felt good to take the situation by the throat. Summer night noises filtered through the screened window, a shrill nocturne. He felt peaceful, remembering the twang of his mother's old country lullaby.

He woke up the next morning with an inspiration and acted on it that very evening, taking the subway uptown to the Barbizon Plaza, where faking prior experience and appealing to the chauvinism of the Sicilian director of banquets and catering he applied for a job as a night room-service waiter.

"I can't work days because I attend classes at Columbia," he told the man who had long graying sideburns and a pencil-thin mustache. "This job would help pay my tuition. You see, Signore Ippolito, mamma scrubs floors in the Woolworth Building." He crossed himself for dramatic effect before adding, "Pappa, you see, took a shell at Vittorio Veneto . . ." He hunched his shoulders and turned palms upward in the ancient gesture of the Stoics. A gift for white lying was essential to a good newspaperman.

Ippolito's black eyes were liquid with compassion. "We will contact you as soon as a place becomes available," he promised Dante, clapping him on the shoulder in a paternal manner.

Dante left the hotel satisfied. He had managed to push from his mind the fear rising from Patsy Secundo's threats. A man had to have courage, after all.

On the subway ride downtown he thought about some basics. Most people plowed through life like oxen, avoiding risk, chasing small comforts. But this wasn't life, it was slow death. He would rather go out in a blaze of glory as cannon fodder like the father he had just invented for Ippolito than be broken under the yoke of false security.

And he thought of his real father, crushed reaching for the grail of simple sustenance. He was determined that this would not happen to him.

Chapter

14

A RELIABLE SOURCE

DANTE stood on the corner of Mulberry and Grand, having his wingtips shined and reading the *Times.* The news that was fit to print included an account of Governor Roosevelt's visit to Tammany Hall, where he delivered a fire-and-brimstoner denouncing big-business trusts that made him sound very much like a man afflicted with Potomac fever. He also read a sports thumbsucker about why the Yanks were trailing the Athletics in the pennant race. The answer could have been summed up in a name: Jimmy Foxx.

His eyes strayed from the newsprint. The street was littered with spent firecrackers, detritus of Independence Day celebrations. He saw the bootblack's cowlick and the flurry of his hands. He decided to make small talk. "Think the Yankees will catch up?" he asked the shoeshine boy.

"Who gives a pig's whistle?" said Tony Coco, smearing on a second coat of polish. "I'm a Dodger fan."

"How about Babe Herman, huh? Leading both leagues, batting over .400."

"Yeah," said the laconic twelve-year-old killjoy.

Dante gave up on him. He glanced around. On the corner Moretti the fruit merchant was selling slices of water-

melon to evening strollers. An old codger in a brown derby
sat in front of the Porto Empedocle Social Club reading a
copy of *Il Progresso* with a magnifying glass in the waning
sunlight. A young hood named Willy Ottone was showing
off his new Packard to a few *lazzaroni.* Dante was relieved
to notice that Patsy wasn't around.

Dante had been poking his finely carved nose around
again, ignoring Patsy's threats to turn him into chopped
meat. At least chopped meat was red-blooded, better than
behaving like a yellow squash. He didn't want to wake up
one morning to discover that somewhere on the bumpy
trolley ride he had misplaced his dream. He knew Patsy's
threats were serious and he feared them. He knew what a
hard and unforgiving place the world could be. But he
feared more the prospect of an empty and meaningless
life, playing it safe until they shoveled earth over him. No,
not for Dante, whose idols were Stephen Crane and his *Red
Badge of Courage* and Richard Harding Davis. Not for
Dante Viola, of ringing name and maybe future fame. Not
on your ever-loving life.

He had managed to unearth a few facts, too, nosing
around the neighborhood. His questions and manner had
been discreet, embroidered with chitchat, cloaked in
obliquities. A patch of info came from the old lady who
sold dago red. A rumor came from a bricklayer who lived
down the hall from Dante. A scrap was overheard in the
illegal tavern on Elizabeth Street. An eliptical tapestry
emerged of Guy Pellegrino and his dealings with a brash
Irisher named Homer "Scoop" Madigan.

It looked more or less like this: Pellegrino wanted to open
a gambling joint in a prime location in Hell's Kitchen,
where Jimmy the Judge had the muscle; Madigan demanded twenty-five percent in tribute; Big Guy balked,
threatened to open up without an okay; Madigan said he'd
get a high police official who's in the Judge's pocket to
close him down; the hot-blooded Big Guy blew his stack,
hired Junior Riccio to ice the two-faced reporter; now the
Sicilian council of elders put Pellegrino on the shitlist for
rubbing out a newspaper reporter without their benedic-

tion (which probably they would not have given anyway since it hurt business).

So, if this version was mostly correct, the Big Guy was in the position of having to protect himself from a pincer movement: Jimmy the Judge wanted his ass; the Sicilian satraps wanted his head.

But—if one credited neighborhood scuttlebutt—Pellegrino might be more than equal to the challenge. The rumormongers painted him in garish colors, an avatar of Attila, ruthless, ambitious, courageous, fear-inspiring, highly intelligent and—well, odd. The word was, he had either a bright future or no future at all.

Then there were whispers, confidential, hushed. Intimations of things too dark to utter aloud concerning Gaetano Pellegrino and his barbarous ways. Taboo subjects. They were not voiced, but hinted at in the arch of an eyebrow, the kissing of a crucifix at the mere mention of his name, the shaking of a hand held limp at the wrist. These gestures had fired Dante's curiosity much more than any facts he had learned about the man.

But he could not seem to get any hard details. The remark of a man in the Elizabeth Street speak echoed in Dante's mind: "Pellegrino makes Mad Dog Coll look like a choirboy."

Tony Coco tapped Dante's ankle and started on the second shoe. Dante made another stab at engaging him in conversation. He blurted out a familiar question directed at kids: "What do you want to be when you grow up, Tony?"

The boy didn't hesitate. "A killer," he said.

Dante was temporarily tongue-tied. "A ladykiller, you mean," he said hopefully.

"Nah," said Tony, fixing Dante with a flinty eye. "I wanna pack a machine gun and kill people."

"You mean you want to be a soldier?"

"Maybe. Maybe I'll just mow 'em down in the streets. Duh-duh-duh-duh-dum. My old man wuz killed," he added, jerking his head. "Right down here on Canal and Lafayette."

"No kidding? Sorry to hear that."

"Yeah, they give him a bellyful of lead maybe two years ago. Sent 'im straight to hell and no parole. I'll fix their wagons someday."

"You know who's responsible?"

"Sure I know. Big Guy Pellegrino's boys done him in. The no-good fuckin' scumbags. When I grow up I'm gonna scatter his brains from here to the Battery. Maybe even before I grow up."

Dante's pulse quickened. He might have found here a source who would talk without being afraid of his own shadow. "Why did they kill your father?" he asked.

The boy tapped Dante's shoe to indicate he had finished shining it. He rested his buttocks on the backs of his heels and asked, "Got a weed?"

Dante reached into his pocket and handed him a Home Run.

"Tanks," said the boy, accepting a light from a match held out by Dante. "They said the old man welched on a gambling debt but that was bullshit. Louie Coco was no deadbeat. They fuckin' liars, is what." He spat out cigarette smoke.

"What was the real reason, then?"

"Aw, you wouldn't believe me nohow. Nobody believes me. But hey, it's the God's honest truth. My mudder told me the whole story and she wouldn't lie. She's practically a saint."

"Try me," said Dante.

"Okay, get this—my old man was rubbed out because he wouldn't play house with Guy Pellegrino."

"Huh? What do you mean, play house?"

"I mean the big bad gangster's queer, that's what I mean. And he fell for my old man like a ton of bricks. Hey, my father was a real handsome guinea, you know? The old lady says she used to have to beat the women off with a stick. Here's the thing: My father did some jobs for Pellegrino. A heist here, a booze run there. You know. How else is a dago just off the boat gonna make a few bucks? But it was all strictly business. Pellegrino, he wants to mix business with funny business. Catch my meaning? Natcherly

the old man says nothin' doing. He told 'im to shove it up
his own keister, if it was long enough. My old man was *all*
man, see?"

Dante was dumbstruck. He wondered how much of this
monologue he could believe. Incredible as it seemed on the
surface, the kid sounded square.

"So the bastard made up an excuse and told his goons to
moider my father. Someday I'll retoin the favor." Tony
Coco's dark eyes smoked at the idea. "When I do it," he
added, "I'll stick the gat up his ass. He might like that."

Dante gave Tony a quarter and filed the conversation
away for future reference. All in all he had to consider the
kid a reliable source. It was hard to picture him inventing
such an outrageous story. But it was also hard to imagine
a homosexual ranking so high in the mob. Still, he supposed it was possible if the mobster inspired great fear and
kept his sex life very discreet. He remembered hearing
that Pellegrino was a bachelor, not that this meant very
much.

At home Dante cooked dinner, spaghetti with oil and garlic. He ate in a kitchen that gleamed with applicances that
he had bought on time—a Frigidaire with chrome deco
insignia and a toaster that cooked two slices of bread at
once. Owning the items filled him with furtive pride. He
suddenly yearned for Clare's platinum presence. He realized that his feeling for her was infatuation disguised as
passion, but the realization wasn't enough to bank the
fires.

He washed down the meal with an amber home-brewed
wine. It had a robust taste and strong kick. He was trying
to work up the nerve to phone Clare to invite her to accompany him to the new Mary Pickford talkie everyone was
gossiping about, *Coquette.* America's Sweetheart had
shorn her blond curls for the picture and shingled her hair
in the modern style to create an image more in tune with
her years. He could call Clare at the office, where, he knew,
she was working late on a feature story about lady tennis

champ Helen Willis. He took another draft of courage from the wineglass. Here he was, he thought with a wry smile, ready to antagonize a ruthless gangster but afraid to ask a dame for a date. Par for the course, eh?

He finally screwed up his moxie and called. To his surprise she readily accepted. He floated on a cloud.

The picture wasn't very good, Dante thought as they came out of the Broadway picture palace and strolled in the sultry night under the electric lamps of the Wrigley's Gum sign in Times Square. But he thought that Mary Pickford had turned in a wonderful performance. "I think she'll win the Academy Award," he predicted.

Clare Parker shrugged her shoulders. She wore a mint green sheath with bone buttons down the front. "At least she's acting her age," she said. "Got a coffin nail?"

Dante stopped and gave her a cigarette. He smiled at her standard wiseacre language and her brass to smoke in the street. She was some dish, he thought, lighting her cigarette. He wished she would take his arm as they walked. But she didn't.

"I'm famished," she said. "Let's go to '21.'"

Panic struck Dante, who was short on cash. "I've eaten already," he said.

"My treat," she added understandingly.

They walked the few blocks to West Fifty-second Street in silence. Inside the club they ordered cocktails and supper. Clare started with a crab salad while Dante nibbled on camembert and seedless white grapes.

"You look delicious, as usual," he said in a low croak.

She dismissed the flattery with a wave. "Oh, you're much prettier than I am," she said.

"No, I'm not!" He looked wounded.

"Yes, you are." She dabbed her mouth with a napkin, drank soda water and asked, "How's Lily?"

He stammered a little, then said, "How'd you find out . . . about us?"

"Silly boy! It's all over town."

Dante looked troubled.

"Oh, don't worry," she added. "Her husband doesn't mind in the least. It gives him the green light to bed down all those Earl Carroll and Ziegfeld girls he chases from sundown to sunup. That is, whenever he isn't traipsing around Europe closing big business deals and chasing French cupcakes."

He reached across the table and covered her hand with his. "It's just a physical attraction," he said. "Nothing more."

When Clare realized he thought she might be jealous she smiled, fluttered her lashes and said, "It's sweet of you to be concerned with my feelings, but believe me, I don't mind if you dally with Lily Curtin. You have to sow your wild oats."

"Aren't you a little jealous?" he asked hopefully.

She considered saying yes for the benefit of his ego but realized that would be crueler in the long run. "No, Dan. I'm not jealous."

"You mean you're not the jealous type," he said, clutching at straws.

"I mean I'm not jealous of you and Lily," she said with a sympathetic look.

He took away his hand. "I'm in love with you, Clare." Said like a confession.

"You most decidedly are not. You only think you are. You really know very little about me. How could you possibly be in love with me?"

"I know everything about you. I've read all your articles. I even went to the library to look up your family history. Scotch and English via Canada. Did you know you had an archbishop of Canterbury on the paternal branch of the family tree? Sixteenth century."

"I'm sure he was a scoundrel too. Your ancestors were building Greek temples and reading philosophy while mine were still wearing animal skins and sniffing each others' behinds. Nothing much has changed, of course. We still wear animal skins—sable and mink—and we secretly wish we had the nerve to sniff each others' behinds."

"Well, the joke's on me. Say what you want. I'll always love you—"

"Don't talk like a chump," she said, speaking from the side of her mouth.

"Why did you agree to come out with me tonight?"

"Because I like you very much, Dan. I enjoy your company." She paused. "And something else . . ."

"What?"

"I wanted to talk to you about Callahan."

Dante's neck reddened under the starched collar. "Well?"

"We both care for him," she said.

"Do we?"

"I think he's in some kind of trouble."

Dante planted a cigarette in the corner of his mouth. "Aw, he's been in trouble since grade school." Sulfur hissed as he struck a match and lit the cigarette. He looked away from her.

Clare refused to be put off. "You notice how strangely he's been acting? Distant, secretive—like he's got something to hide. And he's spending dough like a soldier on leave who's just won the sweeps. Where does he get it?"

Dante signaled the waiter for another glass of soda water. "Maybe he did hit the sweeps. Or a lucky streak on the ponies."

Clare shook her head.

"What's your theory?" asked Dante.

"I have no theory. I just don't like the company he's been keeping."

"Meaning?"

"Look, he's been seen in the speaks conferring with a lot of shady characters."

Dante laughed. "He's a crime reporter, for crying out loud."

She shook her head. "It's different, somehow. And another thing—the other day I went with some friends to Nigger Joe's, the blind pig in Chinatown. He didn't see me but I saw him. He was bending elbows with Roland O'-Hara."

"The big cop we saw in the Pot Still? So?"

"He's a smug-looking bastard with that shock of wavy white hair and that face. The face of a corrupt pope."

"It's Cal's job to interview mugs like that—"

"Is it his job to hand him a fat white envelope? That's what I saw him do, after looking around like a kid about to pee in the holy water."

In troubled silence Dante considered what she was saying. "Could've been anything. Tickets to the fights. Press releases. Invites to the Sigma Delta Chi dinner-dance—"

"Could've been, but the whole picture looks funny. The way he's been lighting his cigars with five-dollar bills and all. He's even been getting his hair cut regularly. I wonder if he's been using the same cologne as Scoop Madigan—"

"Cal would be real pissed to hear you say that."

"Really?" Having finished the crab salad she ordered a French omelette. Meanwhile Dante sipped soda and brooded over the info from another reliable source. Finally he asked, "Well, what can we do?"

"Have a talk with him, Dan. He likes you. He more than likes you. Maybe he'll level with you."

"You care that much?"

"Sure. And so do you."

"He's been avoiding me lately."

"Ever ask yourself why?" She plunged a fork into the omelette, shaking her titian-topped head. "Let's hope I'm wrong about this."

He silently and wholeheartedly agreed.

"Come on, Cal. Are you trying to tell me you're so busy chasing cops-and-robbers stories that we can't get together for an hour or two and compare notes? I thought we were pals."

Silence at the other end of the line as Callahan thought it over. Dante had reached him on Mrs. Brannock's pay phone in the hallway of his apartment house just two days after the movie date with Clare. Now that he was a legman on the police beat Callahan rarely poked his web-veined nose in the local room. He was very hard to track down.

Callahan sighed audibly. "I've got an appointment later tonight," he said. "But I can see you now. Can you hop a cab uptown?"

Dante glanced at his watch. It said seven-ten. "Give me twenty minutes," he said.

Chapter
15

THE FLEA CIRCUS

THEY rendezvoused in front of the severe white Times Building at Forty-second and Broadway, a towering wedge of stone, steel, glass and glazed terra cotta. Callahan, who had stopped at the United Cigar store across the street next door to the Rialto, was late. The guttering sun scintillated off the high copper roofs of the skyscrapers as Callahan pumped his young friend's hand and made excuses. In the distance piped a tugboat on the Hudson.

"What say, kid," said Callahan, "wanna take in a leg show?"

"No thanks."

"There's a good picture playing at the Roxy." Callahan glanced at his pocket watch. "I got just enough time."

"I'd rather talk. Let's go to the Brass Rail for a sandwich."

Callahan patted his paunch. "Ate already kid."

"Since when did that stop you?"

Callahan smirked. "Let's walk."

They strolled west on Forty-second Street, passing an array of movie palaces, novelty stores, burlesque houses, haberdasheries, chop suey joints and taxi-dance halls. The people on the street were as checkered as the surroundings, including panhandlers and racketeers, playboys and procurers, pitchmen and burlesque comics, clerks and rubes. Even priests: Callahan waved hello to Father Francis Duffy, pastor of the nearby Holy Cross Church and a fixture in the area. The padre, strolling under garlands of electric light, was reading his breviary.

The pair of newspapermen stopped in front of Hubert's Museum, an amusement arcade and sideshow. The penny-in-the-slots were showing "She Believed the Window Shade Was Drawn" and "Damsel in the Dentist Chair," among other epics. A hand-painted sign ballyhooed Boroni the Three-Legged Man and the Wild Man of Borneo.

"Hey, let's go see the flea circus," Callahan suggested.

Dante squinted at the portly newsman, thinking he detected a trace of furtiveness under the hail-fellow-well-met exterior. He again noticed, as had Clare, that Callahan was looking pretty dandified for Callahan, dressed in a wing collar, loosely knotted tie and doeskin spats. The seersucker coat bulged at the hip, of course.

"Why don't you want to talk to me? Why are you avoiding it?"

"Can't we talk and watch fleas do tricks at the same time?"

"I guess so."

Callahan clapped him on the shoulder. "Wait'll you get a load of these insects. They're funnier than Harold Lloyd and Charlie Chaplin combined. Hey, they're even funnier than Jimmy Walker."

"That's hard to believe."

"I know," said Callahan, thinking about the Jazz Mayor. "It's hard not to like a gent who tells those bumpkin lawmakers in Albany that they should vote down the Clean Books Bill because 'No woman was ever ruined by a book.'" Callahan laughed. "Remember that one, kid?"

"Before my time."

"Of course," said Callahan, steering him through the turnstile.

The master of ceremonies was a sallow-skinned man wearing a toothbrush mustache and a soiled dickey. He called himself "Professor Colgate" and waved his hands around like Arturo Toscanini. He stood on a wooden platform and spoke into a big metal lollipop of a microphone. He urged onlookers to "Step right up and see a most refined and educational attraction, suitable for young and old, male and female, beggar and prince. Yes indeed, ladies and gentlemen, you won't believe your eyes."

About fifteen spectators gathered around the platform. A sailor in dress whites nudged his mate with an elbow, jerking his head in the direction of two unescorted flappers. The rest of the people rubbernecked around the Professor.

The performers were kept in matchboxes stuffed with cotton. He rigged them up with tiny harnesses and, prodding wayward insects with a toothpick when necessary, put them through their paces behind magnifying-glass windows. Abigail Arthropoda hauled a miniature cannon around the stage. Other cast members skipped rope, ran a carrousel, danced the black bottom and staged a mock Battle of Gettysburg while waving the American and Confederate flags.

When he got the chance Callahan cupped the side of his mouth and asked the Professor, "What d'yuh feed the little bastards?"

The Professor, sizing Callahan up as a man of the world, said in a low tone through clenched teeth, "They eat shit when they're little, blood when they're big."

Callahan laughed, turned to Dante and cracked, "Hey, Abigail looks familiar, doesn't she? I believe she once had a long-term lease on Ivan Bruce's mustache. Correct me if I'm wrong, but I never forget a flea."

"Let's get out of here, Cal," said Dante, impatient to get down to brass tacks.

Callahan put his forefinger to his lips. "You'll hurt the Professor's feelings. Artists are sensitive souls."

The patrons were given the option of paying a dime on the way out, a policy that increased Callahan's admiration of the Professor's style and showmanship. One day he'd write a feature story about the show.

When they reached the street again, night, which had

visited other parts of the city, was banished from Times Square, blazing in the tinsel noon of artificial light.

Callahan suggested, "Let's head over to Mother Superior's."

"How about our talk?"

"We're talking."

"You're ducking me, Callahan."

"Aw," he said, pushing Dante playfully on the chest. "What you need is some snapping pussy."

"And a dose of clap?"

Callahan looked wounded. "Mother's stable of shebas, I'll have you know, are as clean as new-fallen snow. We can have a drink and a chat before going upstairs."

"I don't want to go upstairs."

"You can be my guest," said Callahan, knowing that newspapermen got it free.

"It's not the money, I just don't want to."

"So just tag along."

They hailed a cab and headed downtown.

Mother Superior was delighted to see Callahan and graciously welcomed his companion. "Always glad to see a new face around here, especially one as young and decorative as yours."

They drank Haig & Haig and were serenaded by Mother's parrots and a phonograph playing blues. A grandfather clock tocked away while the grand piano by the front window stood silent.

Mother asked Callahan, "Are you here on business or pleasure?"

He flashed a look at Dante, then smiled at the woman. "A little of both."

"Want me to tell Mazie you're here?"

"Don't trouble yourself."

"I see," she said. The babble of drinkers, games and revelers echoed around them. She preened the embroidered rosettes on her crêpe de chine gown. "If you'll excuse me," she said. "I have housekeeping to do."

The two men stood up and inclined their heads, sat down again on the Duncan Phyfe sofa.

"So what's eating you?" Callahan asked.

"Will you level with me?"

"Don't I always?" Callahan plucked a large purple grape from a bunch on a silver platter on the coffee table. He peeled it carefully with his pocket knife.

"Are you filling Scoop Madigan's shoes, Cal?"

"You don't beat around the bush."

"But you do. What's the answer?"

"Depends on what you mean. I'm covering the crime beat."

"That's not what I mean. You know what I mean."

Callahan tossed the grape into his mouth and started to peel another one. "Scoop was one in a million, see? I could never take his place."

"You said you'd level with me."

"I'm on the level."

"You're being evasive."

"Do you think I'm capable of what you're asking?"

Dante mulled it over. "I'm not sure," he said.

Callahan popped the second grape into his mouth. He got up. "I don't know about you," he said, "but I feel like getting laid."

"You still haven't given me a straight answer."

How could he when he hadn't given himself one? . . . He opened his mouth to speak but was interrupted by the Cain-raising of three ossified sheiks in white dinner coats who stumbled down the staircase. When the racket died down he said, "You want a straight answer, kiddo? I'll give you one: no."

Dante's spirits rose. "That's not banana oil?"

Callahan clasped his heart, mocking offense. "You want a sworn affidavit?"

"Nah, Cal. Your word's jake with me."

"You damn cake-eater. I sure don't know why I have to answer to you." Callahan touched the knot of his tie and combed his hair back at the sides. "Now. Mother's got this here new Betty Coed working for her and I'd like to sample her wares."

"I'll wait here."

"If you want to be a flat tire, that's up to you." As he saluted Dante his tie pin glittered in the light of the chandelier.

Dante settled back to sip Scotch and listen to the blues on the phonograph. As Ethel Waters warbled "Oh Daddy" he looked glum. He badly wanted to believe Callahan. It was as if he had invested his faith in himself in the Bank of Callahan, his first real friend and mentor. Now he inventoried his holdings, and hoped that this trustee of the values of wisdom and honesty had not signed the deal in invisible ink. So the wish was father to the conviction that Callahan had just told him the truth. But doubt still gnawed at the core of him. . . .

Soon Mother Superior came over to him, sat down, crossed her legs and hitched up her dressing gown an inch or two, revealing pink satin pumps. She uncorked a girlish smile and asked, "How do you like my place, Ramon Navarro?"

"It's the bee's knees," he said, looking around the luxurious setting. "Very swanky."

She appraised him closely and jerking her head toward the stairs, asked, "Aren't you in the mood? It's on the house."

"No thanks."

"Don't you like girls?"

"Sure I do."

"You're such a swell-looking sheik I guess you don't need the services of a joint like this, eh? Girls must be falling all over you."

"Not exactly."

"Modest, too." Tilting her head she asked, "Italian?"

"Yes.

"I don't get many Italian boys in here. More's the pity. I think they consider it a mark of honor not to pay. Of course there's exceptions. I count a dago 'legger or two among my regular customers. Pardon the lingo."

The remark had piqued Dante's interest. He played reporter. "You know a fellow called Patsy Secundo?"

"Yeah. I blackballed the weasel."

"Why?"

"I don't mind telling you. He was a perverted son of a bitch. Screwy." She looked around and cupped her mouth. "He wanted to piss on the girls. I mean that literally. I don't put up with that kind of applesauce."

"Lord, I don't blame you."

"Yeah. That mug gave me the heebie-jeebies."

"What about the bosses? You get their business?"

"Who do you have in mind?

"Pellegrino."

"He's never set foot in here."

"Maybe he prefers Polly Adler's," said Dante, playing dumb, probing.

"I doubt it." She squinted at him. "You just curious or do you have professional reasons for your questions?"

"Just curious."

"Your charm has made me forget my holy vow of silence." She rose from the chair. "I have business to attend to. And, as a famous American said, 'Business is the business of America.' "

Dante got up, touched the knot of his tie and bowed from the waist. When she had left he sat down again and marveled at what he'd just heard. It astounded him that some jokers got their kicks from urinating on women. He always figured that Patsy was off his trolley. He just never realized how far off. He supposed this trait helped qualify him for the job as one of Big Guy's torpedoes. . . .

As time passed the room filled with customers and whores of every shape, size and color. The girls all were clothed in revealing dressing gowns and all wore fixed smiles. They reminded Dante of painted artificial flowers. Some girls looked appealingly in Dante's direction, obviously thinking that they wouldn't mind bestowing their favors on a young and handsome customer for a change. One, a fattish girl with sturdy tree trunks for legs, riveted him with less friendly, more speculative eyes.

Dante did not notice the girls' inviting glances or Mazie Rodell's curiosity. He was too engrossed in troubling thoughts about what Mother had told him.

Meanwhile Mazie was wondering who he was and whether he was the man who had come in with Callahan, whose voice she had heard earlier while she was upstairs leaning on a bolster and eating a Ward's cake. Under Mother Superior's slatey gaze she kept her mouth shut, suppressing the urge to ask if he knew where Callahan was.

She would, though, soon find out. The object of her jealousy was upstairs in the new girl's room, putting his clothes back on. Finally he fastened his tie to a starched shirt front with an emerald stickpin.

Chapter

16

ALL WET

A cool summer rain fell on Greenwich Village as Dante Viola did his evening marketing. He wore a raincoat but carried no umbrella as he left the A&P and made a dash for Bleecker Street, where he bought a hunk of smoked provolone and a sausage at Manganaro's cheese store, then scurried across the street for a five-cent round loaf at Zito's bakery. Shoving the bundles under the raincoat, he walked east in the light drizzle. A sudden downpour spurred him to seek shelter under the Sixth Avenue El, where he waited for the rain to ease up before covering the remaining two blocks to his apartment building on the corner of Sullivan Street.

He waited impatiently, eager to get home to hear a favorite broadcast, the Kellogg Radio Town Crier with Alexander Woolcott and Otis Skinner on WOR. The program was scheduled to begin in ten minutes, at seven-thirty.

From his vantage under the El, Dante could see the phaetons and sedans pulling up in front of the awning over the entrance to the Mori Restaurant down the block. A doorman hastened out with an umbrella to protect the diners from the rain and escort them past the restaurant's columned portico. Dante wondered where and when

191

this bloated quest for pleasure and prosperity would end, this putting-on-the-ritz, devil-take-tomorrow, boom-or-bust atmosphere. Surely, he thought, it wouldn't last forever. . . .

Soon the rain abated and Dante shook such thoughts and walked through the mist and gathering twilight to his apartment building. In the vestibule he picked up his mail, then tramped up to his third-floor apartment. He wiped his feet on the doormat and placed the soggy bundles on the kitchen table, removed the raincoat and went to the bathroom to hang it in the shower. He stretched his aching muscles, tired from a full day of writing and editing after nights of either capering with Lily or following up leads in the investigation. In spite of his youth and vigor the pace was taking its toll. He took off his shoes and socks and went to the living room to turn on the radio and hear what was left of the Town Crier program. He sorted the mail until his hand stopped at a letter with a printed return address that read "Barbizon Plaza Hotel."

His heart thumped a little as he tore open the envelope. As he suspected, Mr. Ippolito had written informing him that a vacancy had opened up on the catering staff and that he could start as a room-service waiter early the next week. Shades of Nelly Bly, thought Dante—he was on the brink of becoming an undercover reporter and the idea both thrilled and scared him. He knew the job might be dangerous. He was determined, though, to go through with it, and instantly sat down and wrote Mr. Ippolito accepting the position.

The following Friday Lily called to persuade him to join her in a weekend of hotcha and jazzing. Under her tutelage Dante was developing a taste for bacchic pleasure, and since he knew that time for fun would be scarce from now on he accepted the invitation. That night they hopped into her chauffeur-driven Lincoln Brougham for a tour of the Harlem night spots. The motor car, lacquered forest green with black trim, rode uptown past the mansions and modern high-rises of Park Avenue. The handsome auto had spoked wheels, sweeping fenders, elegant electric side-lamps and a plush upholstered interior roomy and comfortable as a small parlor. Partitioned from the driver by an opaque sliding-glass window, the car afforded plenty of privacy, an advantage randy Lily did not ignore. By the time they had reached the first stop, the Saratoga Club on Lenox Avenue, she and her escort were adjusting their clothes and smoking cigarettes.

From the Saratoga Club, where they dined and danced to Wibert De Paris's syncopated music, they headed for the Alhambra Ballroom on Seventh Avenue, where they gave their dogs another workout, then on to Connie's Inn to hear the hot horn of Father Dip, Louis Armstrong, ogle the high-yaller kootch dancers and swill watered-down booze. Dante was pretty tuckered when they ended up at the Savoy, where Jake Whyte's Missourians were appearing. But Lily never seemed to tire.

In the wee hours they slept on each other's shoulders as the driver whisked them off to Lily's bungalow in Port Washington on Long Island Sound, a private *pied à terre* to which her husband never came. They woke up in the afternoon, ate a hearty brunch and went bathing in the Sound. Lily had a full slate of activities planned. They attended a polo match at Meadowbrook before taking the car into Manhattan to join the celebration in honor of Our Lady of Mount Carmel in Italian Harlem, eating razor clams in the shadow of the massive East River gas tanks. The evening was spent touring the ritzy speaks for which Lily had a stack of membership cards—Tree Club, Cote d'Or, Club Vendome, the Marlboro Club—drinking and dancing till the first glimmer of rosy dawn.

Sunday gave little rest. They went to Jamaica racetrack, Sheepshead Bay for a fish dinner, the Loew's Paradise for a moving picture and back to Manhattan, where Lily wanted to dance again at the Savoy.

But Dante at last begged off. "I'm bushed," he said as the

Brougham's motor purred in the foreground. "I've got a hard day at the office tomorrow, slaving over a hot typewriter—"

Her perfumed hand leapt to his button fly. "Did you say hot and hard?"

"Please, Lily."

"One more time, baby."

One more time.

Afterward, as she touched up her lipstick, she said, "I'll call you later this week."

He hesitated, then said, "No, Lily. I'm going to be awfully busy for a while."

"Don't be screwy, kiddo, no one's ever too busy to have a little fun."

"You don't understand . . ."

She put her compact back into her purse, snapping it shut. "Nerts, Dan," she said. "I'm kind of stuck on you. Don't give me the runaround."

"I'm not giving you the runaround. I like you an awful lot too. But I have business to attend to."

"You *like* me?" She narrowed her eyes. "Why you slippery lounge lizard, you're not two-timing me, are you?"

"Say," he said, sounding annoyed, "since when did I hand you a deed to my person?"

"So, you *are* two-timing me. Who's the dame?"

"There is no dame. But you don't own me—"

"I'll tear her limb from limb." Not smiling.

He flapped his arms in frustration. "I told you it was business . . . undercover work."

"I know what kind of work you do under the covers, kiddo. Why, I taught you every trick in the book and now you want to try them out on some slut? I'll fix your wagon and hers too."

"You're a married woman—"

His cheek stung where her hand left a red imprint.

She tapped the window to get the driver's attention.

"Yes, Mizzuz Ferrand," the man said, having slid open the glass partition.

"Stop the car. The gentleman is getting off here."

"Now, wait a second . . ." They were crossing the High Bridge and it was raining lightly.

The driver took his eyes off the road for a second, glancing into the back seat.

"I said stop the car," Lilly repeated. Mr. Viola is getting off here."

The driver pulled over to the side of the roadway and idled the engine.

Wearing a colossal frown and muttering curses, Dante got out of the car, huddled into the turned-up collar of his dinner jacket and watched the sleek automobile speed away.

As the car cruised under the leafy bluffs of upper Manhattan Lily Ferrand lit a Chesterfield and muttered to herself, "I'll show that cake-eating counterfeit he can't pull the wool over my eyes." But merely thinking about the handsome boy and the way he plucked her strings made her bitter. Swigging bourbon from a hollow cane she kept for such purposes, she racked her brains trying to figure out who her rival might be. Why, she told herself, with his good looks, it might be any siren from here to Hoboken.

Of course, she conceded, he might have been telling her the truth about not having another girl. She drew down the window and let cigarette smoke drift out into the misty night. Now the poor boy had to make his way home through the fog and darkness. She considered telling Bernard to turn back and pick him up, then quickly dismissed the idea. He was probably gone already, having hailed a taxi or something. Besides, he had no right to insinuate that she was a tramp with that married-woman dig. Maybe she would get her father to fire him. The old man would do practically anything for her. Anything, that was, but free her from the twisted cords of his love.

But she really couldn't have Dante fired, she thought, it would destroy the poor darling, and now her vindictive streak warred with feelings of tenderness.

She continued, though, to speculate on the identity of her imagined rival, and suddenly remembered the party at the Parker country house and the way he had danced that evening with Clare, mooning over the bitch, making eyes at her. Of course. He's stuck on the sob sister. She flicked a cigarette butt out the open window.

By the time the car pulled up in front of Mrs. Ferrand's brownstone on Sutton Square Lily was submerged in the stratagems of campaigns of the heart. She did not hear the gentle lapping of the waves on the rocks of the East River shore, or the rumble of traffic over the cantilevered Queensboro Bridge. She did not really see the gracefully fluted wrought-iron fence, the shrubbery and riot of petunias that fronted the oak door of her house. She heard only the murmurs of her jealous heart, saw only the map of her vengeance.

Dante was soaking wet by the time he reached the IRT subway station at Broadway and 168th Street. He shivered in the chill night air. The pot-bellied stove in the station was unlit in summer so he had to suffer discomfort in his wet clothes. He dug in his pockets for a nickel, dropped it in the slot and pushed through the heavy wooden turnstile.

As the train rattled downtown he sat morosely, arms dangling between his knees and thinking about what had happened. A red rose wilted in his buttonhole.

In a way he felt relieved that Lily had given him the heave-ho. It would have been only a matter of time before they had to break it off anyhow. He didn't need the distractions of an affair with everything else that was going on. Yes, he would like to have parted with her on friendly terms, if possible. He was really fond of Lily and he knew he would miss the sex. He was also worried that she might make a nuisance of herself, try to get even in some way. She was no shrinking violet. He might have to watch his step.

It was still raining when he reached his station in Greenwich Village. When he got to his apartment he stripped to the buff, took a warm bath and went, teeth chattering, to bed.

Next morning he woke with a blooming case of influenza and telephoned the office to report in sick.

"Okay, kid, I'll see if I can get hold of Callahan," said Ivan Bruce on the other end of the line.

"Where is he?" asked Dante.

"I was hoping you could tell *me.* Ain't seen hide nor hair of him since I assigned him to follow up another tip that Rudy Valentino had been poisoned."

"Gee, can't you let it die? He croaked three years ago."

"His name still sells newspapers. . . . I'll try Cal's battle-axe of a landlady again. Get well, son." Before hanging up he thought to ask, "How's that other matter coming?"

"Good. Nothing definite to report yet but I'm making headway. I should have a break soon."

"Okay," said Bruce, and hung up.

Dante was determined to nurse himself back to health before the hotel job started. He had very little time to shake the bug, since he had to report to work the following night. He brewed hot tea and drank it with the juice of a lemon. He read novels and magazines, took steaming hot baths and tried to sleep. Browsing through *Collier's* and *Literary Digest,* listening to music on the radio, devouring a serialization of *A Farewell to Arms,* Dante began to feel the poisons draining from his body.

By Tuesday evening when he had to start the hotel job he felt much better, though not tip-top. He hoped he wouldn't suffer a relapse caused by going out so soon but he had to chance it. The evening was windy and dry with high scudding clouds outlined in pink by the setting sun. Dante was a little worried by his lack of experience as a waiter but figured he could cover his tracks pretty well by using the experience he had gotten working as a busboy two summers in City Island when he was a teenager.

At the hotel they outfitted him in a white coat, wing collar and black bow tie. Mr. Ippolito teamed him up with an experienced waiter named Lee Lindenbaum, a middle-aged man given to fathomless silences and unexpected squalls of fatherly advice such as, "Never look at the coffee cup on the tray or you're bound to spill the damn thing." Dante took an instant liking to his partner, a man with an aquiline profile, clear blue eyes and slate gray hair pomaded straight back on the sides and thinning on top. He had mastered the knack of balancing courteous servility with dignity, no mean trick.

Over the next two weeks Dante shook off the illness, wrote obituaries and learned how to set a breakfast tray, fold napkins and balance coffee cups while opening doors. He also managed to hear a few things about a certain privileged guest sequestered in a penthouse suite of the residential hotel. He was registered under the name G. Pell, had all his callers carefully screened and doled out ten-dollar tips, making him a coveted assignment among the room service staff. Lee—although he liked ten-buck tips as well as the next fellow—was not among those waiters who vied for a chance to bring tea trays and dinners to the mysterious Mr. Pell, whose real identity was an open secret. "That guy gives me the willies," Lee said one night.

"Why?" asked Dante, trying to make his interest sound casual.

"Don't know for sure, something about the way he bares them extra-white teeth of his even when he's rapping your knuckles for getting the eggs wrong. And those crisp tenners all the guys are lining up for give me the heebie-jeebies too. They see green, I see red. Blood money."

Dante said nothing. For Lee the comments constituted a rare major oration. They were standing in the steamy hotel kitchen. Lee took out a handkerchief and mopped his high, gleaming brow. "Boy, it's a scorcher today," he said.

The dog days of August crept by. President Hoover refused to commute the death sentence of bootlegger James Alderman, who had rubbed out two Coast Guardsmen in Florida. Riots broke out at the federal pen in Leavenworth. A jut-jawed *pagliaccio* named Benito Mussolini celebrated his forty-fifth birthday in Rome. Babe Ruth slammed his five-hundredth career home-run in Cleveland.

And at the Barbizon Plaza Hotel in midtown Manhattan room-service waiter Dante Viola carried a tray of coffee to a ninth-floor resident when the night headwaiter informed him that his next assignment was to take a high-tea tray up to Mr. Pell's penthouse.

Dante glanced at the coffee cups and spilled them over the headwaiter's razor-creased trousers.

Chapter
17

ROOM SERVICE

DANTE held the ten-spot in both hands, snapping the firm paper, stretching it and studying the pursed-lipped engraving of Alexander Hamilton. Blood money, Lee had called it. It was as much as Dante earned in a day of scribbling obits.

He pocketed the bill and walked over to the service elevator, thinking about his first encounter with the Big Guy, a physical misnomer for Gaetano Pellegrino, a rather delicately built man on the brink of middle age who wore silk dressing gowns and spicy scents, affected the British custom of having high tea and spoke in an urbane, modulated rasp that mingled street life and acquired sophistication. Dante admitted to himself, walking down the corridor to the kitchen, that he had been impressed with Pellegrino as a person and surprised at the incongruities of his style. He seemed to have substance and depth. Something about him also confirmed for Dante Lee Lindenbaum's impressions of profound menace and the reek of moral indifference.

Dante walked along a dark and dingy service corridor, heading toward the kitchen—the hotel's service areas were as squalid as the public places were elegant. The

gilded ornaments, sumptuous carpets, gleaming chandeliers and marble statuary of the lobbies and hallways gave
way to the blistered walls, dirty linoleum and vermin-in-
fested cupboards of the supply rooms and pantries. As he
proceeded Dante kept visualizing Pellegrino's face with its
five o'clock shadow, hooded black eyes and thin, ascetic
lips. He would be, Dante felt, an object of fascination for
aficionados of evil—a rare black gem.

In the kitchen some of the waiters gave him truculent
stares, and he soon learned why. Pellegrino had already
informed the night desk that whenever possible he wanted
the new waiter, Dante, to serve him. The hotel's star
boarder apparently had taken a shine to him. The news
both pleased and troubled Dante.

A spinoff of the moonlighting was that it soon took a toll
on the quality of his work on the obit desk. He got a sharp
memo from Bruce reporting copy-desk complaints about
errors in the hard copy. He considered, then thought better
of reminding Bruce that he was doing double duty. Accepting criticism, he decided, would better his chances of winning the editor's confidence. Nobody, he realized, liked
whiners, even when the whining was justified.

Silence came from Lily Ferrand's direction, at least for
the time being, and although he did miss the sex he was
grateful for the respite.

Meanwhile, tending Pellegrino's domestic needs, he
kept an eye and ear cocked for inside dope to advance the
investigation that Bruce had given him—somewhat reluc-
tantly—the red light to conduct. He passionately wanted to
succeed with this story, not only to advance his career—a
strong motivation, to be sure—but also, dammit, for some
less self-serving reasons. Call him an idealist, but he felt
a man's existence ought to include doing his bit to clean up
the climate of these crazy times, to make a small difference. . . . Why not? In his mind flashed the image of himself
as a boy in gabardine and his mother in fringed shawl and
polka-dot apron picking through the basket of stale bread
for sale on Mulberry Street. And as this remembrance dissolved he pictured himself, dirty-faced, hawking copies of

the New York *World* from a canvas bag slung over his shoulder, the embryonic journalist. Somehow he felt there was a preordained inevitability about his vocation. . . .

With silver tongs he dropped two cubes of sugar into Mr. Pellegrino's teacup.

"Thank you, Dante," the gangster, smelling of talcum, said, raising oval liquid eyes from the newspaper he had been scanning.

Dante inclined his head. "Will there be anything else, Mr. Pell?"

Pellegrino picked up the teaspoon and stirred with a clinking sound. "Yes. I'd like to ask you a question."

Dante stood up straight. His hands grew clammy and his heart thumped. "Yes, sir?"

"Do you read the tabs?"

Now Dante was really worried. Did Pellegrino suspect something? He fought to keep his expression calm and hands steady. "Sometimes," he finally got out.

Pellegrino pointed to the copy of the *Daily Mirror* he was holding. "Some people say these newspapers are a menace to our society. Sort of like a national drug habit. What do you think?"

No dark import there. That the subject happened to be tabloid newspapers was pure coincidence, he told himself.

"I haven't given much thought to the question, Mr. Pell."

Pellegrino picked up in his manicured hand a copy of the *Nation,* a magazine he had been reading earlier. "Don't you think they overdramatize stories and give too much space to crime, divorces, sex scandals, stuff like that?"

"I suppose so." Dante wanted to encourage his attempts at familiarity without betraying too much knowledge of the news business. But he didn't want to seem overly familiar either. They were alone in the parlor adjoining a terrace that overlooked the spangled brilliance of the city. A bodyguard was posted out in the vestibule.

"I understand you're a student at Columbia."

"Yes," said Dante looking directly at Pellegrino. He didn't seem at all effeminate, merely sort of cultured for a bootlegger.

"What are you studying?"

Dante improvised: "Literature."

"English lit?"

"Uh—world literature."

"Then I guess you've read the works of your namesake."

The Divine Comedy, yes."

"La Vita Nuova?"

"No, I haven't read that." He had heard of the work but he knew very little about it and hoped that his ignorance wouldn't give away his lie.

"Ah, his songs of love!" Mr. Big said with a lilt in his raspy voice that gave Dante goose bumps.

Dante coughed. "Will that be all, sir?"

Wearing an ironic smile, Pellegrino nodded. . . .

That was the first time they exchanged more than perfunctory remarks. It would not be the last. During the next few weeks Pellegrino's attitude toward Dante became more and more familiar. He was careful, of course, not to discuss business but seemed to trust him—or at least wanted to trust him. Their conversations were about art, literature, opera, history, not exactly subjects he could explore with his usual associates.

"These chowderheads know only three things," he once told Dante, "cash, baseball and broads."

Pellegrino had many visitors to his suite, most of whom resembled first cousins to the missing link. Pellegrino would entertain them with food and drink served usually by Dante. Sometimes the occasions would be mainly social, and Pellegrino and his guests would sit out on the terrace overlooking Central Park and the geometric skyline, sipping vintage wines from his private stock and eating Italian delicacies delivered from stores on Ninth Avenue.

Pellegrino liked living in the hotel for many reasons besides the luxury services and spectacular views. It provided him complete privacy, buffering him from the outside world with a staff of well-oiled bellboys, telephone operators, room clerks and house dicks. At his bedside he had a private phone with an unlisted number. Entering and leaving the hotel he would mingle with the other guests in the elevators, wearing dark glasses and keeping as low a profile as possible, considering that he was always accompanied by two of his men. In fact, security was kept to a minimum for a hood of his stature. "One can't live like a scared rabbit," he often said.

Dante's shift ended at one P.M. Whatever romantic entanglements the bachelor resident might have had were kept discreet. Even among the staff no rumors circulated. . . . Some speculated that he was asexual. Others had been greased to keep their traps shut.

Once in a while Dante recognized the face of a visitor to Pellegrino's suite from newspaper photos, not only on the crime page but also on the society and political pages. From his ducal fortress overlooking Central Park, Pellegrino manipulated the strings that set in motion events and characters in street life below. Dante considered getting a *Courier* photographer to rig him with a hidden camera to capture on film the mobster's conference with certain pillars of society, but decided it was too risky. For the moment.

"Do you like the opera?" Pellegrino asked Dante one cool evening as Dante served him a sandwich and mineral water on the terrace. The leaves on the trees in the park were tinged with yellow.

"I don't know much about opera, sir."

Pellegrino hiked his eyebrows at this admission by an Italian boy. "They're doing *Rigoletto* at the Metropolitan next week. With Ruffo in the title role. Verdi's best work, along with *Traviata* and *Trovatore,* don't you think?" He didn't actually expect a reply, he was lecturing. "What dramatic power, eh? *Rigoletto*'s like a tidal wave, flooding everything in its way!" His black eyes sought Dante's for confirmation.

"As I said, sir. I know very little about opera—"

"Then it's time you learned. How do you expect a cultured person, a true son of proud Italy 'whose manners still our tardy apish nation limps after in base imitation'? That's Shakespeare, boy."

"Yes, sir."

"I have tickets for opening night. Come with me."

Dante was flustered. "Yes . . . I mean, no, sir, I . . . I have to work—"

"I'll fix that. . . . You know, I first heard Verdi played by organ grinders in the old neighborhood. We couldn't afford to attend the opera. Even then the music made me want to cry with joy and shake my fist at the same time. I knew it was the present expression of the mystery of the soul. Beyond mere words. You will see what I mean. As an Italian man of sensitivity you will understand."

It sounded as much an order as a promise. Dante stood there trying to frame a reply. Why not? It might provide a good opportunity to get information for the story. But what about the possible . . . consequences? Was he getting in over his head? Did he have the moxie to see this through?

Pellegrino continued to rhapsodize and remember. "As a boy twenty-six years ago I stood outside the opera house when the great Caruso made his New York debut in the role of the Duke. While I watched the swells pulling up in their fancy carriages a coachman booted me in the ass, the mick bastard. Said I should get out of the way, I was stinking up the street. Later I sneaked into the alley and heard the opera while I rubbed my butt and swore I'd get even with the dirty crumbbum who kicked me. I also promised myself that some day I'd go first class to any opera I wanted." He looked at Dante. . . . "I kept both promises. Well?"

Dante made a quick decision. "I'd be honored, Mr. Pell."

"Good. Meet me here Wednesday at seven. I'll fix it with Ippolito."

Bone-tired, Dante still had trouble sleeping that night. He got up and poured "for medicinal reasons" a glass of home-brewed marsala. He kept wondering just what Pellegrino had done to avenge himself on the coachman who had kicked him. He also, of course, wondered how he would react if Pellegrino made sexual advances. How far would he go to get the story? Nelly Bly had herself committed to an insane asylum, Stephen Crane fought Spaniards in Cuba, Henry Morton Stanley braved the unknown perils of darkest Africa. How far would Dante Viola go? What unexplored frontiers would *he* cross? Sleep crept up like a footpad. . . .

Next day he almost nodded off at his desk.

Clare Parker snapped her fingers in front of his face. "Dreaming of Greta Garbo?"

He shook himself awake and placed his fingers back on the typewriter keyboard. "Uh-uh."

"Joan Crawford?"

"Nah." He made cow eyes at her. "Next to you those dames look like hags."

She did a mock curtsy. "Sweet of you," she said, planting her ripe rear on the edge of the desk. Her face grew serious. "Have you talked to Cal about the matter I mentioned?"

"Yeah."

She tilted her red-topped head to one side.

His face looked wan under the sickly electric lamps. "He's clean," Dante said, unable to erase the doubtful note from his voice.

"Are you certain?"

"He wouldn't lie to me."

"All you have is his word?"

He stopped typing and looked up at her. "That's all I *need.*" Did he believe that?

"Okay," she said, and peered at him. "You look awfully tired, Dan. You and Lily burning the candle at both ends?" She didn't add, No pun intended.

He was tempted to tell her about the undercover job at the hotel, but thought better of it. "Lily and I aren't seeing each other any more. I've been working. . . ."

" 'My candle burns at both ends; / It will not last the night; / But ah, my foes, and oh, my friends— / It gives a lovely light!' Edna St. Vincent Millay."

"Was that supposed to be a compliment or a warning?"

"You take it the way you want." She craned her neck over the copy in the typewriter. "Whose epitaph are we composing today?"

"Nobody special. Director of the Newark Museum."

"Ah, but I'm sure he was special to somebody."

"What are you working on?" he asked.

"Same old bunkum." She tossed her shingled hair. "I'm profiling a marathon dance contestant who pickles her feet in brine and vinegar to increase her endurance. Contest starts tomorrow in Madison Square Garden."

He shook his head. "How do you come up with these angles?"

"It's easy, dear boy, when you're living in a world gone mad. Do you know that in every marathon I've covered— and I've covered a mess of them—at least one contestant has died of heart failure? But we ballyhoo them all the same. I'd go nuts, too, if I didn't tell myself I'm writing a kind of social satire, a testament for posterity of the insanity of our time."

"That sounds pretty heavy."

"I guess it does. It is."

Dante put his elbow on the desk and propped his chin in his hand, admiring her lively brown eyes. He remembered that he had the upcoming Labor Day weekend off from the hotel and managed to get up the courage to ask her to go to Orchard Beach for the day.

"Sorry," she said, "but I've been assigned to cover the Miss America contest in Atlantic City. I'm taking the train down on Monday. Dreary."

"Yeah, dreary," echoed Dante.

He spent the weekend at home, getting some much-needed rest. He also tried to prepare himself for the awkward prospect of attending the opera with Pellegrino on Wednesday. He didn't know how to handle himself and decided he would just have to rely on instinct. He focused on the opportunity it gave to uncover information, maybe even documentation, for his news story. He tried to keep his eye on the doughnut, not the hole.

When he returned to the hotel Tuesday evening, Lee Lindenbaum and the others gave him fish-eyed looks and the cold shoulder. They undoubtedly had heard through the grapevine that Dante had the next night off to go out

with Pellegrino, and regarded the pretty boy as an unscrupulous golddigger *and* pervert. But they were too
afraid of Pellegrino's well-known anger to say anything.
Dante himself spent the evening finding excuses to avoid
assignments to Pellegrino's suite. Once during a cigarette
break Lee broke the ice by taking Dante aside and saying,
"I hope you know, goddammit, what you're letting yourself
in for, kid."

Dragging on the cigarette, Dante nodded, said nothing.
It hurt him to lose Lee's respect, but that was only one part
of the price he might have to pay.

On the way to the opera house Dante sat alongside Pellegrino on the hand-crushed leather upholstery in the back
seat of the chauffeured Packard while the gangster gave
Dante a thumbnail description of the story of the court
jester, his beloved daughter and the Duke of Mantua. The
husky-voiced synopsis took a fairly long time, and all the
while Dante nodded nervously, fingering the starched fabric of his wing collar and caressing the flower in his buttonhole.

"The Duke's my favorite character, a rogue who gets
away with everything," Pellegrino at last finished, smiling
sidelong at his companion. Dante mumbled something in
reply and studied the burled walnut paneling of the auto's
interior. One of Pellegrino's armed goons sat in the front
seat beside the chauffeur, who also undoubtedly packed a
heater. The goon had gray eyes that constantly flicked
about in all directions. Pellegrino himself seemed perfectly at ease, outwardly oblivious to the possible dangers
of appearing in public while the target of retribution by
the Judge and other underworld factions. Along with a
spicy cologne he exuded the conviction that no Sparafucile
lived who could get to him. The car came to a halt on
Broadway and Fortieth Street, and while the bodyguard
scouted up and down the street, the chauffeur hurried out
of his seat to hold open the door.

Sitting in a private box in the lower tier of the Diamond

Horseshoe that extended in sweeping arcs from the proscenium, Dante found himself gaping at the grandeur of the hall with its generous proportions and finely carved decorations. Smoothing the tails of his evening coat under his rear, Pellegrino sat in the plush red chair and boasted to Dante, "We're right next door to the Roosevelt box. Not too bad, right?"

At curtain rise Pellegrino grew intent, focused on the opera, shutting out everything else. The muscles in his carved cheek twitched. Dante watched his every move.

After the final curtain Pellegrino turned to Dante. "Well?"

"I was . . . very moved."

"Let's talk about it over a nightcap back at my suite. What do you say?"

Dante's throat felt cottony, his gut constricted. The moment of truth was at hand. "Okay," he said in as neutral a voice as he could manage.

"Good." Pellegrino stood and signaled the bodyguard that they were ready to leave. He smiled at Dante and guided him by the elbow out of the box.

As they left, their movements were captured in the twin lenses of an opera glass trained on them from across the auditorium. The observer did not move a muscle until the two men had left the box seats. Removal of the glass revealed two puzzled and icy blue eyes set in a round and pretty face.

Max Ferrand leaned over her shoulder and whispered, "The opera has concluded, my dear. Or hadn't you noticed?"

Lily Ferrand wore a look of calculation mixed with bridled anger. "I'm coming, Max. Hold your damn horses." With a swirl of taffeta she rose to leave.

Chapter

18

TRANSGRESSION AND RETRIBUTION

THEY sat on Morris chairs on the terrace, the city below a collection of glittering baubles on a velvet tray, the night pungent with the smell and feel of nearby Central Park, echoing with the clop of horses drawing carriages and the blare of auto horns as Gaetano Pellegrino's sandpaper voice carried on about the musical, dramatic and political elements of *Rigoletto.*

Pellegrino took a breather to sip cognac.

"If you had given me this lecture before we went," Dante said, meaning it as a compliment, "I would have appreciated it more."

Pellegrino shook his gleaming pompadoured head. "No, I think it's better for virgins to be allowed some spontaneity of reaction."

"Virgins?" Oh God . . .

Pellegrino leaned forward. "I mean you're a virgin when it comes to opera."

"Oh, sure," said Dante, sipping Coca-Cola, and put a hand on his own kneecap to steady it.

Pellegrino pointed to the class of cola. "Wouldn't you like something stronger?"

"No thanks. You mind my asking, how did you learn so much about the opera?"

210

Pellegrino's thin lips formed a small smile. "What you mean to ask is, how does an uneducated 'legger like me know so much about it."

Dante's face turned red. *"No,* I didn't mean that at all—"

"Well, I'll tell you, my old man, he had a beautiful *bel canto,* see? And a passion for Italian opera, which I believe is the deepest expression of our national character. Of our soul, by God. But he was a rotten tailor and a lousy provider. Pasta and beans we had for feast days in our house. Other times we were lucky to get a scrap of bread rubbed with garlic and oil. He taught me two things, the old man: to love opera and avoid poverty like a sin. One was positive, the other negative."

Dante glanced around at the luxurious surroundings. "You learned both well," he said. His glance had taken in the door to Pellegrino's bedroom, a place he had never entered as a waiter and that seemed to be a kind of inner sanctum, off limits to all but a select few. Even the maids were not allowed in except for once each day between ten and eleven in the morning. Maybe only vestal virgins could enter, Dante thought. He guessed that Pellegrino got down to the brass tacks of his far-flung business activities in that room . . . maybe even kept records there. He would like the chance to confirm the hunch but wished he didn't have to risk so much to get it. He'd rather stay a virgin, he thought.

"You know, Verdi considered *Rigoletto* his best opera?" Pellegrino was saying.

"Is that so?"

"I agree with *il Maestro,* although I have a fondness for his earlier works, too. *Attila,* I find especially appealing."

He *would,* thought Dante, marveling again at how the man combined an aesthetic temperament with his vicious trade. He supposed Pellegrino had to be particularly ruthless to survive in his 'profession' considering his—eccentricities.

Pellegrino continued pontificating on the opera. "The music weeps," he said in that distinctive voice of honey and gravel, gesturing with expressive hands. "And the *recitatives* come on you like sudden storms."

"I liked the music," said Dante, "but I did think the drama was sort of farfetched. . . ."

Pellegrino waved his hand. "The plot doesn't matter in grand opera. What matters is the motivation, psychology. You remember in the last act how *Rigoletto* answers the assassin's request for the name of the victim? He says to Sparafucile, 'He is Transgression, I am Retribution.' He sees himself above the law, an instrument of a higher justice. Ah, the jester is truly a man to be reckoned with."

"But he's a failure. His actions lead to his own daughter's death."

Pellegrino shrugged. "The curse of Monterone. We can't escape the force of a curse, the glance of the evil eye. It's in the cards."

"So you're a fatalist?"

Pellegrino showed teeth in a silent smile. "Of course. I'm a Sicilian." He laughed again, displaying his considerable fallen-angel charm, then quickly changed the subject. "Do you have a girlfriend, Dante?"

It was so abrupt Dante couldn't plan a careful answer. "Not at the moment . . ." he said.

Pellegrino grinned. "The lady is fickle, eh? *La donna è mobile.*"

"You guessed it."

Pellegrino hummed the notes of the aria. "I'll bet they're clawing each other's eyes out over you."

"Not exactly."

"Then there's something very wrong with the dames in this town."

Dante saw where this was headed. To cover his nervousness he pretended to stifle a yawn.

"Are you tired?"

"No!" said Dante, now feeling a sudden stab of panic.

"Good." Pellegrino inspected his fingernails. "Would you like to hear a recording I have of Caruso in the role of the Duke of Mantua? It's magnificent."

"Sure," said Dante, trying to disguise his uneasiness.

Pellegrino drained the glass of cognac and rose from the chair. "Excellent," he growled. "Come. The Victrola's in the bedroom."

Dante gripped the arms of the chair as he tried to keep fixed in his mind thoughts of Stephen Crane and Nelly Blye, Lincoln Steffins and Jacob Riis, all the crusading, muckraking journalists he idolized. He got up, in total panic.

"By the way," said Pellegrino as they passed through the terrace door, "what's your last name?"

Dante uttered the first thing that came into his head: "Fuoco. Dante Fuoco." He was thankful he hadn't hesitated but wondered how he'd come up with the Italian word for *fire*. His subconscious was at least working.

"What an interesting name," said Pellegrino, ushering the young man toward the bedroom door.

Over the first violins Dante listened to the tenor voice of Enrico Caruso singing *"Bella figlia dell'amore"* and watched from the corner of his eye how Pellegrino's eyes burned during the long tenor solo. He wondered whether the intensity of his gaze reflected passion for the music or for him. They sat in armchairs on a marble landing near french doors leading to another terrace. Ten paces away stood a large canopied oak bed. Dante quickly looked away from it.

Finally the voice of Rigoletto: *"Gilda! mia Gilda! È morta! Ah! la maledizione!"* and Pellegrino rose to shut off the machine.

"There'll never be another like him. Did you know that Caruso died of pleurisy, *Dante mio!* Fascinating that his lungs betrayed him in the end. One doesn't sing with the vocal cords alone, you know. A powerful respiratory system, the lungs and diaphragm are crucial to a great singer. It's obvious that Caruso, who died young, sacrificed his life to his art. A fair bargain, don't you think? Glory comes high. And anything worth living for is worth dying for."

Pellegrino faced the young man, searing him with his eyes.

Dante was reminded of Callahan's comment about the irony of Rodin freezing to death. In fact he actually agreed with Pellegrino's last statement.

"I have his autograph," Pellegrino said.

"Whose?"

"Caruso's, of course. It's my most prized possession. I nearly froze waiting for him at the stage door without an overcoat. He wrote it for me on a program that I had picked up from the gutter. Would you like to see it?"

"Yes. Sure."

Pellegrino went over to a cylinder-top mahogany secretary near the fireplace and unlocked it. After rummaging in the desk for a moment he came back to where Dante was sitting and showed him the autograph. As Dante studied it while Pellegrino kept on talking, he was busy exploring ways to use this opportunity. What else, he wondered, did Pellegrino keep locked up in that antique desk . . . ?

The chance to find out soon came when Pellegrino excused himself to go to the bathroom.

Dante had to act quickly. He saw them right away in a compartment under the pigeonholes, two bulky morocco-bound ledgers. As he opened them and scanned the writing it soon became apparent that here Pellegrino kept detailed records of his wide-ranging business ventures. As far as he could make out in his nervousness and haste the records included names of agents who had infiltrated companies with federal licenses to manufacture alcohol for "medicinal purposes," locations of stills, breweries, warehouses and labs for cutting whiskey shipments with pure alcohol and caramel coloring, locations of policy banks and their balances, names of hospital officials who would peddle the pure stuff to cut whiskey just off the boat, lists of mom-and-pop bookie operations and horse parlors, houses of joy with mob slot machines, even profit projections from combined industries, including bootlegging, prostitution, gambling, hijacking, jewelry fencing, heists, protection peddling, loansharking, every cottage industry of the outlaw businessman except selling junk, an activity that Pellegrino apparently considered taboo. It came as a shock to Dante that the gangster had relationships with big, legitimate financial institutions which supplied funds—*maybe* unwittingly—that helped fuel the engine of his illegal empire. But the biggest bombshell came at the end of the second ledger—a grease sheet. A list of regular graft payments to prominent cops and political bigwigs. Bingo.

At the sound of the toilet flushing Dante had just enough time to get back to the armchair. Close as a cat's whisker.

Reentering the room, Pellegrino flashed his dazzling white-toothed smile.

Dante tried to control his breathing before he glanced at his wristwatch and said, "I didn't realize it was so late."

The smile froze, but Pellegrino did not press the matter. He was too smart and careful for that. He merely gave an icy nod and said goodnight.

Dante got out of there as quickly as he could.

In another bedroom across town a woman putting on a peach-colored silk nightgown heard a foghorn groan on the East River. She looked through mullioned panes of glass at the wooden boathouses and ramshackle piers of the Fifty-third Street dock, now shrouded in mist. She was feeling intense physical longing, she ached for him, for his flesh, cool agate to the eye, warm clay to the touch, to buck and shudder under him. What the hell had he been doing at the opera house tonight? Who was the man she saw him with? What was going on in the boy's life? Maybe he wasn't as pure and innocent as he'd seemed. Maybe he was a shrewd faker. Maybe he was what his fey appearance suggested, a satyr, a libertine of the urban bosque. If so he had been holding out on her, trifling with her. She was doubly determined not to stand for it.

She turned away from the window and sat down in front of the dressing-table mirror. She applied cold cream to her round fantocine face. She had met more than one Casanova in her time, but this boy was becoming an obsession. It unnerved her. She liked to keep a tight grip on the reins. She didn't like one bit the taste of dust. She didn't like crying herself to sleep. She had stopped doing that a long, long time ago, after about the fifth time her father had tiptoed out of the room with the cute giraffes on the wallpaper, leaving her clutching her Belgian milkmaid rag doll and feeling so desolate that he was gone after having been so close. . . . Of course she hated him now, but she had thought she loved him then, prized his secret endearments. He was a god who would descend from Olympus in the still of the night and make her feel this special pleasure. When he stopped coming to her she felt bereft, relieved but used. She never shed another tear again.

Until now.

Crawling into bed and tugging the linen sheet up to her neck, she decided that the best way to exorcise the obsession was to solve it. And she thought of Sol Famm, a private eye she had once hired to shadow a parlormaid she suspected of filching cash and jewelry. He had done a good job on that case, getting enough of the goods on the girl, an octoroon with a phony British accent, to force her to give most of the loot back or face prosecution. He had been thorough, charged reasonable rates and was discreet. She resolved to call him in the morning as she drifted off to sleep.

Meanwhile on the streets of the city a real-life drama of transgression and retribution broke out, featuring the *Sparafuciles* of Pellegrino and Fitzgerald. First Junior Riccio was released on $100,000 bail, a legal maneuver that no longer could be forestalled, and soon a big shipment of uncut Scotch slated for the Judge's warehouse was hijacked beyond the three-mile limit off the Jersey coast.

Fitzgerald's gang retaliated by snatching off a Bronx streetcorner a hood named Fats Finnegan, a Jew from Rhinebeck with an Irish moniker who was the Big Guy's partner in an upstate brewery. He was held for twenty-five grand ransom. Two days later the money was paid and Fats was returned in one piece.

But the skirmishes continued. A week's take was heisted from one of Pellegrino's policy banks in Harlem. This was followed by a shootout in a Thompson Street pizzeria. Nobody was killed but Footsie O'Keefe's satellite Basil Bianco got winged in the right shoulder.

The police, of course, fumbled around making a few

pinches but their sound and fury signified little. Most of the micks wearing shields were either in Fitzgerald's pocket or on Pellegrino's pad. Their efforts neutralized each other. A few low-ranking hoods from each faction were collared and fed to shysters, who helped them beat the rap. Business as usual. . . .

A roundup of these events was reported in the page-three headline of the newspaper that lay on Dante's desk. The pot seemed to be coming to a boil. Somebody was sure to get hurt, maybe one of the rare honest johns pounding the asphalt out there.

He put aside the page proofs he had been correcting and gazed out of the arched windows of the city room. The sound of Caruso's golden tenor echoed in memory. To the northwest he glimpsed the massive arcade of the Municipal Building straddling Chambers Street and the stream of motor cars flowing across the Brooklyn Bridge. He still was serenaded by the honeyed voice in his memory and thought again about the weird night in Pellegrino's bedroom. Toscanini conducted without a score, Marconi became the youngest senator in the Parliament of the new Italy, Sherwood Anderson had an Italian mother and Charles Ponzi was the most brilliant swindler of all time . . . scraps gleaned from Gaetano Pellegrino, collector of chauvinistic, ethnic miscellany, among other things. It was indeed hard to reconcile this person with the mobster directing the gang war now raging. Dante told himself he had to figure a way to get those records out of the hotel. Which meant getting back inside the desk at least one more time—no mean trick. He had managed to exit the inner sanctum the first time with his so-called virginity intact, thanks to Pellegrino not forcing this issue, probably chalking up his reluctance to the shyness of a novice. He no doubt figured he could afford to bide his time, savor the challenge and ultimate conquest. Subtle as it was, Pellegrino's behavior so far pretty much confirmed the bootblack Tony Coco's version of things.

Meanwhile Dante had taken the service cart to Pellegrino's suite only three or four times, and the Big Guy's reaction to him had been cool and polite, period. The last time he'd gone up there with a tray, only two nights ago, Joe Baccala, the resident troll who guarded the gate, intercepted him at the front door, telling Dante that he would serve Pellegrino and his guests. Later Dante learned from Lee Lindenbaum that a parade of characters whose mugs had beautified many a police blotter had been arriving all day for some kind of big-deal powwow. Something major was brewing and it wasn't near-beer.

As he made his way out to the composing room to stand behind the stone and supervise the typesetting of the obit page, Dante wondered what the big sitdown was all about and how, if at all, it figured in the Madigan puzzle, the Riccio shooting and all the events in their murky wake. Pointing with the stub of a pencil at a widowed line on the proof, Dante handed it to a printer, a wall-eyed, pasty-faced fellow wearing a hearing aid.

On the IRT subway going home from work, his arm dangling from a strap, Dante did not notice the lanky nondescript man across the aisle with his nose stuck in a fishing magazine. When Dante later stopped to admire a pair of doeskin gloves in the window of a haberdasher on Sixth Avenue he did not see the same man's figure reflected there. . . .

Dante continued toward his apartment, where he intended to take a quick shower and change clothes before heading uptown for his shift at the hotel. As he showered and dressed he pondered again how to get his hands on the ledgers, and an idea struck: he would ask photo chief Al Diamond to lend him a tiny camera like the one Tom Howard of the *Daily News* used about two years before to snap Ruth Snyder in the Sing Sing death chamber at the moment she was being fricasseed for plotting with her paramour to bump off her husband. After Al showed him how to work the thing, he wouldn't have to remove the records from Pellegrino's bedroom, just take pictures of the pages and nobody would be the wiser, until they read about it in the *Courier.* Of course, he still had to figure out a way to get his hands on the records long enough to photograph them. He would need to keep the camera handy until Pellegrino went out for the evening, then let himself into the suite with a hotel passkey. Even when he went out, though, Pellegrino usually had a guard posted in the anteroom. Dante would have to figure a way to get around the sentry. . . .

The next day he spoke to Al Diamond about the camera, but the photo editor insisted on authorization from Ivan Bruce. Dante explained to Bruce that he needed it for his undercover work, and since the job was unofficial Bruce seemed not to want to know all the details. As he signed the authorizing memo Bruce said, "Look here, sport, don't stick your neck out too far."

"I won't," promised Dante, taking the memo from him, and wondering how far was too far.

Chapter

19

HANKY PANKY
IN THE STRUGGLE BUGGY

DANTE was in Washington Square looking to hail a taxi.
It was his only night off and he decided to take a respite
from the stresses of late and gate-crash a party being
thrown in Chelsea by some bohemian pal of Lorenzo
Casey, the copyboy. Any bash given the seal of approval by
Casey, a seasoned joy-seeker, was worth trying. Dante
needed to unwind.

But he couldn't locate a cab, and looking at his wristwatch he suddenly realized why. It was just after seven
and the whole nation, including hack drivers, was in sus-
pended animation listening to the new radio sensation of
the NBC network, "Amos 'n' Andy." Ever since the program had debuted the previous month the shopgirls and
shoe clerks had been talking about nothing else. Since the
weather was pleasant and the party wasn't terribly far
away, Dante decided to walk and save two bits.

Heading up Fifth Avenue, he passed the stone stoops and
wrought-iron fences of the Rhinelander townhouses, then
turned west on Eighth Street. Since he didn't know
whether there would be much of anything to eat at the
shindig and he was hungry, he stopped to buy a Hygrade
all-beef frank and an orange drink at a stand in the middle
of the block.

The party was held in a brick mansion across the street from the old armory building on West Twenty-sixth Street. As he climbed the steps toward the front door he noticed Clare Parker's Stutz runabout parked by the curb, and suddenly wondered if maybe Callahan had gotten wind of the party too.

Dante rang the electric chimes and soon joined the maelstrom of music and movement inside the three-story house of host Stuyvesant Marbury, a blueblood and recent Princeton graduate who dabbled in verse and the prevailing cult of gaiety. The music came from a Victrola playing the hot licks of Fats Waller, the tart sound nearly drowned out by the magpies of idle conversation. Dante removed a glass of bubbly from a tray that bobbed through the crowd on the palm of one of the white-coated Negro waiters who navigated the reefs and shoals of the rooms. Casey had touted the party as a big event attended by the swells, sophisticates and infamous alike. He said that even the dapper and diminutive playboy mayor was expected to make an appearance, foregoing his usual stop at Billy La Hiff's Tavern on West Forty-eighth Street. Sipping the decidedly inferior champagne, Dante searched the crowd and failed to spot Jimmy Walker. Of course it was early and the mayor was a notorious latecomer. Probably he was just then donning his spats in his digs at the Mayfair Hotel in Park Avenue. Dante did notice in the crowd a number of famous faces, including the mayor's chum, bandleader Vincent Lopez, Tammany potentate Albert Marinelli, the well-known Negro journalist George S. Schuyler, Ziegfeld girl Mae Murray, publisher Raoul Fleischmann, actress Joyce Barbour and a well-groomed young man who might have passed for a member of the diplomatic corps but whom Dante recognized from news photos as one Francesco Castiglia of East Harlem, also known as Frank Costello, reigning caesar of the one-armed bandits. The galaxy of guests lived up to Casey's billing.

Dante caught sight of Clare leaning against a mantlepiece in the next room and chatting with a silver-haired fellow whom Dante didn't know. He elbowed through the crowd toward them.

"Hello, Dan," she drawled with a tart look at the surroundings. "Welcome to Vanity Fair."

"Yeah," he replied, attempting an equally astringent
tone, "cakes and circuses, right?" He looked inquiringly at
the man standing next to her.

"You'll never guess who this is," she said.

"Let's see—the Maharajah of Magadore?"

"No, but I'll reward you with a kiss anyhow," she said,
planting one on his lips.

"How can I get into this game?" asked the man, sticking
out his hand for Dante to grasp. "Nick Callahan," he
added, introducing himself.

"No kidding? So much for family resemblances. I'm
Dante Viola."

"We used to look more alike. But Johnny got a head start
on ugly and never looked back."

Dante inclined his head. "It's Senator Callahan, isn't it?"

"Only when I'm working."

"When are you working?" asked Clare.

"Whenever I can't avoid it."

"Which is mostly always, when you're a politician," said
Dante. "Cal around?"

Clare nodded toward the winding carved oak staircase.
"Upstairs."

"Happy dust?" asked Dante.

"Sticks, muggles, you name it." She put a scarlet-nailed
forefinger to her lips and said to the legislator. "You won't
tell will you?"

He shook his head and sipped contraband booze.

Dante looked up, hearing noise at the door. More guests
arriving. The party probably had started around six and
would last until dawn when contingents of revelers would
carry the bacchanalia outdoors, bathing in city fountains,
journeying down to the Battery to watch the sunrise,
breaking into the Aquarium to steal alligator eggs and
drop them into the sewer system. Others might, as novelist
Scott Fitzgerald was supposed to have done, cap the festivi-
ties with a visit to the morgue to view the corpses. A gener-
ation that refused to call it a night, as someone said.

"Quite a gathering," said Dante, again surveying the

crowd, a mixture of what Texas Guinan dubbed "big but-
ter-and-egg men," junkies, prostitutes, gigolos, aesthetes,
rum-runners and gawkers.

"All this madcap pleasure-hunting," said Clare. "It gets
tedious."

"You could always leave," said Nick, his tone somehow
avoiding the implication that he wanted her to.

"I'm addicted to it," she said. "I suppose we're all hop-
heads of whoopee. But soon the Devil will call in his markers," she concluded with a mock-sibylline air.

"The piper must be paid, eh?" said Nick. He shook his
head. "I don't believe in that."

"No?" said Clare. "What's your philosophy, then?"

"The good die young," said Nick.

Dante, getting into the spirit of things, was about to offer
a homily of his own when he felt a clap on the shoulder
and turned to face John Joseph Callahan.

"I see you've met my big brother," Callahan said.

"Hi, Cal," Dante said, searchlighting Cal's red-veined
eyeballs. He hadn't spoken more than two words to Callahan since the night at Mother Superior's. While he didn't
quite admit it to himself, he was inhibited by the vague
distrust he felt for him. "Aren't you going a little fast?"
Dante said. "The night's still young."

"Has the mayor arrived yet?" asked Callahan.

Clare shook her head. "You'll know when he's coming by
the squeak of his shoes."

"How was the Miss America contest?" he asked.

"Pageant, dear heart. Oh, I feel sorry for those floozies in
their fancy celanese Violet Ray swimsuits. I've never seen
so many knock-kneed dames in one place in my life."

"I prefer them pigeon-toed," said Callahan. "Easier ac-
cess."

Clare gave Callahan a light slap on the cheek. "Hey, why
don't they have a *Mr.* America contest?"

Dante coughed, smoothing back his shiny center-parted
hair.

"Why, Mr. Bleecker Street here would be sure to cop first
prize," she said, smiling at Dante.

"The country's not ready for it," said Nick.

Callahan cornered Dante. "Hear you been jazzing the boss' daughter. Didn't your mother ever tell you not to shit where you eat?"

"Look who's talking," said Dante.

"Look here, sport, I know she's a hot number, but you could have quiff lined up around the block. Play it smart."

"Thanks for the advice, but I've already broken it off with Lily."

"Out of the frying pan, huh? Now you have to worry about the fury of that woman scorned. Lots of luck."

"I didn't scorn her."

"Does she see it that way?"

"I can't speak for her."

"I'll lay you odds she doesn't."

"I'm not a gambler."

"Then you shouldn't have started up with her in the first place."

"Hey, I don't want to discuss it, Cal."

"Don't say I didn't warn you, kiddo."

Couples had started dancing. Fox-trot. Black bottom. Shuffle. Tango. The castle walk.

Dante fought with the impulse to tell him that he was still digging into the Pellegrino story, but he didn't know if he could trust him any more, and the doubt depressed him. He had always counted on Cal for advice. Now he was on his own, more or less.

He probed: "Say, you must be a busy beaver these days, Cal."

"How's that?"

"All the fireworks between Pellegrino and Fitzgerald."

Callahan shot him a dark look.

"You're a crime reporter, right?" Dante added.

"Right . . . that guinea maniac, some say he was the one who bumped off Rothstein."

"Why do you call him a maniac? He's a killer, for sure, but a maniac? Isn't that too easy?"

"What do you know about it?"

Dante hesitated, then said, "Just what I read in the papers."

Callahan looked at him. "I hope you're keeping your

nose clean. I hope you're not sticking your neck out."

"Me? Nah."

"Remember—the yarn's on the spike."

"Sure," Dante said.

The side of beef known as Callahan's face assumed a deeply troubled expression. "I've heard some wild tales lately about this joker Pellegrino. Nasty stuff."

"No kidding? Like what?"

Sidling through the crowd, they passed through the kitchen and stepped out into a postage-stamp-sized backyard. The odor of dying geraniums and impatiens filled the September night air. They sat on a stone bench. Callahan reached down and scooped up dirt from the ground. He hurled it at a nearby birdbath. "Let me tell you something," he said. "The hoods around here have some pretty inventive ways of separating body from soul. I mean, besides the obvious ones like ventilating your ass with a tommy gun. Some of them like the scenic route, see? They pitch a pineapple through the transom of your john while you're taking a dump, giving you two explosions for the price of one. Or they wire your car with a stick and roast you alive. Sometimes they toss you over the side of a boat with your feet encased in cement overshoes. They can batter you into unconsciousness, then arrange a hemp necktie so that you strangle yourself when you come to. But hey, from what I hear, these artists look like pikers next to Pellegrino."

"You sound like an expert," said Dante, looking sidelong at him. "Dead is dead, isn't it?"

"I'm told that mug Pellegrino eats liver."

"A good source of iron."

Callahan made a face. "You know that I mean. And that's not the worst of it," whispered Callahan, laying it on. "He prefers, if possible, to do it while the victim is still alive."

Later Clare introduced Callahan to the host, Stuyvesant Marbury, to whom Callahan took an instant dislike, a phony aesthete with a too-flawless face and the handshake of a wet dishrag. While Clare and Marbury compared notes on friends in the Social Register, Callahan looked over the guests, a mixture of famous faces and bohemian oddballs. He eyed a pretty deb who stood near the winding staircase powdering her knees above her turned-down hose.

Another spectator also ogled her. Nick Callahan. Just the man his brother wanted to talk to.

Excusing himself, Callahan left Clare to Marbury and crossed the room.

"I gate-crashed," he said to his older brother. "What's your excuse?"

"I have a weakness for bad champagne."

Callahan looked again at the girl powdering her knees. "And for vamps in silk stockings?"

"I've never made a secret of that."

"How've you been?" Callahan asked.

"Fine. You?"

"Well, I was on the city editor's shitlist for a while. He didn't exactly appreciate my three days' AWOL when I was running errands for the Judge. But I'm back on the track now."

Callahan frowned at the memory. He had been exiled for two weeks to writing captions about marathon dances and Gloria Swanson lookalike contests and covering meetings of the Bureau of Gas and Electricity (the sessions contained plenty of gas but little electricity). He had known that if he didn't get back on the crime beat soon he would land in the Judge's dog house, a very bad place and not helpful for his project of staying in good inside. So he had kept himself on his best behavior, punching the clock, cutting down on the sauce. With September the city editor's mood had softened and he put Callahan back on the crime beat. He was determined to reward Bruce with a scoop. Maybe Nick could help him out.

Callahan said, "I could use a scoop. Something to cement my rehabilitation. Any scuttlebutt?"

"I hear things," Nick said.

"Well?"

Nick wore a teasing smile. "I'm not in the habit of leak-ing info to news reporters."

Callahan got a mental glimpse of Nick when they were boys, tantalizing his brother by holding back a share of his bag of rock candy. He always managed to have treasures cached under the pillow; turkish taffy from the Jersey shore; tintypes of semi-nude Gibson girls.

"Be a sport, Nick."

Nick studied the champagne glass. "I can see the head-line."

"I'm all ears."

Nick raised his hand, scintillating with precious stones set in precious metal. " 'Gangland Chiefs Hold National Convention. Sign Truce.' "

"You missed your calling. You shoulda been on the copy desk."

Nick shook his head. "Not enough do-re-mi."

"When did all this happen?"

"It's *going* to happen. Next week in Atlantic City."

"Tell more."

Nick looked around, then drew closer to his brother. "Hey, the boys are getting wise. Like Rockefeller and J.P. Morgan, they're smart. They know how competition drives up operating costs. And the strong-arm stuff—the hits, the vendettas, the blood feuds that nobody remembers how they got started. Bad for business. So the major gangs are planning this national convention, see? Like the captains of industry. They'll carve up territory, name a board of directors and swear to settle disputes peaceful-like. No more tommy-gun diplomacy."

"Who'll be chairman?"

"Probably Charlie Lucky."

"Lucania?"

"They call him Luciano now. These goombahs change their names every hour on the hour." He sniffed the air. "Anybody steps out of line, the shit hits the fan."

"Including Fitzgerald and Pellegrino?"

"Especially them. Smart arrangement. It'll mean more profits all around."

Callahan looked skeptical. "Hey, no truce is gonna hand-cuff a hothead wop like Pellegrino. Or Jimmy the Judge, for that matter."

"We'll see," said Nick. "Anyway, you got your exclusive."

"When can I use it?"

"Right *after* the convention. I'll give you the word. Of course you'll have to attribute the story in vague ways."

"Yeah. 'Reliable sources.' They won't mind my publish-ing it?"

"Nah. It's good publicity. And they understand you got a job to do." Clare was approaching and Nick cautioned, "Mum's the word." He switched on the artificial light of his charm. "Did I ever tell you, Miss Parker, what a big fan I am of your feature articles? I loved the piece on Lillian Boyer, that stunt flier."

"Thanks, Senator," she said. "And while we're throwing bouquets around, may I say that you're much better-look-ing than your newspaper photos?"

"They never do justice to my wonderful coloring," he said.

"Yeah, red, white and blue," said Callahan. "Red face, white hair, blue eyes." He hummed the opening bars of "Stars and Stripes Forever."

"Nice going, Johnny boy. Can I use that in my campaign literature?"

"No charge," said Callahan.

The mayor never showed up. As the night wore on the party grew wilder, fueled by junk, hootch and harum-sca-rum lust. Necking parties formed in the garden, bedrooms and hallways. Hip flasks were brandished under every nose. Sugar daddies in formal attire played horsie-back with young flappers. Dante submitted, drank several glasses of bad champagne and other beverages but turned down the tea and snow offered to him. More than one horny sheba threw herself at him, but Dante was too reti-cent, preoccupied and drunk to take advantage. He had lost track of Clare and the Callahan brothers. Images kept surfacing of Pellegrino's grotesque fetish. Callahan had said he did it for ritual purposes, to incorporate the courage and strength of his dead enemies and strike terror in the hearts of his living ones. Like some primitive shaman in Sumatra or somewhere. The party's atmosphere of abandon now lent an air of unreality—or maybe heightened reality—to the ugly pictures sparked by Cal's disclosure.

Then he saw Clare and Cal in the pantry off the kitchen. She had her hand at his fly, stroking. Dante turned his face away and hurried off to look for another drink. He was confronted by a pretty girl with a strawberry smear of bright lipstick on her face and two glasses of champagne in her fists. She handed a glass to Dante, shouting something inaudible at him. He nodded numbly, they locked arms and stumbled into the pulsing mass of revelers.

The first thing Dante saw as he surfaced to consciousness was the claw foot of a bathtub two inches from his nose. It was a mystery to his befogged brain how he had ended up on the bathroom tiles and what he had been doing there. Staggering to his feet he wobbled over to the transom window and gazed out at the still inky sky. He doused his face with tap water and left the bathroom, running a blockade of bodies and debris to find the front door.

Outside, the birds of the city gave a fanfare to dawn. He looked up and down the street, and wondering again if he should take a cab or walk, he noticed Clare's runabout still parked in front. He turned up the collar of his coat, plunged his hands into his pockets and began walking. As he passed the automobile he couldn't help hearing the telltale soughing. His eyes were drawn like magnets to the sight. Quickly he turned away, choking down the misery.

Clare and Callahan copulated on the seat of her car to the matinal ragtime of birds. One thing had led to another, goaded by the gods of grape, hemp, poppy and coca.

Should he feel self-reproach for this too, given what he knew to be Dante's infatuation? In a strict technical sense he was not betraying his young friend. Dante had no lien on Clare. But since when were matters of the heart strictly technical? Callahan felt like a Judas, and that was enough to make him one.

Afterward Clare straightened her marigold hair and adjusted her clothing as the slow bleach of dawn seeped into the city.

Chapter

20

WATCH THE BIRDIE

DANTE woke at midday and sulked around the apartment, nursing a big head while he waited until it was time to go to work at the hotel. He drank a pot of strong black coffee and tried to keep the ugly images at bay. He failed.

The weather, recently autumnal, had turned steamy again. He looked out the window toward the Sixth Avenue El. The air was stagnant. Like the moral climate of this time and place. The image returned: Cal's heaving half-moons, luminous in the dawn. Clare's salacious grimace, her chin lodged on his mossy shoulder. Dante drove his fist into the plaster wall, then shook his aching hand.

He went to the bedroom to look at his file of news clips of important stories. Research might help ease the pain. Soon he was reading the *Mirror*'s account, dated November 5, 1928, of Arnold Rothstein's rubout in the Park Central Hotel. The mob chieftain was shot during a card game and lived for two days before checking out. He declined to finger his killer or killers, observing the First Commandment of gangland, Thou Shalt Not Squeal. The cops never unraveled the mystery of his shooting. Not officially, anyway. Dante remembered that the case cast long shadows over police headquarters, the political clubhouses, even the courthouses, the Municipal Building and, yes, City Hall. He remembered also that Rothstein, like Pellegrino, kept records, prompting this search through the clipping file.

As he poured over the scissored-out articles he remembered once hearing in the city room (had it been Joe Cyriax or Scoop Madigan himself who said it?) that Rothstein's mouthpiece had described his client as "a mouse standing in a doorway waiting for his cheese." Well, who didn't in this day and age? The Cities of the Plain seemed to have risen from the ashes. Boom times, muttered Dante. Bankers, bootleggers, industrialists, publishers—everybody was hopping on the gravy train. Or was it an express train to hell? Even shoe salesmen and stenographers were buying stocks at margin, basking in the general mindless optimism.

Dante lay the clippings aside and thought about Rothstein's private files, the ones that had been seized by the authorities right after his death. He recalled hearing through the local-room grapevine that the files held explosive information but the general public never got wind of it. It was hushed up. Dante knew that he couldn't entrust Pellegrino's files to the police or even to the district attorney, if he ever managed to copy them. He would, he decided, take them straight to Ivan Bruce, an honest man, whatever else he was.

When Dante went to work that night he carried the latest model vest-pocket Leica that he had requisitioned from the photo department. Diamond, the photo editor, had given him a crash course on how to operate the 35mm camera with high aperture lens. It was small enough to fit comfortably in his uniform jacket without bulging at the hip. But night after night no opportunity came to use it. Either Pellegrino or one of his torpedoes was always around. Dante tried to be patient.

Meanwhile Pellegrino kept making overtures to Dante, inviting him to restaurants, the theater, the fights. Dante found alibis and excuses, but was also afraid to alienate the gangster. One day he could put him off no longer and accepted the invitation to Aqueduct Race Track. At least this was more man-to-man activity than going to the opera. And this time Dante intended to find an excuse not to go back with him to the hotel afterward.

Pellegrino backed a loser in the Brooklyn Handicap, dropping a bundle, but it didn't seem to faze him. Over soft drinks in the clubhouse he asked Dante to join him for dinner.

Dante invented a lie. "Sorry, Mr. Pell, but my mother's ill and I have to go home to take care of her."

Pellegrino clucked his tongue. Italians, even barbaric ones, approved of filial devotion. "Please call me Guy. I'm sorry to hear that. What's wrong with her?"

"Uh . . . her heart."

"Have you a doctor? I know an excellent cardiac specialist—"

"Oh no, it's . . . it's not that bad. I mean, we have a doctor already. Thanks anyhow."

Pellegrino shrugged and finished his ginger ale. "Okay, I'll take you home. Where do you live?"

"You mustn't bother."

"No bother at all. Where do you live?"

"Bleecker Street."

Pellegrino signaled to Joe Baccala to get the car and bring it around to the back door of the clubhouse.

On the ride back from Queens Pellegrino and Dante sat silently in the back seat. Crossing the Williamsburg Bridge, Pellegrino took two cigarettes from a silver case etched with a dolphin design and offered one to Dante. As he took the cigarette their fingers grazed. Pellegrino smiled.

"Do you know you're a beautiful boy, Dante?"

Dante coughed, terror-stricken.

Pellegrino patted him on the knee. "You're a man, too. You're part man and part boy. One of the secrets of your charm, eh?"

Dante cleared his throat again and looked out the window at the Orchard Street pushcart market. Ranging many blocks north and south of Delancey Street, the market fea-

tured Jewish peddlers hawking the bounty of their hands
and toil: fruits, vegetables, bread, bagels, pickles, boiled
chick peas, knishes of groats and mashed potatoes. When
they stopped for a traffic light a melange of wonderful
aromas wafted into the car. "Doesn't that smell good," said
Dante, anxious to change the subject.

"I want to buy you something," Pellegrino said.

"No, please," said Dante, "I was just—"

"Nonsense." Pellegrino leaned forward and ordered the
driver to stop the car, then barked instructions to Joe Baccala, who nodded, got out of the car and came back a few
minutes later with brown bags filled with an assortment of
neighborhood delicacies.

"For your mamma," said Pellegrino, handing Dante the
shopping bags. Pellegrino's dark brown eyes, shaded by
the brim of his black homburg, were shining.

The car started up again, turned right on Cleveland
Place and went north on Lafayette Street. Pellegrino's
hand returned to Dante's knee.

Dante struggled against showing the revulsion he felt. "I
live right over there," he said, pointing as the car approached Bleecker and Sullivan streets. The car stopped in
front of his apartment building. Peeling paint on the
bricks. Black cross-hatches of fire escape on the facade.

"Well, here we are," he said nervously, repeating himself.

"Don't forget your packages," said Pellegrino with an
ironic smile. The hand that had rested on Dante's knee
now played with the knot of its owner's tie.

"I won't. Thanks again." He gripped the twisted paper
handles of the shopping bags.

"I hope your mother feels better soon."

"I'm sure she will. Thank you, Guy. Goodnight. I'll see
you soon."

Dante got out of the car and stood on the lamplit sidewalk. As he leaned in to shut the door behind him Pellegrino crooked a finger at him. Dante leaned in further.

Pellegrino grabbed the young man's face in both hands
and kissed him on the mouth. The car sped away.

Dante, rooted to the concrete, watched the car vanish down the street. Finally he wiped his mouth with the back of his hand and spat on the sidewalk.

A lean figure slouched in a shadowed alley across the cobblestones.

Dante hurriedly turned away and entered the apartment building. Before going upstairs he gave away the groceries to the janitor's wife, who had six kids.

The next day at the office he got a telephone call from Lily Ferrand.

"I miss your loving, honey bun," she said.

"Don't talk that way, Lily."

"All's forgiven if you promise to come see me tonight. Max is out of town again."

"I can't."

"Have a heart.

"I said I can't, I'm busy."

Her voice grew metallic. "Busy doing what, lover boy? Butt-fucking your fairy godfather?"

Which stopped him cold. "I've no idea what you're talking about—"

"I'll bet you don't. What do you take me for, a dumb dora?" He could hear her labored breathing on the other end of the line. "Boy, you had me bamboozled. First I thought you were two-timing me with that skinny bitch Clare Parker. I never figured you for a homo."

"I'm not a homo!"

She sighed. "Hey, stick with me, baby, and I'll convert you. I got more holes than fellers. Look, if you're made for love in all directions I can accept that. Just save a piece for me. Don't freeze me out."

"You've got this all wrong, Lily. All wrong."

"Prove it. See me tonight."

Dante wavered, but what was the point? "That won't prove anything," he said. "Sorry, but I can't."

Silence. Then: "I'll fix your fucking wagon. And his too!"

Pigeons pranced like big-bosomed dowagers at Dante's feet as he sat brooding on a park bench. He was under Augustus Saint-Gaudens' equestrian statue of General William Tecumseh Sherman at the Plaza entrance to Central Park. He glanced at the horse-drawn carriages parked on the corner of Fifty-ninth and Fifth and let his gaze sweep over the green mansard roofs of the surrounding luxury hotels, the terraced wedding-cake apartment houses reflected in the brackish pond. He ate a hotdog before work at the hotel, plotting a way to steal unobserved into Pellegrino's bedroom.

After weeks Dante finally thought he had the chance. Pellegrino had taken an unexpected trip out of town (to Atlantic City, it was rumored). But Joe Baccala remained posted at the door to the suite, leaving cupcake crumbs and assorted detritus all over the Turkish carpets. How to lure the slavering watchdog from the door? A passing tart in a cloche hat gave him an inspiration. But he would need an accomplice, maybe two.

During a lull in the work shift he cornered Lee Lindenbaum. Like the other hotel employees Lee had been cool to him since his association with Pellegrino had become grist for the gossip mill. Now Lee and Dante were smoking cigarettes in the alley near the service entrance. "I need a favor, Lee," Dante said.

"Yeah?"

"Look, I'm not what you think I am."

"What do I think you are?"

"A conniving, mercenary pansy. You're wrong but—"

Lee looked away. "None of my business."

"I need your help with something. . . ."

Lee studied Dante's face. At least he was curious. "Doing what?"

"I want to get his man Baccala away from his guard post for about a half hour. I need to get into Pellegrino's bedroom."

"What the hell for? You wanna pull a job, stick up a gas station. It's a lot healthier."

"I'm not a thief."

Lee peered at him even more closely, then smoothed

back the gray sides of his hair, gleaming with brilliantine. "You a member of a rival gang?" he asked.

"No."

"A cop?"

"No again."

Lee prided himself on an ability to read people's facial expressions. It was a conceit that he had lived by for fifty-three years, had never let him down, he believed.

"Okay then, what *is* your racket?"

Dante decided to be completely honest with Lee. To level with him and hope the truth was the best argument. "I'm a newspaper reporter, Lee. . . ."

Lee looked skeptical. "They take 'em outta grade school now?"

"Never mind my looks: I am telling you the truth."

Lee, reading and believing, squashed the cigarette under his heel. "So? What do you want from me?"

"Nothing that will get you in the least bit of a jam. Mainly I need information. You know all the ropes around here."

"Such as?"

"Hookers work the hotel, right?"

"They work every hotel."

"How do I find one?"

"You that desperate? Come on. Guy with your looks shouldn't have to pay—"

"I don't mean for me. I mean for that goombah Baccala. And I want the lady to make him think she's doing it not for dough but because she's got to have him. I want her to seduce him. I'll pay."

"You don't want a prostitute, you want an award-winning actress."

"I *want* her to get him out of the suite for a while."

"It'll cost."

"How much?"

"Fifty bucks, I'd say."

"That's a lot of green."

"Like I said, she has to be an actress and actresses come high. Good ones, anyway."

"Aren't all actresses whores of a sort?"

Lee shrugged. "I've heard said that all women are actresses—"

"And I've heard said all women are whores."

"Excluding your mother and mine," Lee added with a smile.

Dante decided to approach Ivan Bruce for advance expenses. He would make the pitch tomorrow. "Okay, then, fifty bucks," he said.

Lee nodded. "There's this chambermaid named Melba. Moonlights on her rump."

"Attractive enough?"

"Got a pair of shakers on her make a dead man drool. Don't worry. She'll take care of him."

"Where'll she take him?"

"Not too far. There's a walk-in linen closet down the hall. It's private. Once she's got him steamed, she shouldn't have much trouble getting him there." Lee looked at his watch. "Break's over. When's all this supposed to happen?"

"Soon as possible. Tomorrow night?"

Lee buttoned his coat, nodded.

The next day Bruce put up a little squawk but signed the expense sheet. At the hotel kitchen Dante handed Lee two twenties and a ten. "All set?" he asked.

"All set," said Lee, pocketing the money.

"I'm glad the Big Guy hasn't come back yet. I hope you get a piece of this, Lee."

"I take ten, if it's all the same to you."

"Sure."

"Melba's been filled in. She's gonna bag him at ten tonight when you're on your break. That'll give you the green light to take care of business, whatever that is. If she hits a snag she'll send me word through the dumbwaiter. We got a system set up."

"You're partners? You've done this kind of thing before?"

Lee shook his head. "I don't ask you questions, so don't ask me."

"Bad habit," conceded Dante.

Lee grunted. "Look, kid, be careful."

"I will." He grasped Lee's hand. "Thanks for your help. I won't forget it."

"Go peddle your papers," said Lee, and sauntered back to the kitchen.

The hours dragged as Dante went about his work. He had actually become a fairly proficient room-service waiter and was even starting to earn good tips. His trays were always impeccably arranged and his manner efficient, discreet and courteous. Ippolito and the other managers treated him with kid gloves because of his perceived relationship with the big shot in the penthouse. Dante not only took up routine orders of coffee, tea, soft drinks, late dinners and snacks but also learned a thing or two about steering visiting firemen to speaks, package stores, burlycue shows and houses of joy—services many transient guests had come to expect of bellboys and waiters.

Finally his break time came. He waited five minutes before taking the elevator up to the floor two stories below the penthouse. He climbed the stairs the rest of the way. At the door of Pellegrino's suite he checked out both ends of the hallway to make sure nobody was around, then rapped lightly on the door in case something had gone wrong and the torpedo was still inside. No reply. He fit the passkey into the latch.

The anteroom was littered with girlie magazines, discarded cellophane wrappers and empty sarsaparilla bottles. When the boss was away. . . . Dante smiled to himself. It also looked like Baccala had left in a hurry.

He entered the drawing room, crossed in front of the steps leading to the terrace and jiggled the knob of the bedroom door. Locked. He tried the passkey he had used on the front door but, as he feared, it didn't fit. There were five more keys on the ring and he began trying them one by one. The fourth one fit.

He switched on a floor lamp and checked his watch: 10:10. He had to work fast. Patting the Leica in his pocket, he crossed over to the desk. As he suspected, the cylinder top was locked. He might jimmy it with something but that would tip off Pellegrino that somebody had fiddled with his files. So what? The last person he'd suspect was Dante, right? Besides, by the time Pellegrino discovered the files had been broken into it would be too late. He would have quit the job and be out of there. Of course, the coincidence would point a finger in his direction. . . . Okay, that was just the way it had to be, the risks were there and he'd weighed them. He looked around for an instrument to break open the desk, and found it by the fireplace—a brass andiron with a hooked end.

Five more minutes to pry open the rolltop, trying not to damage the desk, but the moulding cracked and a piece of marquetry fell off.

The ledgers lay inside.

Quickly he followed Al Diamond's instructions on using the camera with available light. He brought over a floor lamp, removed the shade and beamed the light directly on the ledgers. He calculated the settings and propped the camera on a stack of books to hold it steady. He photographed every page. The whole operation took only seven more minutes. He had time to spare. His forehead glistened with sweat.

He put the ledgers back into the desk and tried to lock the cylinder again. It held, more or less . . . there was a crack of space at the top that the owner, he hoped, might not notice right away. He put everything in the room back in its proper place.

It was 10:25 as he shoved the camera back into his pocket. Ten seconds later he heard the front door to the suite open and slam shut.

Quickly Dante switched off the lights.

Chapter

21

THE BROKEN FLOWER

DANTE Viola froze.

Fear shot through him, blockading his throat. He listened to the sounds on the other side of the bedroom door.

Apparently Joe Baccala had little staying power. Dante tasted iron. He knew he had to act. He padded over the carpet to the door and pressed his ear against it. He heard a cough, the rustling of a magazine.

He slumped to the floor. Two minutes more and he would have been out of there. It might have been worse, though: Baccala could have surprised him as he came out of the bedroom. He tried to calm himself and think. Chances were Baccala would not enter the locked bedroom and Dante was fairly certain that he had left no sign of his entry outside. Had he locked the front door behind him? He didn't remember. If not, Joe Baccala probably thought he himself had left it unlocked or he would have become suspicious and searched the rooms. There was nothing Dante could do now but wait and hope for the opportunity to sneak out unseen. Maybe Baccala would go out for a breath of air; it was a clear, snappy autumn night. Maybe he would go to the john and stay in long enough for Dante to make his getaway. Maybe, after his exertions in the linen closet, he would fall asleep on the sofa.

Within an hour this did happen. Dante could hear his tuneless wheezing that carried to the bedroom. He got to his feet, prayed that Baccala was as heavy a sleeper as the *basso profundo* of his snoring indicated. He was scared of venturing out there but this might be his only chance. If Baccala woke up he would say he thought he'd rung for room service. He hoped it would not come to that. Before taking the next step he crossed himself.

As stealthily as a ghost he revolved the knob of the bedroom door, opened it and stepped into the living room. He closed the door quietly and with the passkey locked the bedroom door. Looking ahead he saw the open door to the vestibule spilling a pool of electric light on the carpet. Joe's snoring was major. As his eyes got accustomed to the semi-darkness he inventoried the objects in his path to make sure he wouldn't trip over anything.

He started to advance. Near the vestibule entrance he hugged the wall with his back and inched along until he could see Baccala's bovine face and bulky form sprawled on the couch. The man was dressed in shirtsleeves, necktie loosened, shoes kicked off. A revolver was tucked into the waistband of his trousers, and a copy of the *Police Gazette* lay at his feet.

Dante swallowed, trying to get the crab apple out of his throat. Ten feet lay between him and freedom. He was mightily tempted to move quickly and get it over with, but that would increase the chances of making noise. He worried about the sound of his own labored breathing. Surely, though, Joe's snuffling drowned it out.

Holding his breath and not looking back, Dante moved to the front door. His hand froze on the brass knob. The sleeper moved. After a terrifying moment the snoring resumed. He had been shifting position. His back to the sleeping man, Dante revolved the doorknob.

Seconds later he was in the hotel corridor, mopping his forehead, feeling the exhilaration of huge relief. He walked over and buzzed the elevator. . . .

"What the hell happened to you?" asked Lee, who ran into Dante in the lobby.

"Close call. Your friend Melba works too damn fast.

"She burned the toast, eh?" Lee shaded his mouth with his hand. "Night manager's fit to be tied. He's been looking high and low for you."

After what he'd just been through the wrath of the night manager held little terror for Dante. "Who gives a hoot?" he said.

The next morning Dante gave the roll of film to Al Diamond to be developed. He decided not to tell Ivan Bruce about his coup until he had time to study the records and consider his next move. Given the prevailing climate he knew there was a chance that the newspaper would be reluctant to publish such explosive information, especially without double-checking. Dante, realizing he was a novice at breaking big stories like this one, decided he needed advice from an old hand, a mentor. Could he take a chance and show the material to John Joseph Callahan? . . .

Later that day Dante phoned Ippolito to quit the hotel job.

"You can't just up and quit on me," said the annoyed voice on the other end of the line. "You owe me two weeks' notice at least. I'm short-handed and this is a busy time. There's a lotta exhibitions in town, the National Funeral Directors at the Grand Central Palace for one. There's a motor boat show and the rodeo. Hey, we're booked solid. Come on, kid."

Dante thought it over. He didn't like to leave Ippolito in the lurch, the man had been nice to him. And staying on would divert suspicion if Pellegrino got wise to the broken desk. Also, Dante really liked having the extra money. Two weeks would pass quickly. . . . "Okay, I'll give it two more weeks," he said.

"Thanks, Dante." After a moment's silence Mr. Ippolito said, "They tell me you disappeared for over an hour last night. What happened?"

"I fell asleep."

"Sure, kid, between the legs of that peroxide blonde

widow on the tenth floor?" He sighed. "I don't really blame you, kid. Nowadays the women, they're bold. Worse than the men, for crying out loud. I know it's hard to turn it down when they wave it in your face."

Dante, grateful, said nothing to discredit this version of events. He felt proud, and more than usually secure about his future in the news business.

That night, in the locker room where he changed into his waiter's uniform, Lee Lindenbaum approached Dante with a conspiratorial look. "Guess who came back today," he said.

Dante frowned. "Pellegrino."

Lee nodded, lacing a shoe. "Right."

"No sweat," said Dante.

"Thought you were quitting."

"Ippolito asked me to hang around for two weeks."

"I'd say you're a glutton for punishment."

"Can Melba be trusted to keep her mouth shut?"

"Sure. She just can't be trusted to keep her legs together. Hey, the bodyguard's not about to tell his boss he left the post for a hunk of nookie, is he? You're in the clear."

Dante nodded as he buttoned up the white coat.

Lee smiled at him. "Melba said she'd like to meet you."

"I can't afford it."

"I think she wants to give you a freebie."

"No thanks."

"Don't worry, she's clean. She gives all customers a short-arms inspection before taking them to town."

"Not interested."

"Why not? Hey, she's worth a tumble, take it from me."

"I guess I just don't like going with prostitutes."

"You don't have to *take* her anywhere." Lee sighed, adding, "Ah, to have the luxury of turning it down."

"Tell her thanks, anyway. Make up some story, okay?"

"I could say what everybody else is thinking. That you're a pansy."

"You don't have to go that far."

"Anyhow, don't worry about it. She ain't the sensitive type." Lee had finished dressing. "See yuh around."

In spite of Lee's assurances, Dante was apprehensive as he went about his duties that night. Finally, just after nine, he got the call he had been expecting and dreading. The night-shift headwaiter, an oily Alsatian named Gustave, gave him the order: "Open-faced veal sandwiches with horseradish sauce for Monsieur Pell and guest. No dally-dilly. And no get lost, hmmm?"

He picked up the tray in the kitchen, put it on the cart and rolled it to the elevators. Watching the bronze arrows that indicated what floors the elevator was passing, he checked himself out. He was fairly composed, confident he could act in a natural way with Pellegrino. In the gilt mirror that hung on the section of wall between the two elevators he glimpsed his own face, serene enough.

He rapped on the door to the suite.

"Okay," came a voice from inside.

A dull eye appeared at a crack in the door, Cyclops screening thunderbolts. Joe Baccala swung it open. He grunted and jerked his ink-smudged finger toward the living-room door, sat down again on the sofa, sticking his squashed nose into a magazine. Dante went over to the next door and rapped again.

"Just a second," came Pellegrino's familiar gravel sound. The door opened.

The gangster was attired in a foulard silk dressing gown and antelope slippers. His thick animal shock of hair was slick with water and oil and his gold incisor glinted in a ready smile.

"Dante, how good to see you," said with feeling. "Please come in."

"Thank you, Mr. Pell," he said, rolling the cart into the room. "Welcome home."

Pellegrino frowned. "You *must* call me Guy," he said.

The guest was sitting in a wing chair with his back to the door. Bluish wisps of cigarette smoke haloed his head. Pellegrino motioned to Dante with his right hand. "Over here, kid. Put everything on the coffee table."

Dante rolled the cart in front of the guest's suede wing-tips. Without raising his eyes he removed the sandwich plates from the tray and placed them over paper doilies on the coffee table. When he finally looked up at the guest he felt like he'd been kicked in the chest by a mule.

Patsy Secundo's weaselly face showed surprise. "What's this prick doing here?"

"Relax, Patsy," said Pellegrino. "This here's my regular waiter, Dante Fuoco."

"Bullshit. You mean, Dante Fucko. This here is Danny Viola, the newspaper guy. You remember—your *paesano.*"

Pellegrino's face iced over. "You're crazy, mistaken—"

"Mistaken, my ass," said Patsy. "I went to grade school with this meatball. And remember, we had a heart-to-heart not too long ago. What're yuh doing here, Danny, getting a scoop?" Patsy got up from the chair and rocked on the balls of his feet, arms loosely poised away from his sides.

Dante, who had bent over to lay down the sandwich plates, now straightened up. Cold sweat beaded his high smooth forehead. He tried to breathe, to control his bucking emotions.

Pellegrino, dangerously calm, was silent for a moment, then finally said, "Well, Dante?"

Dante looked toward the door. Should he make a run for it? How would he get past Baccala? Maybe he should just try strolling out of there. They wouldn't risk bumping off another newspaper reporter. Or would they? Did he have the courage to test his theory?

"Well?"

"I . . . I got fired from my newspaper job, Mr. Pell, this is the only way I could make a living." The story sounded lame even to Dante's ears. He was too scared to be creative.

"I thought you were a student at Columbia," Pellegrino said.

"I was. I mean, I used to be until I ran out of tuition money."

"You said your name was Fuoco."

"It was my mother's maiden name. . . ."

"The bastard's been spying on you," said Patsy, reaching into his coat. "Lemme take him out."

Pellegrino put a hand on his associate's arm. "Remember Atlantic City? The new rules?" He turned to Dante. "I would love to believe you, Dante *mio*. But even for a news monkey you're a terrible liar."

"Yah," said Patsy, "this horse's ass really's got it coming to him. He's one dumb goombah." Patsy got out a revolver and fitted it with a silencer. "Lemme give him one between those baby blues, okay, boss? Then I give the carcass the treatment. Feed him to the furnace. Break his bones with a hammer. Be like he never was born. Okay?"

"Put it away, Patsy," Pellegrino ordered.

Patsy, clearly unhappy, unhooked the silencer and put the hardware back into his pocket.

Dante felt his knees knock together.

"I do believe he's gonna piss his pants," said Patsy.

"Shut up." Pellegrino was concentrating. "Look, it's one thing to ice a reporter who was really one of us. It's another thing to ice a reporter doing his job as a reporter. Especially an angel like this one. No, we'd have the whole town down on our necks."

"So we're gonna let the prick walk?"

"I didn't say that, Patsy." Pellegrino's gritty voice assumed an odd melodic lilt, then he barked toward the vestibule, "Joe, get in here."

Joe Baccala waddled in and stood there, ready for orders.

From the pocket of his dressing gown Pellegrino took out a .45 automatic. He held it idly at his side. "Go dig up a length of strong rope somewhere and bring it to me," he ordered Baccala.

"Where'm I gonna get it?"

"How do I know? Use that pea brain of yours for something once in your life. Now get out of here. Patsy, watch the door."

As Joe Baccala departed Patsy went to stand guard. Pellegrino waved the pistol at the chair that Patsy had vacated. "Sit," he told Dante.

Dante was a little more composed now that he knew they didn't intend to kill him.

Pellegrino sat across from him on the sofa. He crossed his legs and the dressing gown parted, revealing a naked knee and ankle bristling with black hair. A smile played about his thin red lips. His eyes were intense.

They sat there in silence until Baccala came back with the rope. "Found a hardware store open on Fifty-sixth Street," he said, puffing.

"Thanks, Einstein," said Pellegrino. "Now go back to your post and stay there. Tell Patsy I want him."

"Yeah, Boss."

When Patsy arrived Pellegrino said, "Close the door behind you, Patsy boy. Close it tight."

Patsy did as told and lounged with his back against the door, a glimmer of dawning awareness on his chinless face.

"Joe doesn't understand this kind of thing like you do, Patsy," Pellegrino went on. "Get the rope."

Patsy nodded, wearing a broad smile, strode across the room and picked up the rope from a side table.

"Now tie his hands in front, very securely, put him on his knees and hogtie him face down on the coffee table."

Dante realized he had relaxed too soon. He began to sweat and gasp for breath. Tears came.

Pellegrino spoke. "You see, Patsy, we might not be able to kill the stoolie but we can punish him. Oh yes . . . and the beauty part is we can do it so that he won't ever tell a soul what happened. Will you, Dante *mio?*"

Dante's face was pushed against the cold marble of the table.

"And we can have some fun while we're at it," added Pellegrino. "Some real swell fun." So saying, Pellegrino jerked his head at Patsy, who went over to Dante's quivering body, reached under to unbuckle the kid's belt, and pulled down his trousers and undershorts.

Dante squeezed his eyes shut. He feared losing total control. He wanted to scream, no sound came out. He tried to remember the words to his schoolboy prayers. Gaetano Pellegrino untied the sash of his silk dressing gown.

PART
THREE

Chapter

22

SPIKED AGAIN

My country 'tis of thee,
I come from Italy,
My name is Joe.
I own a barber shop,
They call me Joe the Wop,
I killed an Irish cop
In the good old U.S.A.

THE parody he remembered from his boyhood kept running through Dante's head. As far as he knew it had no rational connection to anything. It just kept playing over and over in his brain like a broken gramophone record.

For the last two days he had called in sick to the paper. Most of the time he just stared out of his apartment window. When he slept it was with awful nightmares. He drank nothing but water, ate nothing but dry bread. Sometimes he listened to music on the radio. Mostly he just sat on a hard wooden chair by the window and looked at the slate sky. He did not bathe, change clothes or answer the telephone. Would he ever feel clean again? He doubted it.

But by the second evening his mood had at least improved from black to blue. He put on a jacket and took a long walk down to Columbus Park, scuffling dry leaves on the pavement. He watched Chinese and Italian kids playing handball. Once, the rubber ball landed near his feet and he threw it back. They thanked him. It was the first positive act he'd been able to manage.

He looked around. It surprised him that the world seemed normal—people were going about their business under a guttering orange October sun. Children squealed at their games. Old men chewed on corncob pipes, their broad gestures and rosy noses giving them a buffoonish look. What had happened to him had no reflection in the flow of life.

Sitting in the park, for the moment his spirits stopped careening from despair to anger to numbness. Maybe he'd inherited the fatalism of his Sicilian ancestors.

For sure he had inherited their lust for revenge.

He felt a pang of hunger. A sign of life.

He walked to a bistro on Mulberry Street and ordered spaghetti and home-brewed dago red that the proprietors served openly, having greased the rumpot cop on the beat. The idea of Prohibition was incomprehensible to people of European blood. It seemed a national folly of a comic-opera nature, an insanity. He ate slowly, savoring each bite and contemplating his revenge.

He would survive his shame, he felt, if . . . Pellegrino and Secundo had to be punished. And he, Dante, had to play the major role in their punishment. This had been his goal, of course, even before he had a personal stake in the matter. Now the ante was raised.

He caught a glimpse of his reflection in the cafe window. His hair was disheveled, no flower adorned his lapel. The ditty resurfaced: *"My country 'tis of thee, I come from Italy . . ."*

He finished the meal, paid the bill and left.

Next day he returned to work and got the prints of Pellegrino's ledgers back from the photo editor. He felt a tremor of excitement as he held the key to his retribution. He stored the prints in his briefcase and returned to his desk to finish writing the obituary of an Episcopal minister in Queens.

Lily Ferrand stopped in front of the hardware store on Third Avenue to marvel at the clutter of objects in the display window and metal bins on the sidewalk. A sign advertised a sale on tools and hawked "Paints—Varnishes and Oils. Brushes of All Kinds at Low Prices." In the window were hung toilet seats, electric fans, bird cages, kitchen knives, claw hammers, lanterns, hot plates, potato peelers, handsaws, scales. Arrayed on the sidewalk were light bulbs, hatchets, shovels, nails, twine, solvents, detergents, auto jacks, gas stoves, hack saws, putty knives. Lily figured such a store would carry what she wanted, and went inside.

"Do you sell muriatic acid?" she asked the clerk, a man with lank wheat-colored hair and five o'clock shadow. Her appearance caused a minor stir among the male customers and clerks. It did not displease her to feel their eyes rake her from turbaned head to saucy rear to silk-stockinged legs to ankle-strap heels. She flounced her curls, wet her bee-stung lips and waited for his answer.

"What strength?"

"I'm not sure."

He rolled his eyes at the men. "What do you wanna use it for?"

"To take rust off of bathroom tiles. You see, I just moved into a new apartment. I guess it should be very strong. The tiles are in really bad shape." She smiled.

"How about twenty percent?" he asked.

"That sounds just fine."

He vanished into the back room and returned with a bottle. "You ain't doing the job yourself, are you?"

She hesitated, then said, "No. Why?"

"I was gonna warn you to be very careful. Whoever does the job should wear rubber gloves and try not to spatter it on the skin when he mixes it with water."

"Oh, you mix it with water?"

He groaned at her ignorance. "Of course, lady. Full-strength, it'll corrode the tile."

"I see." She unclasped her purse. "How much do I owe you?"

After she paid he put the bottle in a brown paper bag and handed it over. "Come back *any* time," he said.

She sashayed out, climbed into a cab, giving bystanders a glimpse of bright white flesh above the rolled-down stocking, gave the driver her address and started to hum, "Shaking the Blues Away."

At home she put away the acid, stripped to the buff and ran a bath. She sank into a tub lined with Italian ceramic and facing a picture-window overlooking the East River. Soaking in the tub she went over her plan, and was interrupted by a rap at the bathroom door, the maid announcing a telephone call from her father, Major Curtin. Lily took the call in the bath on a phone with a long cord.

"Hello, Daddy, what is it?"

The Major harumphed, his most eloquent form of expression. "Don't use that tone with me, Lily."

"What are you going to do—have me court-martialed?"

He cleared his throat. "I hear Max is out of town again."

"So?"

"Where is he this time?"

"Brussels. At least that's what he said. What do your military scouts tell you?"

"Don't be facetious, young lady."

"You mean you don't have any Brussels scouts." She laughed at her own cleverness. "I favor them *au gratin.*"

"What the hell are you talking about?"

"Never mind."

"Are you free for dinner tonight?"

She sloshed water over her pink tummy. "Sorry, I have plans."

"I'd like to talk to you."

"You're talking to me now."

"I want to talk to you *face to face.*"

She pictured his toothbrush mustache bobbing as he

spoke. What a ridiculous popinjay he was, she thought. She marveled that so many grown men, so many important men in business, politics and the military quaked in his presence.

"What do you want to talk about?"

"I think you know."

"I really have no idea," she said, lying. He was probably calling from the office and worried about his secretary eavesdropping. Even from a lonely peak of the Himalayas he would have a blimpish aversion to being blunt with his daughter on *the* subject.

"Your affairs," he managed.

She hooted with laughter.

"You have the gall to react this way? Why, they're snickering about you all over town. I won't stand for it, Lily. I can't even walk into my club without somebody making a double entendre. I'm not used to being the object of gossip and ridicule. Let me tell you something—"

"Sure," she interrupted. "It's not my reputation you're worried about. It's yours."

"I care about *both* our reputations. And the family name."

"The family name? As if you yourself haven't already tarnished that golden thing."

"Me? I'll have you know—"

"I'm not talking about your silly medals. What about your shady business deals? What about the way you run that rag you call a newspaper? And what about—Oh for God's sake, do I have to go on?"

"Rubbish," he said, but in a quieter tone.

"You also have a nerve talking about *my* affairs."

"Lily, I warn you—"

"Don't you think both mother and I knew about your tarts? Let's see if I can count them without an abacus. There was the Viennese governess, the secretary from Jersey City, the Cuban chili pepper. God, father, you must have worn out the zipper on your cavalry twills."

"How dare you—"

"I'm just a shaving off the old block." Holding the telephone in the crook of her neck she got out of the tub and wrapped a towel around her rear.

"Lily, it's different with a man—"

"So I'm told."

"I still want to talk to you."

"How about Thursday?"

"Can't, dammit. I'm going to Chicago for the World Series."

"Flying?"

"No, I'm taking the sleeper."

"Then I'll see you when you get back. Ta-ta."

"Wait a minute."

"Yes?"

He hesitated, then asked, "Who's this Dante Viola?" He made the name sound like smelly cheese.

"You ought to know. He works for you."

"I can't be personally acquainted with every mail clerk or copyboy."

"He writes obituaries."

"Well, he'll be unemployed damn soon unless he knows what's good for him."

"Don't worry, Daddy," she said, mixing anger, remorse and determination on the same vocal palette. "That won't be necessary." She sat in a wicker chair and rubbed her knees with the towel.

"Why do you always get mixed up with these low-bred slum boys?"

"You think the so-called aristocrat you hand-picked for me as a husband is better? Lemme tell you, Major, he has certain habits of body and mind that make the slum boys, as you call them, seem like knights of the round table."

"I'm not interested in the intimacies of your marital state."

"No? It might make good copy for the shopgirls and streetcar conductors who buy the *Courier.*"

He coughed. "Nothing wrong with putting out a newspaper that has mass appeal. I mean, James Gordon Bennett, Pulitzer, Hearst—"

"Mass appeal? Right?"

"Yes. And if you'd ever shown a shred of interest in the paper I'd have given you a job."

"Newspaper work is not my cup of poison, Daddy. For one thing, it would ruin my manicure."

"Clare Parker seems to do all right."

"I'll thank you not to mention that bitch's name to me. If that crotch-sniffing hack's your idea of a model newspaperwoman, I'll—"

"Where did you learn such gutter language?"

"From the Ivy Leaguers, Daddy. Not from the slum boys, I assure you."

"Well, don't use such language to me."

"Yes, sir. Sorry, sir. Right face, left face, to the rear, march."

He hung up.

She smiled, rose and toweled her hair, standing naked in front of the picture window. She stretched her plump body and watched the motor cars crawl along the East River Drive. Again she thought of Dante: "If I can't have that gorgeous slum boy, I'll see to it no other girl will want him."

Dante stopped at the A&P to buy a steak. Colleagues at work had remarked on his pallor and listlessness, he said he had the flu. At home he was aware that he was crawling out of the mental abyss. What happened had not been his fault, on a *rational* level he knew this. But it wasn't enough. He had been stained, violated. It could never be scoured away.

After dinner he went to the bedroom to study the ledgers. He shook his head in amazement: the names on the grease sheet would fill both a city register and a social register. Explosive stuff. One name in particular made him catch his breath—State Senator Nick Callahan.

He put the records aside and stared at the clutter of objects on his desk, wondering if Cal knew about his brother's shenanigans. They were cut from the same bolt of cloth, weren't they? He pushed away the thought and closed the books. He would not go to Cal first, he would show the documents to Ivan tomorrow and ask permission to break the story. No good reason to wait. Would his coup make him a reporter? Did that matter any more? Printing the truth mattered, damn it. It always had, but even more so now.

Dante sat down at the desk across from Ivan Bruce and gave a quick glance around the city room. He handed Bruce the documents. "I believe this will knock your socks off."

Bruce read. From time to time his eyes actually bugged as his whistled and shook his head. "You got another copy of this?" he finally said.

"Yes."

"Keep it in a very safe place. This one's going upstairs to the Major."

Bruce took a cigar box from his desk drawer, extracted a stogie and stuck it in Dante's mouth. "Have a cigar, kid. You earned it."

The cigar was still wrapped in cellophane. Dante took it out of his mouth. "I don't smoke cigars," he said, still unable to play the game.

On the other side of the city room Callahan, chewing the rag end of a stogie, read the news of Wall Street. Not long ago the headlines had been booming about how the markets had hit an all-time high. General Electric had posted at 396, AT&T at 304, U.S. Steel at 271—stratospheric numbers. But yesterday stocks had taken a big dip before rallying. Speculators were showing signs of nervousness over the increase of margin calls from brokers. Mood? Skittish, to say the least. In Chicago, Callahan read, somebody had lobbed a stink bomb into three brokerage offices. He wagged his head. Real pineapples were next. Ah, it was all Greek to him, Callahan thought. He liked to gamble as much as the next sucker, but he also liked to see the sweat on the horse's rump, the color of the red ace in the hole. Stock-market speculation was too abstract for his money.

Somebody tapped him on the shoulder.

"Take a look at this," said Bruce, handing him the copy of the documents that Dante had given him. "Thought you might want to see what your protegé has been up to. Especially since he's horning in on your territory." He meant the crime beat.

Callahan's curiosity had been stoked good. As he read Callahan spat cigar shreds, his expression running the gamut from detachment to interest to alarm. "How'd the kid get this?" he finally asked.

"Hot as a firecracker, right?"

"I'll say!"

"It's Pellegrino's palm-oil list."

"I figured that much out for myself." He repeated, "How'd he get it?"

"That's his business. The kid's got moxie, eh?"

"I thought the investigation was on the shelf." Callahan couldn't help burning.

"I looked the other way while Dante did this on his own. This is not the Madigan story, anyhow. This is a lot bigger. Ought to bring down every pillar in Sodom, right?"

"Bravo," said Callahan without enthusiasm. "Maybe he'll win the Pulitzer."

"You noticed a familiar name?" Bruce asked.

"I saw a lot of familiar names."

"One in particular?"

"Yeah." Leaning back in the chair Callahan, on second thought, allowed a grudging admiration for his protegé. Quite a coup to get this yard of goods and live to tell about it. So he had the balls for this racket, after all. But now I'm in a jam, Callahan thought, thinking on his double-life. And thinking on it, he realized this was the time to tell Bruce what he'd been doing and why, pool their notes and research. So how come the cat stole his tongue?

"I wanted you to see it before I sent it upstairs to the Major," Bruce added.

"Why?"

"Well, it involves your brother. I thought I owed you that, I got you into this business. . . ."

"What if I asked you not to run it?"

Bruce shook his head.

Callahan dropped the paper on the desk. "You want my blessing? *Benedicat vos omnipotens Deus.*"

But the benediction struck a hollow chord. Nick might be a rouge, a rat. But the Callahan boys hailed from Hell's Kitchen. And Nick still was his brother.

"What's that mumbo-jumbo mean?"

"It's Latin for lots of luck and be my guest. Question is, will the old man publish it?"

"He has to. It's a blockbuster story."

"A lot of the Major's fellow clubmen are on that list," Callahan pointed out. Was that observation self-serving? "Then there's the threat of libel suits. Piece of paper proves nothing, you know."

"It's more than a piece of paper with names on it. It has dates, places, dollar amounts, favors requested, favors received. It cites chapter and verse. The last pages describe in detail each guy's guilty secret, the thing Pellegrino can use to blackmail him with if he steps out of line. They're not gonna sue and air all this dirty linen in court."

"Happy hunting," said Callahan, partly crossing his fingers, partly really meaning it.

She gave Callahan a stinging slap on the cheek. "Try that on for size, you fat prick," said Mazie Rodell, avenging angel in a flowered kimono.

He resisted the impulse to rub his cheek. "What gives?"

"You want another one?" she asked, cocking her hand.

"You must have me confused with one of your other clients. Like that alderman from the East Side. I hear he enjoys getting slugged around."

"Take a hike," she ordered.

He looked from side to side in mock confusion. "Am I mistaken or isn't this here establishment what is known in the vernacular as a cathouse?"

"Beat it, Callahan. You know that Mother Superior lets us veto johns we can't stomach. Well, I can't stomach you.

As far as you're concerned from now there's a padlock on
my twat. Why don't you try Betty Coed again?"

He fidgeted with the brim of his fedora and arranged his
features in a puzzled expression. "Uh—I wonder if I might
pose a question: what the *fuck* did I do?"

"Don't play dumb, Callahan."

"I assure you, I'm not."

"Go wet your weenie somewheres else, see? Poke that
amachoor, why don't you? The newspaper gal. I hope she
gives you a colony of crabs and a triple dose of clap, you
moron with a hard-on."

Callahan curled his lip. "Hey, you talk as if I gave you my
fraternity pin."

Were those tears she was blinking back?

"Just because I'm a pro you think I got no feelings. I used
to trust you, Callahan. No more."

He collapsed on the love seat by the bay window. "Come
on, Maze. You at least owe me an explanation."

"I owe you shit. Get your ass off that sofa."

He got up. "I'm not gonna beg."

"Good. The door's that slab of wood over there with the
brass knob on it. You know what brass is, don't you? It's
what your so-called heart is made of."

"Been nice knowing you," he said sadly, shuffling toward
the door.

She winced. "Likewise," she said in a suddenly subdued
tone.

He closed the door behind him, descended the carpeted
stairs and left the house. He walked the streets aimlessly,
stucco-faced, fists clenched. He passed a Catholic church
just off Sixth Avenue where steeple bells tolled, summon-
ing parishioners to novena and confession. He quickened
his pace.

Callahan proceeded to make the rounds, taking the cure
for tonsillitis, flouting Title II, Section 3 of the National
Prohibition Act. At Perroquet he bumped into Joe Cyriax,
who had an overripe fan dancer on his arm.

"This is Clementine, my girl," Cyriax announced.

Calling her a girl was like calling a raisin a grape. But

Callahan, playing the cavalier, bowed. "Delighted to meet you, Clem." He turned to Cyriax. "Hey Joe, you never told me you had a daughter."

Cyriax punched Callahan in the shoulder. "G'wan, yuh stumblebum. Have a drink with us."

"Must be the Palmolive soap," conjectured Clementine, fluffing a lock of unruly hair.

"Don't mind if I do," said Callahan, and joined them at their table. After ordering a round Cyriax and Clementine lit up Chesterfields while Callahan fumigated the place with a manila. They made small talk on various subjects—a Yankee rookie named Leo Durocher, the marriage of Fanny Brice and Billy Rose, Mule Haas' game-winning ninth-inning homer for Philadelphia in the fifth game of the World Series. Then Cyriax got down to brass tacks.

"Heard you took over Scoop's spot on the cops-and-robbers beat," he said, squinting at Callahan.

Callahan kept mum. He remembered that it was Cyriax who had pinched the emerald stickpin from Madigan. He was glad he wasn't wearing his own souvenir from the Judge tonight.

Cyriax's broad grin showed chasms of missing teeth. "Whatever happened to that undercover job you was working?" he asked.

Callahan swallowed some hootch. "It got spiked. They said it was all smoke, no fire."

"What about that little item of jewelry?"

Callahan looked ignorant. "Huh?"

"You know, the stickpin."

"Oh." He looked idly around the room. "The Judge and Scoop grew up together. They were pals, see? Hey, Joe, are all your friends altar boys?"

Cyriax looked at Clementine. "Didn't I tell you he was a card?" He returned to Callahan. "Nah, they ain't all altar boys. But you can't tell me Scoop wasn't on the take."

"It's your opinion."

"How about you?"

"What do you mean?"

"I mean, got any more scoops on the burner? That was

a swell take-out last week on the Atlantic City convention. Read like it was full of inside dope."

"Hey, I'm an old alley cat. I've got my sources."

"Sure."

"You're making a point?"

Cyriax turned to Clementine. "Couldn't your face use a little more powder and rouge?"

Her dazed expression evaporated. "You really think so, Joey?"

"I mean blow for a minute. Get your butt to the little girl's room."

She got up quickly. "Sure, Joey," and teetered off on high heels and ball-bearing hips.

A touch of malice marked Cyriax's grin. "Cut me in, pal. I can be of service."

Callahan sighed. Was his double-life so obvious that a half-wit like Cyriax had doped it out? "I don't know what you're talking about."

"Sure you do."

"I can guess, though. And I'll tell you this: you're way off base." Was he really?

A flicker of doubt shadowed Cyriax's byzantine face, then vanished. "Why be so greedy?"

"Shine that light somewhere else, Demosthenes."

"Huh?" said Cyriax, puzzled as Callahan hoped he'd be. "What're you talking about? I had an uncle named Demosthenes."

Callahan went home, a wad of cotton in his head and matters to mull over. What would he do about Cyriax's overture? How would he deal with publication of the grease sheet? He got into his pajamas and tried to decide whether to tip off his brother. Blood might be thicker than water, but was it thicker than printer's ink? The encounters with Mazie and Cyriax gnawed at him. More and more, he began to feel like what in his heart he knew he'd become. Curling up in a cradle of self-loathing, he went to sleep.

Meanwhile, a couple of days passed before Dante worked up the nerve to approach Bruce. "Any word?" he asked the editor.

An unusual look crossed Bruce's face. Embarrassment? He turned his thumb down.

"You mean the publisher refuses to run the story?"

Bruce nodded. "Says he's afraid of libel actions."

"You *buy* that?"

"He says pictures of written records prove nothing. Too hot to handle." Bruce shuffled papers.

Dante collapsed into a swivel chair. "You don't know what I went through—"

"Sorry, kid."

"It's a cover-up."

"If you could get confirmation for a backup source he wouldn't be able to weasel out."

"Sure, confirmation. I'll just approach a crooked judge or alderman and ask him when he started taking graft."

"There are ways. . . . I'll give you carte blanche to work on it."

Dante again wondered if he wasn't in over his head, one green cub reporter against the big shots. David without even a slingshot. He glared at Bruce. "Wasn't it an act of conscience you said made you desert the Hearst flagship?"

"Don't tell me I'm about to get a lecture from a kid reporter wet behind the ears."

"Ah, what good would it do?"

Bruce scratched his mustache and shook his head. "We all get handed a limited supply of acts of conscience, see? I shot my wad some time ago."

Dante pressed: "Can I talk to him? Man to man? Face to face?"

"Who?"

"The Major."

"He's not gonna change his mind."

"What harm would it do to try?"

"He won't agree to see you."

"Why not?"

"For one thing, you're on his shitlist."

"His shitlist? He doesn't know me from Adam."

"Wanna bet?"

"What're you talking about?"

"Ask your girlfriend," said Ivan Bruce.

Dante shut his mouth at that one. At least for the time being, the grease-sheet story stayed on the spike.

Chapter

23

THE ACID TEST

ONE Sunday evening Gaetano Pellegrino cleaned his .38 revolver while listening to Leopold Stokowski conducting the Philadelphia Orchestra on the Philco Hour. He wore gray flannels, white cotton shirt and black cashmere cardigan. His dark slicked-back hair gleamed like an otter's coat. He appeared calm but under the surface his emotions bubbled.

Patsy Secundo entered the room, followed by Joe Baccala.

"I came right away, Guy," said Patsy, looking worried. Joe Baccala hulked in the background.

Pellegrino was especially scornful of Baccala. "We gotta do something about this. And quick."

Patsy patted his hip where a belly gun was tucked into his belt under the cocoa-colored jacket. "Don't worry. You know I'm handy with the eraser."

"Too handy, you moron. I tell you again, remember the new rules. Remember the pledge we took in Atlantic City."

Patsy feared Pellegrino but it stung his pride to be dressed down, especially in the presence of a half-wit like Baccala.

Pellegrino studied the dusky skyline. "We gotta come up with something else."

266

"Right, boss," said Baccala, trying for points.

"Quiet. If you'd done your job right we wouldn't be in this mess." Pellegrino squeezed shut his eyes and lost himself in the Bach fugue on the radio.

"Maybe he don't have nothing," suggested Patsy. "Ever think of that?"

"The latch was broken and he's a paid busybody. He copied the records."

"Then how come they ain't wrote anything yet?" asked Patsy.

"I don't know," said Pellegrino, "but I don't want to wait around to find out."

"Right," said Baccala.

Pellegrino finished wiping down the revolver. "Patsy, you arrange a meeting with Mr. Pretty Boy."

"You think he'll come?"

"Yes."

"I don't know. He's gotta be pretty steamed at us."

"He'll come," said Pellegrino. "Make it a public place where he'll feel safe. The Oak Room."

"Okay. What reason do I give?"

"Say we have an exclusive story for him. Leave it at that. Hey, he's a nosey newsman. They got ink for blood and minestrone for brains. He'll come, I'll tell you. Never mind what happened."

Patsy sat down in a leather chair by the fireplace. Baccala remained standing. "What's the gimmick, Guy?"

"Nothing special." The music rose to a crescendo. "You know who wrote this music?"

Patsy shrugged. "Some guinea?"

"A German. Johann Sebastian Bach."

"I like Rudy Vallee," said Patsy.

Pellegrino winced.

"How we gonna convince the little prick to hand back the copies?" Patsy asked.

Pellegrino rubbed his thumb over his forefinger and middle finger. "Money."

Patsy looked doubtful.

"Every man has his price."

"Too bad it has to cost," said Patsy, who hated nothing more than parting with cash.

"Yeah," said Pellegrino. "I'd much rather carve out the cocksucker's liver."

Dante was jolted awake by the sound of a jackhammer, dissolving a dream that featured Pellegrino and Secundo putting a crown of thorns on his head. Sitting up, he marveled at how he even dreamed in tabloid style.

He got out of bed and went over to the window. Workers were digging up the street, repairing electrical lines, he speculated. Conveyors of juice to electric toasters, and electric chairs.

He brewed and drank black coffee, ate a slice of dry bread, showered and dressed for work. He was no longer meticulous about his appearance. The shirts, though clean, were not ironed and starched. The ties and vests often had food stains. The suits were rumpled. He didn't bother to buy a flower for his lapel.

At the office he found a telephone message from Patsy Secundo. He sat down heavily, balling up the slip of paper in his fist. What did they want? Did he have the guts to return the call?

The city room was calm between deadlines. Ace rewriteman Matt Carpenter was making follow-up phone calls about a divorcee whose decapitated body was found in the Bronx. Two copyboys pitched pennies against the divider that marked off the wire room. A printer in a squared-off paper hat argued baseball with the sports editor. Pigeons warbled on the window ledge.

Dante reached for the telephone.

After work he went home and dressed—more carefully than usual—for the rendezvous at the Oak Room. He changed into a freshly pressed camel-brown wool suit with peaked lapels, an eggshell shirt and dark brown bow tie. He fingered oil into the thick waves of his hair and combed it neatly. On the way to the trolley stop he dropped by Mrs. Califate's flower shop and bought a yellow gardenia for his lapel—the short-lived flower that now was his favorite blossom.

Riding uptown he sat on a cane seat and gazed at the city scenes. The streetcar rattled through the heart of the Fourteenth Street shopping district and the center of the needlecraft trade around lower Fifth Avenue, then went on north toward Central Park. Dante tried to settle his nerves. Was he undergoing some test? He wondered why he was being so reckless. For sure he didn't believe that malarkey Patsy gave him about having a news tip for him. Still, there was a slight chance that it was true . . . and printer's ink acted like opium in the bloodstream. Whatever, it was devilishly hard to kick the habit by going cold turkey.

At Fortieth Street he saw something odd: a man casting the line of a fishing rod from the upper balcony of the five-and-dime.

He hopped off the trolley at Fifth and Fifty-eighth and stood under a shedding maple near the white stone Fountain of Abundance. He glanced up at the surrounding residential hotels—the Plaza, Pierre, Sherry Netherland, Savoy Plaza. He almost turned and went home but conquered the impulse and crossed the street.

The headwaiter led him to Pellegrino's table. Dante sat down without a word or a nod. He remembered a quote from Shaw: "Silence is the most perfect expression of scorn."

"Want something to eat or drink?" Pellegrino asked.

Dante shook his head.

Pellegrino and Patsy sat with their backs to the wall. Dante did not see Baccala but he would have given odds he was nearby. He felt blood rush to his face but his nerves were steady. Contempt for the men across the table overwhelmed the rising anger.

"Suit yourself," said Pellegrino, and offered a cigarette.

Again Dante shook his head.

"I think he's mad at us, Patsy."

Dante refused to be baited.

"Don't pout like that, kid, it hurts your good looks."

Dante forgot Shaw's advice. "Go fuck yourself," he said.

Patsy tensed.

Pellegrino gave a smile. "I don't have to. I prefer other people doing the job."

Dante kept silence. Scoring points would bring him no satisfaction.

Pellegrino leaned across the table. "Don't tell me you didn't *enjoy* our last encounter. . . ."

Dante pushed back the chair and stood.

"I'd stick around if I were you."

Dante hesitated. Remember, he told himself, you've come to hear what they have to say. Looking around he spotted Joe Baccala sitting on a stool about fifteen feet away from them near the door to the kitchen.

"Why don't you cut the bullshit and get to the point?" Dante said. "This isn't the opera."

Pellegrino's face hardened. "I think you know what this is about."

"I'm not sure I do."

"You would've made a good yegg, kid. You've got the soul of a con man."

"Come on," said Dante.

"Watch your mouth," from Patsy.

Pellegrino patted the henchman's forearm. "Let him blow off steam, no skin off my ass." He looked at Dante. "I found the busted latch, I know what you did. You ought to have better manners than to poke that fine Italian nose where it doesn't belong."

"I got a nose for news," Dante said. What more could they take from him? His life was worth nothing anymore if he didn't avenge himself.

"Ah . . . you wanted to get ahead at my expense, eh?"

"I wanted to expose you."

Pellegrino took a drag on the cigarette. "You got a nose for news, huh? You also got a nose for horseshit. How come I don't see any big stories in your paper about all this?"

"Wait."

"You're bluffing," Pellegrino said, sitting back in his chair. "I think your bosses are running scared. Maybe they don't trust a punk like you. Or maybe they got their hands in too many tills themselves to throw stones at other people."

"You willing to take that chance?"

"Could be."

"Then why'd you ask me here?"

Pellegrino snuffed out the cigarette in an ashtray. "Maybe because I got a crush on you."

Dante started to get up again.

"Stay put," Pellegrino commanded.

Dante sat down slowly. See this through, he told himself.

"I'll give you five G's for the pictures."

Dante cupped his ear.

"Okay, ten."

Dante frowned at the ceiling, toying with the man he hated more than anyone or anything.

Patsy's hands vanished under the table.

Pellegrino leaned back. "Okay, sweetie, how much?"

"You think it's just price, don't you?"

"Isn't it?"

Now Dante's face was hard and cold. "I'd rather dance at your execution than have two million dollars," he said.

Pellegrino lit another cigarette. "You should live so long. Okay, kid, you drive a hard bargain. Fifty G's. Final offer."

Dante leaned across the table. "Shove it," he said, then felt a muzzle of cold steel in his groin.

Pellegrino wagged his head. "You should have taken the money, kid."

Dante slumped in the chair. "Even you can't get away with killing me here. In public. You know that."

"Wanna bet? You're a real dangerous fellow. You also got a pair of *coglioni* on you, I'll say that for you."

"You can't kill me, you'd be signing your own death warrant, breaking the rules of the council—"

"I'll just have to explain to them the magnitude of the danger you pose. No time to get permission, see?"

Patsy spoke now: "Get up. Walk out, real natural, like."

Dante gripped the arms of the chair, glanced around the crowded room. "I'm not moving."

"I'll finish you right here," said Patsy.

"No."

"You really do have big stones," said Pellegrino.

Suddenly Dante hollered, "Waiter!"

A tall man with bright red hair pattered across the room. "Where's the gents, please?" Dante asked.

The waiter opened his mouth to give directions when Pellegrino produced a hundred-dollar bill. "Get lost, Carlo. We got business here."

The waiter took the money and quickly withdrew.

Pellegrino buttoned his coat and leaned across the table. "Listen, Dante, I'm giving you one more chance." He looked at Patsy, then back at the reporter. "Patsy will shoot you if I tell him to. He's very loyal. He knows that I got ways of getting him on a steamship to South America before the bulls can pick him up. He knows the mouth-pieces would spring him on bail. Even if he had to do time he knows we've greased every warden and screw from here to Ossining. Hard time for him would be living in a country club. You're sunk, kid. So come across."

Dante tried playing for time. "All right," he said. "You win."

Pellegrino tapped his own head. "Now you're talking. You got brains plus balls."

Patsy tucked the gun back into his belt. He showed his disappointment.

"You brought the copies with you?" Pellegrino asked.

"No. There are two sets, one in my apartment, the other at the office. Along with the negatives."

"Anybody else wise to them?"

Dante shook his head.

"You better not be lying."

"The photo editor developed the prints but he didn't know what he was looking at."

"You mean to tell me you didn't show them to an editor?"

"I was holding off. Lots of times we wait until we have

a string tied around a story before showing it to the desk. I had more research to do." Dante was making it up as he went along. He hoped it would hang together. Plates and silverware tinkled and clattered in the background. "I also wanted to wait for a news lull. You know—a time when my story would have its biggest impact. Making a big splash is what wins prizes."

Pellegrino seemed satisfied. Anyway, he held most of the cards. "All right, let's go get the photos and the negatives."

"Right now? Can't I bring them to you somewhere?"

"You think you're dealing with a rube off the boat? *Get moving.*"

"If you come with me to the office you'll only attract suspicion."

"I'll worry about that," said Pellegrino. "Let's go."

The trio rose from the table. Across the room Joe Baccala hopped off the stool.

Dante now cursed his own recklessness. He didn't so much mind dying, but to die unavenged? He decided to watch for the best chance and make a run for it.

Suddenly Patsy grabbed one of his elbows while Joe grabbed the other, and Pellegrino led the way.

They walked through the lobby. It was not crowded as Dante had hoped. A family of prosperous hayseeds checked in at the reservation desk, a fat man in an out-dated homburg, his skinny wife and two overweight children. Dante also noticed a man wearing a fedora, reading a newspaper and sitting in a leather chair, cigar clamped in his mouth. He had house dick written all over him.

Before Dante could figure out a plan to get the man's attention they were heading through the revolving door of the hotel entrance. They reached the landing of the stone steps leading to the street. A doorman, dressed like a tin-horn generalissimo, tipped his cap. A light rain could be seen slanting in the arc of the electric lamps.

She came out of the shadows then, a spectral figure in a navy trench coat and beret. Dante noticed her first and froze like one of the griffons adorning the hotel facade. The men at his elbows glared at him.

Pellegrino stopped and turned around, wondering what was delaying them. Raindrops sequined the black velvet collar of his coat.

She spoke and acted in the same instant. "Let's see how you like this brand of after-shave lotion," she said, hurling the liquid from the bottle. Like quicksilver it floated in the air, a frozen moment of molecular beauty, swirling, swirling.

Dante ducked.

Patsy Secundo screamed and clutched his face.

Pellegrino's revolver sounded twice, flashing blue in the night.

Lily Ferrand, astounded, slumped dead on the stone steps.

Chapter

24

INK AND BLOOD

MATT Carpenter was yanked off the Bronx decapitation story to write about the killing of the publisher's daughter. It was—to say the least—a delicate assignment. But he was a pro and knew how to handle it. Cigarette ash powdering the space bar of the typewriter, he wrote the yarn straight down the middle. Balanced. Objective.

There were big holes in the story but holes never troubled Carpenter if he had enough wool to keep weaving. And he was so skillful the reader never noticed the gaps. He was a rare bird who could peck out copy without a backward glance or a spasm of self-doubt. To him writer's block was an exotic disease that afflicted others. Hottentots, maybe. Not Matthew Carpenter. He had written more—potboilers—than he'd read in his lifetime, and when his fingers hit the keys of a writing machine a symbiotic connection formed. A casual observer could not tell where flesh ended and metal began. His hat had a greasy sweatband and was a size too small for his head. He made a habit of scratching his bulbous nose after every sentence. Otherwise he was a whirling dervish of the hunt-and-peck brigade. Oil him with bourbon and a modest Christmas bonus and he worked every time, motor idling between editions.

275

Before rolling in the final take he lit another cigarette. The story, like any other murder story, was slugged *Slay*. It got no special treatment. He took the cigarette out of his mouth, swigged coffee and finished writing the story. He typed "—30—" on the bottom of the page of copy paper.

These were some of the words the compositors set into type under the headline, PUBLISHER'S DAUGHTER SLAIN BY GANGSTER OUTSIDE PLAZA HOTEL:

A beautiful Manhattan socialite, daughter of this newspaper's publisher, was shot and killed last night by a reputed bootlegger in a bizarre incident outside the Plaza Hotel.

The blood of Lily Ferrand, daughter of Major Carlos Curtin and wife of international financier Max Ferrand, mingled with raindrops on the hotel steps after she allegedly hurled acid in the face of another bootlegger, Pasquale Secundo of Manhattan, according to detectives investigating the tragic shooting. Eyewitnesses reported that she had been shot twice at close range by Gaetano "Big Guy" Pellegrino, known in law-enforcement circles as a rising star in the gangster firmament.

The hotel doctor, called to the scene, pronounced the woman dead. Both bullets struck her in the heart, the coroner later said. Also on the scene were Giuseppe Baccala, a Pellegrino henchman who has been held for questioning, and Dante Viola, a *Courier* employee known both to Mrs. Ferrand and the alleged gunman. Pellegrino surrendered to police without offering resistance. He was taken in handcuffs to the Tombs in lower Manhattan to await arraignment.

Secundo was rushed to the emergency room of a nearby hospital. His condition was unknown at press time.

Pellegrino's attorney, Jacob Tinker, expressed confidence that his client would be released. "Mr. Pellegrino is a respectable businessman," Tinker told reporters. "He acted purely in self-defense. The woman was obviously deranged."

Major Curtin declined comment. Mr. Ferrand was on business in Tangier and unavailable for comment. Police and other sources declined to speculate about why Lily Ferrand had thrown the acid. . . .

The pages rolled off the Hoe Company presses. The papers were bundled off the conveyor belts, loaded into delivery trucks and driven to newsstands. The *Courier* scooped all competitors, and circulation skyrocketed by 100,000 extra copies.

Dante sat at Ivan Bruce's desk behind the glass half-partition.

"Looks bad," said Bruce, shaking his head. "It looks, kid, like you were consorting with gangsters."

"Of course I was consorting with gangsters. I'm a newspaperman after a story."

"Your wop name doesn't help matters."

"Look, I've explained. You know how it happened. Let me write the story. The *whole* story." But Dante had not told Bruce everything. He had left out what happened the night Patsy unmasked him as a newspaper reporter to Pellegrino. He would *never* tell anyone about that.

Bruce looked at the floor. "My hands are tied."

"But you're the editor—"

"Hey, I'm not as young as I used to be. It's easy to be principled when you got the world by the tail. But I'm running out of options."

Dante suddenly saw Bruce as a man on the brink of old age. It was a shock. He had always regarded the city editor as in charge, a man in his prime. Dante had the young man's irrational illusion that people were locked into a certain age. A wild idea struck him. "Why not let me have a go at it?" he said.

"Have a go at what?"

"Convincing the Major to let us print the story."

"You said that once before, remember?"

Dante remembered Bruce telling him that he was on the publisher's shitlist for getting mixed up with his daughter. But now Lily was dead. . . . "Besides," said Bruce, "it'd be like putting a mouse in the lion's den."

"Well, what have we got to lose? Maybe Lily's death has changed the old man. . . ."

Dante, haggard but determined, entered Major Curtin's outer office and approached the receptionist.

"My name is Dante Viola. I work for this newspaper. I have no appointment but I want to see the Major."

She wore a fixed smile. "I'm afraid that's impossible."

He nodded his head at the intercom on her desk. "Would you mind just pressing that little button and asking him? Again, the name's Viola. I believe he'll see me."

She picked up a pencil and pad. "I'm afraid I can't do that but if you'll just leave your name with me—*Hey.*"

He had burst through the wooden gate and was opening the massive door to the publisher's private office.

Major Curtin had been standing on the far side of the large room by the picture window, studying the boats that furrowed the East River. His busy gray eyebrows and toothbrush mustache twitched at the interruption. "What the hell?"

"I'm sorry, sir," said the receptionist, "I couldn't stop him. He ran right in without permission."

"I'm Dante Viola."

Major Curtin was silent for a moment, then said, "You can leave us, Miss Jordan."

The publisher went to his desk and sat down heavily. His eyes, ringed by pouches, had a haunted look. The desk top was uncluttered. The desk held the intercom, a wooden In box containing a small amount of paperwork, a blotter and inkstand, a bronze figure that Dante recognized, thanks to his Jesuit training, as representing the Fall of Phaeton, a copy of the *Courier* and a framed photograph of Lily Curtin Ferrand, at which the father now gazed.

"What do you want?" Curtin asked in a dull voice.

"I want to make sure the man who killed Lily is punished," said Dante, gripping the edge of the desk and leaning toward the publisher, who sat rock-still. "I want to break the story that will help put him behind bars. Along with the rest of the grafters. Sir, I want to do my job—print the truth."

Curtin looked up sharply, staring like a hoot owl. "The truth," he said in a tone of sarcasm. Then his voice went flat. "Leave me alone."

Dante groped for more words. "Look, sir, you can think of it as a memorial to Lily. . . ."

Curtin snorted. At whom or what? At himself or his daughter? At the notion of truth? He again looked at the photo. "Lily was a troubled woman," he said wearily. "Wild, reckless." He squinted at Dante. "What do you know about this acid-throwing business?"

"Well . . . she meant to throw it at me."

"I thought so. You're really to blame for all this."

"I wouldn't say that—"

Curtin got up, locked his thumbs behind his back and gazed out the window, avoiding eye contact with Dante. "She could never control her emotions, just like her mother. No self-discipline. . . ."

Without being asked to, Dante sat down and racked his brains for a rhetorical wedge, staring at the father who could only criticize in the face of his daughter's death. His own father, faced with similar circumstances, would have moved heaven and earth to get even with the killer of his offspring. This man belonged to a different species.

"Sir . . . we have a professional obligation to run this story—"

"You dare lecture *me* about such matters?"

"Respectfully, sir."

The Major softened. "We need . . . we need confirmation. Something harder than photographs of records. Photos obtained illegally, I might add."

"Sir, this newspaper and its competition have printed big stories based on information half as solid as this. You read the documents, we got the goods on them. Deputy police commissioner, two state senators, three aldermen, three magistrates, a city clerk. Hands deep in the till. And we wouldn't have to stretch the ball of yarn too far to incriminate that fellow who sits across the street in City Hall. Others too. Those records show where the drops were made, who the bagmen were, the dollar amounts of the deals. Even the quid pro quos are set down."

"But no *hard* proof."

Dante took a deep breath. "We're not prosecutors, sir,

we're journalists. They wouldn't dare sue for libel, they know we're publishing the truth—"

"Look here, young man, I never even heard of you before a few days ago. You expect me to risk the reputation, the future of this newspaper, on your say-so?"

"Please reconsider . . ."

"I do admire your guts. And your persistence. It's obvious you're ambitious as well. All fine qualities in a young newspaperman. You'll go far on the *Courier* . . . if you're patient."

"You can't kill this story, you just *can't.*"

Curtin sat down again, exhaling wearily. "I have a son, you know. Haven't seen or heard from him in years. I'm told he's living on a Spanish island somewhere. Ibiza, or something like that. A disappointment, a great disappointment. . . ." It was like he was talking to himself.

Dante ignored it, kept to his one note. "Let me write the story, please."

Curtin lost patience. "I won't hear another word about it. Now if you'll excuse me I have some matters to attend to—"

Dante couldn't stand any more. "You're in bed with them too, aren't you?"

"What? Don't be ridiculous."

"They help you handle labor troubles—"

"You goddamn little upstart, I'll—"

"I'm going to take the story to the *Bugle.*"

"Get the hell out of my office."

"I'm going, Major Curtin. But you haven't heard the last of this, I swear it."

The Major's round face had turned crimson. "Clean out your desk, stop at the cashier's on the way out. You're *fired.*"

Gaetano Pellegrino went before a magistrate the next morning and was freed on $25,000 bail. Legal experts in the press room predicted that no indictment would be handed up by the grand jury since Pellegrino had a valid permit for the weapon and it seemed an obvious case of self-defense. Patsy Secundo, reporters learned, would be in the hospital a long time but was expected to survive. In the future his rodent face would convey even more menace, with grotesque scars from hairline to chin and the loss of sight in his left eye.

As Pellegrino returned to his aerie at the Barbizon Plaza, Dante, jobless now, made the rounds of local rooms, trying to convince editors to print the story. Often he couldn't even get past the cynical gatekeepers, accustomed to unknown writers peddling farfetched stories and paranoids prophesying apocalyptic nonsense. He tried the *Bugle,* the Hearst papers, the other tabloids. Stone walls. Maybe it was because he had no big reputation as a reporter. Maybe the Major as head of the local publishers association had had him blackballed. Maybe both, and even worse. Dante's illusions about journalism, already strained, were quickly evaporating.

He went home and tossed the documents on the kitchen table. He'd been too busy to absorb fully the shock of being fired. He had always used visions of his future as a newspaper reporter to fill the void created by his unhappy history. Now he faced the present, without nostalgia or hope.

He took off his clothes and fell into a deep, dark well of sleep.

Ten hours later he woke up shivering without a blanket—it had fallen to the floor. He must have been thrashing around in his sleep but he had no recollection of any dreams, bad or otherwise. He had surfaced from a nullity of sleep.

To what? To renewed thoughts of revenge? There was nothing but revenge to live for now.

Friends? He had none. Callahan, Ivan Bruce, Clare Parker—each in his fashion had abandoned him to the wolves. Did he even have the stomach for revenge? Was he some damn delicate flower?

It was the demeaning thought of himself as a flower that sparked a plan involving Mrs. Califate and her dark herbalist arts.

Chapter
25

MUSQUASH ROOT

NICK Callahan sent a fancy chariot and chauffeur around to pick up his brother and bring him out to Oyster Bay. The car headed away from the gorgeous pink sunset, and Callahan slept the entire trip out.

Electric lamps illuminated the flagstone path leading to the front door of State Senator Callahan's six-bedroom colonial mansion on a bluff overlooking the harbor. What sparkling pixie dust floated in the wake of political poltroonery, Callahan thought as he entered the house, and smiled at his own blarney.

His brother gripped Callahan's hand.

"Welcome, Johnny boy," Nick said, beaming with pride.

Callahan took a slow look around. The foyer was paved with slabs of green marble. Burnished oak paneling shone in the candlelight. A circular stairway with fluted oak bannisters led to the second floor. A crystal chandelier chimed in the drafty entranceway.

"From Hell's Kitchen to hell's drawing room," said Callahan.

"Show some manners. You like it?"

"I've seen worse."

"That's a fact," said Nick. "Here, let me take your hat and coat."

"Butler's night off?"

"Take it easy, Johnny. For your information, we have a maid, no butler. She's in the kitchen with Julia."

Callahan followed Nick into a baronial-size living room with a mix of modern and antique furniture. A fireplace crackled invitingly. They sat on a sofa in front of the fire and Nick poured four fingers of Irish whiskey into two crystal glasses. Callahan let the liquor bite his tongue before he asked, "Where are the kids?"

Nick made a face. "Gwen's at college. Dominick's knocking up the farmer's daughter, or something like that."

"Chip off the old block?"

"I wish. I earn dough, he spends it." Suddenly he looked up. "Hey, ain't that something how your old girlfriend got cooled?"

"I wouldn't call her my old girlfriend."

"What then? Your old roll in the hay?"

Callahan tossed off the drink, got up and went over to the fireplace. It was made of chalk-white limestone. "Give her a break. She's minding her own business pushing up daisies."

"Relax," said Nick. "After all I'm not exactly blaspheming the Blessed Mother."

Callahan studied the blue-tipped flames. He never really liked Lily, he thought, but he did feel a twinge of mourning. Or was he mourning for something else?

Nick shook his head. "That was sure a weird one. What you newspaper guys won't do for a streamer."

"What do you mean by that?"

"What was your friend Viola doing there? And what was Mrs. Ferrand doing sprinkling acid around like holy water at benediction? Strange bedfellows, I'd say."

"Maybe."

"What's the dope?"

"Nothing mysterious. It's the old story of the green-eyed monster."

Nick looked puzzled. "She was jealous? Jealous of who?"

"You're such a smart guy. Figure it out."

"Come to think of it, I've heard stories about Pellegrino. But your friend Viola? He a little funny too?"

"Nah. He was just running down a story."

Nick laced his fingers together and rested them on his trim midsection. "I figured Secundo got it by accident."

"Hear he's a scumbag anyhow."

Nick tried to say it casually. . . . "What kind of story was it anyway, Johnny?"

"Huh?"

"What kind of story was your friend . . . developing? He have anything on Pellegrino?"

Callahan, sitting down again, loosened his necktie. "I don't know."

"Bullshit."

Callahan started to protest but thought better of it and kept his mouth shut.

Nick said, "I know about those pictures your little pal took. I know about the grease sheet, see? Whose side are you on anyway?"

Callahan glared, but it was a question he'd asked himself more than once over the last weeks. "I'm on John Joseph Callahan's side," he said.

"Then do *your* side a favor. Bring me those papers and we'll pitch them into the fireplace. If the story gets published we're all up the creek. Including you, Johnny boy."

"The Judge would like nothing better than to see Pellegrino go up the river."

"Not this way, not if the whole house of cards comes down."

Callahan took another drink. Nick was right there. The web of corruption was so widespread and intermeshed that the story would reverberate through the criminal and political worlds. There was one catch, though, that Nick might not fully be aware of—the damn newspaper refused to print the story.

"The Major has spiked the damn thing anyhow," he said to Nick.

"But we can't take the chance that it will stay on the spike. The old fool may change his mind. And what if your pal peddles it to another paper or magazine? What if that screwball Bernarr MacFadden gets wind of it? No telling what *he* might do. We can't take the chance."

"Well, what can I do about it?"

"Get those documents away from your pal. By hook or crook, see?" He wasn't aware of the pun.

Callahan managed a bleak smile. "That sort of thing's out of my line."

"No more it isn't. Sorry, brother, but you have no choice."

"What?"

"Judge's orders." Nick reached across and patted his brother on the knee. "Get 'em back like a good boy."

"Screw you."

"Stop being a ding-dong. Wanna end up like Madigan? Sorry to say so, Johnny boy, but that can be arranged."

"I don't ride merry-go-rounds." Smart ass.

"What do you think this world is? Shut up and have another drink."

Callahan stared into the fire. He had some conscience left, he hadn't been sucked in all the way. He could bail out whenever he wanted to. Who said it? "We are condemned to everlasting redemption. . . ." He pictured the face of the German boy, now merging with Dante's face.

Next morning when he left the apartment Dante's red necktie was cockeyed, his garterless socks sagged around the ankles. Dark circles pouched his eyes. As he headed for Mrs. Califate's flower shop wind skittered trash in the gutters. He jaywalked, paid no attention to the Yellow Cab that honked at him.

Lily was dead. He was at least partly responsible, and it looked like Pellegrino would get off scot-free. Somehow he had to take action, brake this runaway roller-coaster. Get back his self-respect. Maybe he no longer had a future as a newspaperman but he still had his past, his Sicilian heritage, didn't he?

Unspeakable acts required drastic action. His ancestors had faced every hardship, from bloodthirsty Saracens to starvation. Would he be too weak to use the old formula—wash away shame with blood?

No. He would go to Mrs. Califate, the jolly witch who practiced the black arts of the old country.

When she saw him enter the store the woman seemed taken aback.

"Whatsa matter with my bestuh customer?"

"I need your help," he said in Italian.

"That's clear," said the woman, also in the native tongue, clucking and making the sign of the cross.

He closed the door behind him, shutting out the sounds of Baxter Street. His shoulders were slumped as he rehearsed a speech that turned out to be unnecessary . . . she had already divined his mission.

"It's too bad you have no mother," she declared out of nowhere. "You could be as rich as cream but your heart is a beggar without a mother." She held out a pudgy hand. "Come."

He followed her through a door that led to the rear of the store, down a narrow corridor and into a dazzlingly bright backyard greenhouse. She motioned him to sit in a wicker chair. He marveled at the place, at the lush plants and flowers covering every inch of space, devouring carbon dioxide from the air and filling it with the perfumes of the earth.

She sat down across from him in an identical chair and folded her hands in her aproned lap.

"Un affare del cuore, no?" she said. "It's a matter of the heart that makes your face look like Ash Wednesday."

Dante considered lying to her but quickly rejected the idea, deciding that her intuition was too sharp. "No."

Her eyes had a knowing glint. "Then it could only be one other thing that makes you so pale and limp, like a rag doll. You crave a special food. *La vendetta.*"

He nodded.

She began to weep, which he thought was odd. "Why are you crying?"

"Doesn't the occasion require it?"

"I suppose so. Yes."

She got up from the chair and beckoned him to follow.

Their bodies brushed the tendrils of plants that reached out promiscuously from every corner and cranny. They stopped before one that had small whitish, heavily scented blossoms. She took up a pair of shears from a nearby table and cut one plant off at the stem. An oily yellow sap flowed.

"What is it?" he asked.

"You don't need to know." She smiled, the caricature of a smile. "Always the journalist, eh? You must have all the facts."

"Yes," he said, although he didn't consider himself a journalist anymore. "All the facts, yes."

"The fabulists say that the Devil dresses in black and has a silver nose. These are facts."

He pressed: "What is this plant?" Dante suddenly was doubtful.

Mrs. Califate peered at him. "Your cause is just, and this is the only way?"

"Yes."

"You must pay me something."

"How much?"

She shrugged.

He had brought twenty dollars with him. "I'll give you fifteen dollars."

"Give me ten."

Thinking about Pellegrino, his ruthlessness, his perversions, hardened him. The cause was just and this was the only way, he echoed to himself. He handed over the money. Sunlight gilded the musquash root.

She put the cash in her apron pocket and signaled him to stay. "I will be back right away," she said, and left the greenhouse with the cutting.

He realized he already felt better for having acted to take control. He lit a cigarette and waited for the woman to return with the brew that would, to his way of thinking, restore the balance. Suddenly, unaccountably, he thought of his mother. He remembered how she would give him spiced mulled wine and bitter chestnuts, saying that they would give him strength and understanding. And he thought of his father oiling his handlebar mustache and urging his son, whatever else, never to shrink from the requirements of honor.

Mrs. Califate reappeared and handed him the preparation in a tiny vial. He kissed her hand and put the vial in his pocket. Before he left the shop she gave him a gardenia for his lapel.

Chapter
26

THE BEAR BARES ITS FANGS

HAMILTON Terry's newsstand stood only about half a mile from the colonnaded building on Broad Street where the speculators had been grabbing the tail of the bull market. In spirit and sympathy, though, Ham was miles away. He shook his head sadly as he stacked the morning papers bearing the gloomy headlines of Friday, October 25, 1929.

It seemed the whole world had caught the gambling fever, he reflected in his private world of darkness. Everyone had been buying on margin, making hay while the sun shone. It had been a gold-rush atmosphere. Why, Ham even knew taxi drivers and waiters in Harlem who had stopped patronizing Frank Costello's policy banks to take a flyer with their hard-earned bucks on the stock market. Meanwhile, every Jack and Jane bought new-fangled gadgets on the installment plan and lived it up like there was no tomorrow.

And with the boom the city was growing like Topsy too. Old John D. had just announced plans to build an ultramodern "City of Radio" on land leased from Columbia University bounded by Fifth and Sixth avenues, between Forty-eighth and Fifty-first streets. Further downtown on Thirty-fourth Street builders planned to raze the Waldorf-

Astoria Hotel to make way for the tallest building in the world. The newspapers said it would soar to 102 stories and be topped off by a mooring mast for dirigibles . . .

It all had seemed as phony to Ham as the metal slugs some lowdown customers dropped in his cigar box. Well, now it seemed the buzzards were coming home to roost. The walls of Jericho were tumbling down.

If one read the newspapers—and Ham did, second-hand, of course—it wasn't really clear how bad the situation was. The bankers, industrialists and politicians were double-talking as usual and the headlines reflected the mixed messages. Industrialist John J. Raskob was quoted saying this was a good time to buy stocks at bargain-basement rates. The market nosedive prompted shadow government Democratic senators to call for an investigation of the Federal Reserve system and legislation to bridle the runaway horse of credit. On the other hand President Hoover made a statement saying that everything was hunky-dory. "The fundamental business of the country, that is, production and distribution of commodities, is on a sound and prosperous basis."

Sounded to Ham like the old story about the doctor declaring the operation a success although the patient died.

A rally before the gong sounded at close of trading day, October 24, kept "the hounds of panic at bay." But it didn't stop some smaller partners in U. S. prosperity from dumping shares and a few larger captains of industry from leaping off window ledges around town. One millionaire, reported missing by his wife in Mount Vernon, was last seen by a friend Thursday evening muttering to himself on Broadway as he tore strips of ticker tape into confetti and scattered it to the four winds.

Callahan, at Aqueduct Race Track, did a similar thing to his parimutuel betting stubs at the end of the ninth race. His wallet was lighter by 190 smackers. The wind out of his sails, he sat on a bench and frowned at the cloudless sky. He scanned the newspaper. The experts all predicted the market would bounce back next week. Win or lose, he was glad he sank his money into horseflesh instead of ticker tape. He trusted touts and his own mitt-reading far more than the windbags of Washington and the swamis of Wall Street.

He squandered his last few bucks on a Checker Cab to Manhattan. On the trip from Rockaway he gave further thought to Nick's request that he get his hands on the grease sheet. Would he go that low to save even his brother's neck? Or was it now his own neck he was worried about? Or both? What about journalism's high-minded code of ethics? Dante, who took it seriously . . . his protege, of sorts . . . had been fired for believing in it and acting on it. And the story had stayed on the spike. Breast-beating wouldn't do much good if the Major lacked the spine to go public. Should he sacrifice Nick's ass and his neck under these circumstances . . .? Hell, the world wouldn't come to an end if he made discretion the better part of valor and, like they said, lived to fight another day. It seemed a winning argument, as it was meant to be. After all, he had only himself to convince.

So he would pinch the documents. The question was how. Shouldn't be too difficult. After all, he was a trained snoop.

He reached the *Courier* building just as the day shift was changing into the night shift. Fitch still worked the elevator lever. The runt's face looked ghostly gray.

"What's your problem?" asked Callahan, removing the tattered stogie from his mouth. "You look like your best friend died."

The elevator operator shook his head. "Worse than that. Andes Copper and American Zinc," he said. "Going up. The elevator, I mean."

Callahan raised his eyes to the heavens. "Everybody's a tycoon!"

"The zinc fell seventy pernts," said Fitch. *"Seventy* fucking pernts! Copper took a nosedive too. I can't meet margin. I'm sunk."

"Sorry, pal," said Callahan, getting off at his floor. "But

you should be used to ups and downs." Cheap shot, he knew.

Entering the city room, Callahan looked around. The drama desk was a beehive. Eva Le Gallienne was opening in *The Sea Gull* at the Civic Repertory Theater. The rewrite crew was just settling in for the trick, with reams of copy paper, sharpened pencils and dulled senses. Ivan Bruce was still at his desk. He looked tired.

Callahan approached him. "Don't tell me you play the stock market too."

"Nah, I play the banjo."

"Well, you've still got your great sense of humor. You also look like you've been through the wars."

"Hey, putting out a newspaper any time is nerve-wracking. I've got the stock market going haywire and the publisher going off his trolley. Does that explain things?"

"It does."

Bruce sat down at the desk and massaged his head. "I'm getting old," he said. "I don't have it for the big stories any more. Doesn't seem to stir up the juices the way it used to." He gripped the edge of the desk and leaned in. "I'm tired of thinking in four-column, ninety-six-point bold type. 'Maine Explodes,' 'Titanic Sinks,' 'War Declared,' 'Armistice Signed,' 'Kaiser Flees,' 'Harding Dies,' 'Marcus Garvey Arrested,' 'Lindy Lands.' I even dream in snappy headlines. Enough's enough."

Callahan sat down across from him. "The word's *jaded.* Never thought it would happen to you, Ivan."

"Neither did I." He glanced at Callahan's lopsided face. "What're you doing here at this hour?"

"Licking my wounds. Went to the track today."

"Weren't you supposed to be working?"

"That's why I'm here now. Got a few irons in the fire, a few phone calls to make. Why don't you call it a night?"

"Yeah, guess I will." He stood up and grabbed his hat, coat and scarf off a tree by the desk.

"What's really eating you?" Callahan asked.

Bruce hesitated. "I don't like sitting on stories. Especially big-time exclusives. It gives me piles. When I spike a big one on the orders of a yellow-bellied publisher it's time to hang 'em up."

"Stop beating your breast, Ivan. Everybody has to practice the dark art of compromise once in a while. Just to survive. Don't be so hard on yourself." Who was he talking to, really?

Bruce squared a trilby on his well-thatched head. "It's not my conscience, I'm no angel. It's feeling so damn frustrated. News is where I live. Hell, newspapermen don't have consciences. You ought to know that."

"Yeah," said Callahan.

After Bruce left, Callahan sat in the chair at the editor's desk and remembered Dante telling him that there were two copies of Pellegrino's records. Trying to look casual about it, he searched Bruce's drawers, hoping any onlookers would think he was looking for something he had a right to, like a blank expense chit or an assignment memo. Under a souvenir matrix of the page heralding Dempsey's knockout of Firpo he found what he was looking for. He had to hope that Bruce would not notice too soon that they were missing. Meantime he would figure out an alibi.

He walked across the room to the obit desk, home turf where he didn't have to worry about looking like a snoop or a thief. He was betting Dante hadn't cleaned out his desk yet, not wanting to face the finality of his firing. Besides, Dante was no doubt like most newspapermen, notoriously sloppy about documents and notes, including important ones. No matter how big or small the story, the news reporter's paper wrapped fish within a day. Rummaging, he whistled with studied casualness. Copy pencils, carbons, reference books, old notebooks, galleys, fonts, rules . . . everything in a jumble. Callahan had a new insight into Dante's character . . . neat and orderly on the outside but his closets and drawers were as screwed up as the next man's.

Callahan came up empty. He sat down and gave the matter some thought. The Judge would have to be satisfied with one copy *and* the negatives. He reached into the bottom drawer of the desk he used to occupy as obit chief and

took out a bottle of French brandy he had been saving for
an emergency. It wasn't for himself. Al Diamond, the
photo editor, was known to have a taste for exotic booze. He
was also known to have few scruples. And since the story
had been killed . . . Callahan hitched up his suspenders and
left the city room, headed for the photo lab and the negs.

Dante was in a hurry but since he didn't have enough
money for a cab he took the subway uptown to the hotel.
The worried expressions of his fellow passengers reading
the papers about Wall Street didn't register. He was thinking about what he had learned from a trip to the local
library to research the efforts of musquash root on the
victim. He pictured Pellegrino, savored the unpretty details. It would take only about fifteen minutes. He would
get nauseous, salivate, suffer emesis, whatever that was,
convulsions and finally death. Dante had only one regret—
he would not be around to witness it.

The gangster affected such blighty habits as drinking
high tea. He was a creature of habit too—a salmon swimming upstream to spawn and die. Except his spawn was
filth. Well, he would spawn no more.

Dante got off the subway near Columbus Circle and
walked crosstown. It should not be difficult. He knew the
room-service routine. Pretending to renew acquaintances,
he would chat with Lee Lindenbaum and slip the poison
into the tea. *La Commedia e finita.* One bug squashed.
"And so I am revenged," said the wronged one.

"Geez, what're you doing back?" Lee said as Dante walked
into the kitchen. It was break time, the doldrums when
nobody else was around.

"Can't I visit an old friend?" said Dante.

"Sure. Glad to see yuh," said Lee, looking around nervously. "But we gotta be kinda quiet like. You won't win no
popularity contests around here."

Dante smiled and clapped his friend on the shoulder.
"How you doing, Lee?"

"Pretty good, pretty good. Hey, Melba's still got the hots for you." He surveyed Dante head to foot. "Say, what's the matter, pal? You're not your usual dapper self."

"I been down some lately."

"Yeah, I read about it," Lee said, referring to Lily's death. "What was that all about? Don't tell me you were boffing that society dame."

"Someday, Lee, I'll tell you the whole story." He looked up to the ceiling. "How's the star boarder?"

"Back to normal. Which is abnormal. He didn't spend much time in the clink, did he?" Lee arranged a few wedges of haddock on toast on a tray. "Matter of fact, I was just preparing his tea." Lee raised his pinky aloft and affected a snooty expression.

Dante's throat clogged. He eyed the copper samovar on the tray. "Sure, sure, I remember. He has tea every evening at about this time. You taking it up?"

"Yeah. I know what you're thinking, I ain't his type."

Dante chuckled, faking a casual air as he tried to contrive a way to do what he had to do without arousing Lee's suspicions. He considered enlisting him as a conspirator but quickly rejected the idea. He would probably refuse and it wouldn't be fair. Anyhow, Dante knew he was destined to do this alone.

Abruptly Dante staged a coughing fit.

"Hey," said Lee, grabbing him by the shoulders. "You okay?"

Red-faced, Dante got out: "Still got that stash of hootch?"

"Sure."

"I could use a swig."

"Right away, follow me to the locker room."

Dante braced himself on the edge of the table. "No, please, you go get it. I don't want you to get in hot water, I'll wait here in case the call-buzzer rings."

Lee peered anxiously at him. "Okay. Be back in a flash."

As soon as Lee was out of sight Dante went to work. He looked quickly around, removed the vial from his coat pocket and poured the contents into the samovar. Oddly he felt neither exhilarated, relieved, frightened or satisfied. Mostly he felt drained of his own emotional poison, like the incriminating vial he shoved back into his pocket.

Lee returned with a pint of rye that Dante swigged straight from the bottle. He made a face.

"Thanks," he said, pressing the cork back in with his palm and handing the bottle back.

"Something you ate?" Lee asked.

"No."

"Ah, it's the coffin nails. Happens to me too. Feeling better now?"

"Much. Thanks, Lee. Thanks for everything . . ."

"Don't mention it, kiddo."

They chatted a while longer, touching on subjects from the mysteries of the plummeting stock market to the debate between insurance and auto executives over whether cars should be manufactured to go over thirty-five miles an hour.

"Listen, you better get back to work," Dante finally said, waved goodbye and quickly left the hotel.

Dry leaves crunched under his feet on Central Park West as he again visualized the death rattle of the man he so hated. His cherubic mouth was set in a tight line. He felt no remorse about sending the devil straight to hell. In fact, for the first time since he had been defiled, he felt almost clean again.

Lee Lindenbaum returned to work, placing lemon wedges and a vase of tea roses on Mr. Pell's tray. He thought about the gangster's night-owl routines. Since Pell usually slept until early afternoon his clock of activities and meals was moved back a few hours. When most guests had dinner he had high tea, and when most guests went to bed he had supper. The staff didn't mind the quirks of scheduling because Pell tipped so handsomely. Actually Lee felt uneasy about taking the tips, he considered them blood money. But the kids always seemed to grow out of their clothes and needed new schoolbooks and God knew what all. He had to admit he looked forward to the ten-spot he would get.

He sat down now to rest for a few minutes. He was tired,

having suffered insomina the night before. The peptic ulcer was acting up again. He wondered why, like clockwork, the damn thing bothered him only in the spring and autumn. He had forgotten to take his glass of warm milk before bed. The doc had told him to avoid cigarettes, coffee and "stressful situations." Lee, lighting up a Camel, had one word for this prescription: impossible. Hey, he lived in New York City in the twentieth century, not in some Tibetan monastery. Between drags of the cigarette he popped an antacid tablet into his mouth.

When the night crew returned from their break to prepare dinner trays, Lee sighed, snuffed out the butt and picked up Pell's tea tray.

Gustave, the night manager, stopped him.

"Don't bother with that," the Alsatian said. "Mr. Pell's already gone out for the evening."

Lee muttered in disappointment. He had been counting on that ten bucks. He put the tray back on the counter and sat down again. The doc had warned him, don't get too upset over minor things. It only made the ulcer worse. And his lack of sleep didn't help. How would he get through the rest of the night without nodding off? He needed a stimulant. Well, Mr. Pell won't mind, he thought, as he proceeded to pour himself a cup of tea from the samovar.

Chapter

27

SECOND THOUGHTS

CALLAHAN scanned the articles in the pile of morning dailies that littered his breakfast table. The papers were saying that Thursday's market plunge had run its course and that the situation had returned to normal. According to one subhead, there was "No 'Catastrophe' Seen." He sank his fork into a pancake and continued to read.

ONLY YAWNS RECALL BIG DAY IN WALL ST, said the headline in one reputable broadsheet. Callahan scratched under his armpit. Another article described how phone, cable and radio use Thursday had broken all records. Still another reported a big recovery in the price of bank stocks. Business leaders parroted reassuring statements. Things were looking up. Callahan gave a Bronx jeer and swigged coffee.

While eating he telephoned Nick, whose outlook was not so rosy. Many clients of the so-called brokerage house he and O'Hara ran had been clamoring for them to sell. But in most cases Nick had bucketed the stock ages ago, claiming that the certificates were held by the banks who had lent money to buy on margin. Now the piper was grousing to be paid.

"Cold, hard, green, crisp cash," said Nick. "That's what

everybody and his mother wants to lay his mitts on now. And they'll pay through the nose for it in promissory notes. Got any spare greenbacks collecting dust, brother?"

"Some gag, Nick. You got a great sense of humor. You didn't dabble yourself, did you?"

"Hah! I took a bath."

"Well, don't jump out the window yet. The experts are saying the market's gonna bounce back."

"Don't hold your breath."

"I'll keep my fingers crossed."

"And rub your rabbit's foot. O'Hara needed twenty grand to cover his margin."

"Did he come up with it?"

"Yeah."

"How?"

"How do you think? The Judge gave it to him."

"No strings attached?"

Nick let out a sour laugh.

"I guess the big boys aren't hurting," said Callahan. "As usual."

"In a way they're sitting pretty because they got lots of cash. They hold the unions, the garment business, the politicians, even some bankers by the short hairs. But in other ways they're gonna be hurting too."

"How?"

"If the bottom falls out the hootch trade will suffer. Some of the other stuff too—gambling, prostitution. The numbers racket may be okay. Even in bad times—maybe especially in bad times—people throw a few pennies down on a number. Gives them a reason to live."

"Sad. How about the south of France, Nick?"

"A dream postponed."

Callahan clucked his tongue.

"Hope you have good news for me," Nick said.

"I do." And not so good for what was left of his second thoughts.

"Got them in your possession?"

"Yes. Also the negatives."

"I trust you, Johnny boy. Now make a little bonfire. I'll

tell the Judge everything's taken care of. Do it immediately."

"I will. . . ."

"That didn't sound too convincing. Look here, kid, you double-cross the Judge and both our gooses are cooked."

"I know that, don't worry."

"I do worry. One never knows when the would-be priest in you is gonna surface again."

"The priest is long dead."

"That's the spirit."

Callahan hung up and stared at the phone for a few seconds, then went to his coat on the wall peg and searched the breast pocket. He took the stuff to the washstand and sink, rummaging in his pockets for matches. He planned to make a fire in the sink, didn't want to burn the building down. He held the papers tightly in his fist.

He just couldn't do it. Not right away, anyhow. He stashed the negatives and copy in his dresser drawer under raggedy pin-striped undershorts and sock garters, lit his first cigar of the day and got dressed.

He had his Saturday all planned. He would head over to West Street and give the once-over to the struggle buggies in the General Motors window. He had been toying with the notion of buying a snappy roadster. Nothing too ostentatious, of course; didn't pay to attract attention. Later he had a date to play miniature golf with Clare at Brighton Beach. After dinner they would head uptown to catch Mamie Smith and her Jazz Hounds, bend the elbow and let nature take her course. He squared the old fedora on his haystack head and glanced in the mirror. How come he didn't like what he saw?

On the walk over to the car dealer he wondered what she would make of his extracurricular activities. At least she didn't make moral judgments about people, wasn't the stone-casting type. She was, all in all, good to have around. A terrific bed partner who made no emotional demands. Why, then, did the relationship seem to trouble him? As Nick said, one never knew when the would-be priest would surface. . . .

Crossing Sixth Avenue, he did a little evasive dance as a city bus nearly steamrollered his toes, and on the sidewalk he gave the driver the fingeroo, the aboriginal ritual of the Manhattan Islander.

Clare was unusually cool to him. Of course her manner was usually more tart than sweet, but this afternoon Callahan detected a difference as they sat on a boardwalk bench facing the gently scalloped ocean, the sun in a cool pastel sky.

"You whipped my ass," said Callahan.

Clare drank from a Coke bottle and smoked a cigarette. "You know us debs," she said, "we're weaned on golf, tennis, all those aristocratic games."

He laughed, removing cellophane from a cigar. They listened to the soughing of the sea. To the west reared the frames of the Ferris wheel and roller-coaster, giant toys against the perfect sky.

"Want to ride the horses in Steeplechase Park?" he asked.

She exhaled a stream of blue smoke. "No thanks."

"Shoot the Chutes?"

She shook her head.

"Then let's get a hotdog."

"Maybe later."

"Something eating you, Clare?"

She turned and looked hard at him. She wore a cloche hat at a jaunty angle and a coat with a fur collar. Her brown eyes smoldered. "Want to call it quits?" she asked.

"Call what quits?" He bit down on the cigar.

"That's the problem. You have to ask. Me and you, I mean. Whatever it is we're doing."

"Why? Something the matter?"

She snorted. "Nah." She stared back at the sea. She finished the cola and threw the empty bottle onto the beach.

"Okay, then. Why can't we leave things the way they are?"

"Because I don't want to."

He shrugged and smoked as she eyed him obliquely. They both knew that if she walked away he would not squawk or make even a passing gesture to sentiment. Or would he? Callahan felt odd, like he had lost his compass.

She bit her lip. "I've decided to quit my job."

He looked up, really surprised. "No! Hey, you'd die without a byline. You love this racket—"

"I'm renting an apartment in Paris." She turned full-face to him. "Don't scoff at it. I've decided to try my hand at short stories, maybe a novel. I'm tired of writing garbage-can linings."

"That's nice," he said in a monotone.

"Don't you wish me luck?"

"Luck."

"Try to control your enthusiasm."

He uncorked a real smile. "I mean it."

She glanced down at the boardwalk. "Are you upset that I'm leaving?"

"Sure. But listen, kiddo, you gotta live your own life—"

She covered his knuckles with her hands. "You want some advice?"

"What? You writing a lovelorn column?"

"Get back on track, Cal. You weren't cut out to play Faust."

"Hey, wiseacre. I really don't know what you're gabbing about—"

"Yes you do." She tightened her grip on his hand. "At least promise to think about what I'm saying."

He turned to her. "Let's make this a big night, huh? Let's go for broke."

"Okay."

They walked all the way to Coney, then strolled along the Bowery. The narrow street was studded with speakeasies and echoed with the cries of bankers, even on a late October afternoon.

"Here you go, ladies and gentlemen, everybody wins, three balls for a dime," growled a ruddy-faced midget wearing a battered derby.

Callahan knocked down two milk bottles and walked

away with kewpie doll. He handed it to Clare, and already
felt a void. He knew damn well he would miss her. He
wondered if he loved Clare Parker. Who did he love, come
to think of it? Did he love Nick? Probably not. It was hard
to define his feelings for his brother but he certainly
wouldn't call them love. He had all but forgotten what it
had been like to love his parents. That was so long ago. Lily
Curtin? No. Did he love John Joseph Callahan? Like him?
Tolerate him? Hate him? He decided not to risk the answers. Nobody was offering a kewpie doll for the right
ones.

He might love a ghost, he concluded. The ghost of Beethoven. And maybe a guinea named Dante. But enough to
do what was right?

Clare hooked her arm in his as they strolled past wax
museums, side shows, penny arcades, fortune tellers, high
strikers and shooting galleries. The rumble of the roller-
coaster, the squeal of kids and the piping of the calliope all
rang through the air. The scents of salt air, mustard and
manure mingled. They stopped at a speakeasy in a clap-
board shack behind a hootchy-kootchy palace and drank
beer.

"Al Capone used to be a bouncer here," Cal told her.

"You're a font of useless information," she said. They sat
at a round picnic table.

He winced. "Okay, what's the beef?"

She looked up at him. "I'm sorry." She groped for words.
"The old man took a licking Thursday. Between Allied
Chemical and American Shipbuilding he's about to cash
in his chips."

"That's tough. I hope he won't slash his wrists or leap off
a skyscraper."

"He's not the type. I guess he'll rise from the ashes. He
always seems to."

"Sure," he said, swigging foamy beer.

She gave him a look. "We Parkers are survivors."

"Sure."

She was silent, composing her thoughts, then blurted it
out. "Come with me, Cal."

"What? Where? To Luna Park?"

"No, damn you. Paris."

He gripped the handle of the beer mug, seemed seriously to consider the idea. Finally he said, "No, it's too far from Aqueduct."

"They've got racetracks in France."

"I can't pronounce the names."

She inspected her fingernails. Her usual poise deserted her. Then, "Ask me to stay."

He gazed at the beer mug. He coughed. "Hey, how about that hotdog?"

"How about fuck you, Callahan," she said, grabbing her handbag and getting up from the chair. "Fuck you *twice*." She turned and strode out the door of the speakeasy.

Six beers later Callahan left, half-stumbling down the midway. Must be Go Fuck Yourself Callahan Week, he muttered. First Maze, now Clare. Well, screw them too, and he bought a ticket to the Steeplechase gravity ride. Afterward he laughed at the flappers whose skirts were whipped above the waist by jets of compressed air coming out of the floorboards. Hey, he almost punched a dwarf in a clown outfit who swatted him on the rear with a slapstick. But before he could uncork the blow another little man shocked him with an electric prod. Bystanders laughed. He kept his temper. Did he detect an air of forced merriment? Season was drawing to a close in more ways than one. Let 'em have their fun. Winter was right around the corner. And the twenties had only sixty-six more days to roar.

He paid fifty cents to watch a strong man wrestle a shark in a water tank. Screw them too. He took a tunnel ride and ate a frozen custard.

The sun sank, emblazoning Norton's Point. People still thronged the boardwalk. He ate corn-on-the-cob that stuck to his bridgework. On Surf Avenue he paid a buck for a ticket to a strip show. Nothing like bumps and grinds to get a man's mind off hearts and flowers. But the overweight strippers with their dimpled cottage-cheese flanks only made matters worse. Mental comparisons with Clare. As the third performer peeled down to g-string and bra he laced his fingers across his paunch and frowned.

He felt a tap on his shoulder.

"Enjoying the show, pal?" the man behind him said.

"Well, if it isn't Lieutenant Mitchell. I never figured you for a dirty old man."

"Homicide detectives like to get hard-ons too," said Mitchell.

"Say, you gotta be real deprived to get a hard-on in this joint. Anyhow, I thought you guys got your boners from viewing corpses."

The detective jerked his thumb toward the stage. "What do you think those are?"

"Pipe down," said a voice in the back row.

Arnie Mitchell glared at him, the bellyacher backed down. Mitchell turned to Callahan. "Seen enough for one night?"

"Yeah."

"Then let's blow."

Hoots and catcalls accompanied them as their exiting blocked the views of men behind them. The stripper on stage, a gum-snapper with blue-black hair and a web of blue veins on her breasts, gave them a look-to-kill. When he reached the aisle Callahan bowed from the waist and the catcalls crescendoed.

On the street the detective offered Callahan a cigarette. He turned it down, taking out a cigar instead.

"Manilas, huh?" said Mitchell, looking sideways at Callahan.

"Yeah, what of it?"

"Nothing." Mitchell lit their smokes. "Let's take a little walk, eh?"

They headed west on Surf Avenue, huddling into their coats against gusts off the ocean. The tips of their smokes glowed in the gathering night. When they stopped in front of Tilyou's El Dorado Carrousel the gumshoe's face looked weary. He nodded toward the merry-go-round, rigged with a menagerie of ornately carved animals and boats and chariots embossed with fancy crests and fleurs-de-lis.

"Whatever happened to the Scoop Madigan investigation?" Mitchell asked.

"I could ask you the same thing."

Mitchell's shoulders sagged. "I'm still searching for that honest man."

"Have you tried Staten Island?"

Mitchell smoked silently.

" 'Murder on the Merry-Go-Round.' " He laughed.

"What's funny?"

Mitchell shrugged, looked the reporter up and down. "You look prosperous."

"The ponies have been kicking up the old turf pretty good."

"I never took you for a chalk-eater, playing the favorites."

"I've been hitting the long shots."

"Well, that can't last," observed Mitchell, flicking away the cigarette. He laughed again, a wintry sound.

"What's funny?"

"Well, you see—I went to a mitt joint tonight down the street a ways. This crone, she looked at my palm and said I was gonna run into an old friend tonight, who would need my help. Now that made me sit up and take notice because it wasn't your usual malarkey about how you're gonna inherit five million from an old maid aunt or meet the girl of your dreams. It was an odd fortune she told."

"I didn't know you went in for fortune tellers, Arnie."

"You know, all cops are superstitious."

"How much did she soak you for?"

Mitchell shrugged. "She was pretty sharp." The detective smiled and dropped this thread of conversation.

"I'm happy to hear you think of me as a friend," said Callahan, gazing at the revolving wooden horses, red-nostriled, angry-looking. "Should we get a drink somewhere?"

Mitchell raised his hand. "I've taken the oath."

"No kidding?"

They sat on a green-slatted bench. "Doctor's orders."

"Tough luck. What do you do for kicks?"

"I whip my dog with a garrison belt." Mitchell coughed

and lit another cigarette. "I also get a kick out of collaring murderous bootleggers—when the boys upstairs let me."

"And reading Dickens?"

"Now and then."

"Paid off the mortgage yet?"

"You kidding?" He gave Callahan a careful look. "How about you?"

"I rent. You know that."

"Hey, pal, you can have a lien on other things besides your house. More important things."

"I'm square with the world," said Callahan, examining the end of his stogie.

"You look different than the last time I saw you."

"Yeah, I look better-dressed, better-fed, and less horny, right?"

The butt dangled from the detective's thin lips. "Not exactly."

Callahan was impatient to blow away the fog. "Stop mincing words, Arnie. I've known enough priests to be able to tell when a sermon's coming."

"Okay. Here goes . . . you used to look sloppy, disreputable, boozy, gluttonous, but also sort of innocent. Like a choir boy who'd fallen into a mud puddle."

"And now?"

"I don't know, Cal. But you sure don't look too innocent anymore. And you owe them, Cal. You owe them. What happens when they call in the markers?"

"I can take care of myself."

Mitchell laughed. "What stronger breastplate than a heart untainted?' "

"Huh?"

"The man from Stratford."

Callahan groaned. "First Dickens, now Shakespeare. Spare me."

"Sermon's over, pal," said Mitchell, rising from the bench. "Blame it on the mitt reader."

The detective walked off into the mist that drifted in from the sea to mantle the boardwalk, leaving Callahan on the bench with his aromatic cigar and unwelcome thoughts. Two brush offs in about three hours, he reflected. Not bad for a tinhorn soul-seller.

He dragged his ass over to the subway station refreshment stand, where he had a Nedick's and a hotdog. The Sunday papers were out. He picked up a copy and read as he ate. He had to shoo away too mangy blisters and a grifter who wanted to palm off paste as "real sparklers." First he read the sports pages, then the news section, still filled with optimistic reports from Wall Street. He glanced at a four-head about some room-service waiter mysteriously poisoned at the Barbizon Plaza.

He folded the newspaper and thought about Mitchell and Mazie and Clare. And Cyriax's overture. What did they want from him? If he didn't watch his ass he'd soon be a dead hero. At least he had money now and the prospect of more—so why, he asked himself, did he feel so deep-down miserable?

A busboy in a soiled white campaign cap wiped the counter in front of Callahan. The boy had hazel eyes and a wispy blond mustache. Callahan was startled by a false shock of recognition. He bundled up the newspaper and went home.

Next morning he knew what he was going to do. It would put his ass in a sling but so what? You only live once. You've got to die sooner or later. Might as well go out swinging.

Chapter

28

SACRED COW

BRAWNY Phil Blanchard sat on a grimy leather sofa with the stuffing leaking out. He was in a cramped cubicle just off the composing room where the printers came to snooze, play cards, shoot the breeze, tell off-color jokes and generally get away from the clatter of the linotype machines and the pressure-cooker of deadlines.

The room had a telephone (used mostly to call bookies), a water cooler filled with bathtub gin, a bulletin board tacked with shop-steward memos and pinups of flappers unflapped and—saving grace—a small transom window through which Blanchard could now see a full moon sailing through frothy clouds across the late October sky.

He thumbed through a girlie magazine, muttering to himself. He was in a foul mood because his gout was acting up and he had just learned that his only daughter was dating a wop musician. But the biliousness did not show on the head printer's finely carved face. He wore his usual look of serenity, a large man secure in his small niche in the world. Blanchard consulted his wristwatch, a birthday gift from the daughter who now betrayed him with a smooth-talking greaseball. Six minutes to five on the morning of October 29, 1929. Time to get off his duff and start putting out the first edition of the paper, slated to come off the rotaries at seven.

He had to meet with the makeup editor and copy cutter, check the banks, chases, forms and fonts, peruse the layouts for make-overs, and confer with Ivan Bruce and the managing editor about musts and sacred cows. He got up from the couch, testing his gouty foot on the pine floor. He refused to wince at the pain. There was work to be done.

Blanchard strode into the composing room, where machines did all the talking. He read a few "see copy" notes on dropped lines. He checked dummies snagged on meat hooks over the stones. He read galleys for any marked "rush," "must" or "must kill." Nothing special this morning.

Though he never got past the eighth grade, Blanchard, like most veteran printers, was a well-informed, even lettered person who, after many years of reading copy upside down and right-side up, could tell you the precise location of Cape Horn, knew that Charlie Chaplin's middle name was Spencer, could cite the exact address of Jimmy Walker's boyhood home on St. Luke's Place, and could tell you when John Dos Passos had published *Manhattan Transfer,* among other things. Few people knew of Blanchard's range of knowledge, though, for the man was like a mountain, big and silent.

He lumbered across the composing room and entered the city room, making a sour effort to stop thinking about his daughter's boyfriend. Maybe he could free his mood from the tug of the full moon. As he approached the news editor's desk Blanchard glanced across the room and saw Callahan at the typewriter. The composing-room foreman wondered what the crime reporter was doing at work so early in the morning. It was his usual time for bending elbows, not flexing fingers. Blanchard planted a Home Run cigarette in his mouth.

Callahan stopped typing. He took out a handkerchief and dabbed at the sweat on his forehead. Why this exhilara-

tion? he wondered. What was the label Mother Superior
had stuck on him? An incurable newspaper reporter. That
must be it. . . .

Radiators hissed with steam heat. He read over the sentence he had just composed, and nodded. He continued
writing the story, slugged "GRAFT—for Tues."

He smiled. This was his penance, his five "Our Father's",
five "Hail Mary's" and sincere; "Act of Contrition." Bless
him, Father, for he has sinned. Sinned against the ghost of
John Peter Zenger. Sinned against Dante Viola. Sinned
against all the budding Beethovens of the world. This time
the punchline would be—Beethoven won. Penance meant
making things right. He batted out the story, minting the
jazzy tabloid phrases of his penance.

He typed *more* at the bottom of the page and rolled the
fourth take into the typewriter. It would be a long piece
under a top head three columns wide, 42–point. The lead
would be set in bold pica. Callahan planned to write the
head and subheads himself, naturally, since he would
have to make a detour around the copy desk and every
other link in the editorial production chain. Ah, he was
plotting the journalistic equivalent of sneaking into the
Tower of London, but he was determined. He had a convincing argument in the pocket of his jacket hanging over
the chair. It had the name Colt engraved on the handle.

The sleeping giant—the composing room—stirred. The
ranks of linotypes shuddered and spat a stream of alpha-
bet soup. Galleys were filled with blocks of type. They were
inked, proofed and put on stones to await fixes, adds and
inserts. Copyboys trekked from city room to copy-cutter to
proof room and back. Agate tables were filled with stock
quotes, death notices, shipping news, race results. Little
letters spelling life and death. The tables were locked up
for the back pages.

At twenty-minute intervals page forms were locked up
and brought from the stones to pressure machines to make
matrixes—the impressions of type on papier-mâché

sheets. The mats were taken to stereotypists, who made metal casts of pages that were later clamped to the rotary presses.

Meanwhile the makeup editor and staff had trooped out to the composing room with dummies of the front pages. The tempo quickened. Whenever a page was ready the makeup editor, sallow-faced, sleepy-eyed, ordered a printer to tighten the screws on the frame, clamping the type firmly in place. He nodded to a printer who picked up a mallet and pounded the surface, making sure no stray lines poked up. Deadline was near.

Phil Blanchard walked over to the page-one form, left blank till the last possible minute. " 'Stox' for wood again?" he asked the makeup editor.

"What else?" said the man. He handed Blanchard the dummy. "I'll be back in a few minutes."

Blanchard leaned against the stone and studied the dummy.

"Hey, Phil," said a familiar voice, "I got a sacred cow for yuh. A must from the publisher. Railroad it through, will you?"

Blanchard took the hard copy from Callahan, glanced at it, then looked skeptically at him. "How come this is the first I've heard of it?"

"Old man just called down. It's been in the when room for a week."

"Bullshit. Since when do CGOs go on page one? And I know the overset like the back of my hand. What are you trying to pull, Cal? How come the makeup editor didn't mention it? Why isn't it on the copy-cutter's list? I wasn't born yesterday."

Callahan sighed heavily and took out the pearl-handled belly gun. He showed it to Blanchard and concealed it again. He said, "It goes on page one, it jumps to three." He handed over another sheet of paper. "Here's the head. I'll walk you through the makeup without a dummy. Let's find a typist." He paused. "I'll use it, Phil. I don't want to but I'll use it if I have to."

"Have you gone fucking bananas?"

"I showed you the gun. You're in the clear. I take all the blame. Let's find a typist."

"Let me smell your breath."

"I couldn't be more sober." He fondled the pistol in his pants pocket.

Blanchard's Mount Rushmore face flickered with indecision. "What the hell," he finally said, and, followed by Callahan, brought the copy to a linotypist. Along the way he asked, "What makes you think you're gonna get away with this?"

"No problem. As long as I got you working for me, Phil."

"It's a good yarn," conceded Blanchard.

"The gospel according to John Joseph Callahan."

Blanchard handed the copy over to an owlish, balding compositor who wore bifocals. "Put them fancy fingers to work, Melvin. This one may put you in the history books."

The linotypist's morose expression stayed unchanged. "Okay, Phil."

Soon Blanchard and Callahan were hunkered over the page-one chase. The printer placed the type in the rectangular iron frame, fingers moving at blurring speed, putting lead rules between lines.

"How's that?" he asked Callahan.

"Fine."

"Hey, what's going on?" said Ivan Bruce, approaching on his gimp stick. He had arrived to oversee lockup.

Blanchard hunched his massive shoulders. "Ask your ace crime reporter."

Bruce looked at Callahan, confusion showing.

Callahan sighed and again showed the pistol.

"What the hell's that?"

"It's a gun, Ivan. A loudmouth gun. It says we run the story. I'll use it if I have to."

Bruce laughed nervously. "Jesus, Cal . . . why, we print the news, we don't make it." Trying to stall for time.

"Tell that to Madigan and Viola." Callahan put the gun back into his pocket, keeping his finger on the trigger.

Bruce still looked incredulous, frozen by indecision.

"We don't have much time before headline, Ivan."

"Can I see a proof?" Bruce finally said.

Blanchard handed him a galley.

Bruce read, then: "Very good job, Cal. A barn-burner. Punchy prose, authoritative tone. Lots of hard facts and neatly qualified conclusions. You want a byline?"

"Put the kid's name on it. He earned it."

"He's been fired."

"I said, put his name on it. With this beat he can write his own ticket with another paper."

Bruce asked, "How come you're sticking your neck out like this?"

Callahan's boiled-potato face showed no emotion. "Let's call it an Act of Contrition."

"You Catholics: always fucking up, then beating your breasts." He frowned at Callahan. "This'll probably cost me my job, you know."

"It will probably cost me more than that," noted Callahan. "Just blame the whole thing on me and the belly gun."

Bruce glanced at Blanchard, then faced Callahan. He stuck out his hand. "Give me the gun, Cal."

Callahan's face reddened, his finger caressed the trigger. "I . . . I mean it, Ivan. I'm not fooling. Run the story or—"

Bruce's hand remained outstretched, fingers wiggling. "The gun, Cal. It's a helluva gesture, but you know you can't go through with it."

And Callahan knew he was right. He reached into his pocket and handed over the gun.

Bruce turned to the head printer, confounding smile on his face. "Okay, Phil, lock 'er up."

Callahan looked dumbstruck.

"Come again?" asked Blanchard.

"Just a second," Bruce said, scribbling on memo paper. He called over a copyboy and gave him instructions. "Don't want to forget the kid's byline."

When the type came back Bruce handed it to the head printer. *"Now* lock 'er up."

The foreman shrugged, inserted the line of type and picked up the mallet. "You're the boss," he said.

Bruce laughed. "For the time being." He turned to Callahan. "So? Maybe your craziness is catching."

Blanchard, muscles twitching in his face, pounded the type into place and tightened the screws. He was feeling great.

The day that dawned a few hours later would come to be known around the world as Black Tuesday.

Chapter
29

THE FLY ON THE WALL

DANTE Viola, unaware of his role in the remarkable events taking place at the *Courier,* studied the dregs of coffee in the cup. Soon he was watching a housefly slowly circling the rim. He followed the insect's movements with a mindless intensity, spellbound until the scavenger flew away.

He felt numb, detached from his predicament, an outsider viewing his own life. At moments he was startled by mundane things taking place in another universe—horns honking, rain falling, a housefly taking off.

The fly reminded Dante of Walter Lippmann's comparison of a newspaper reporter to a fly on the wall, a symbol of the objective observer. He looked at the newspaper clipping on the table. He hadn't followed this code. He crumpled the clip reporting the poisoning of a room-service waiter. He reached into his pocket and produced Clare's letter and reread her farewell words. He wished her well. She had treated him square. Not that it mattered much. Very little did now.

He got up and went to the bathroom. The act of relieving himself struck him as absurd. Repetition to what end? Back in the living room he sat on the sofa and absently took

316

inventory. Clare's leaving, Cal's betrayals, Lee's death, his fault, and, of course, the defilement by Pellegrino. Shame had a mindless, inexorable quality. It was just *there.* He looked out the window at the sun rising. He stared for a long time at it.

At least nobody could stop him now. He was in complete control for once. Success was certain. Meddlers and well-meaning people might postpone it, but they couldn't prevent it if he was determined. And he was.

The sun now straddled the city, a squalid place. Good riddance. One thing was certain—it would be easy to part from the bipeds who prowled this planet. And no torment in hell could exceed what he'd known here. What demons could rival the leering faces of Pellegrino and Secundo branded in his memory?

And Lee Lindenbaum, what of him?

He saw the fly again, motionless on the window shade. He was sure it was the same fly. It took off and buzzed against the pane. The fly ate feces and felt no shame. Why did he feel shame? He must be lower than a fly.

It was time. He returned to the bathroom, where he got a towel and stuffed it into the crack under the front door. He went to each room, taking off screens and closing all windows. The bathroom transom opened on an air shaft. He closed it.

In the bedroom he studied the sepia photo of his parents. His father had cropped hair, a handlebar mustache and piercing eyes. His mother was dark and demure. She wouldn't look at the camera lens. Her face, shiny as a copper penny, had a tender quality. He turned away.

He entered the kitchen, walked over to the gas stove and turned on the jets. A faint hissing. He left the kitchen door open and returned to the living room.

He lay down on the couch. It would not take long. It would not even be painful. It would be like a river crossing. He noticed that stuffing was coming out of the couch.

He began to feel light-headed. He was sinking into a well. He saw the fly swoop from the windowpane to the ledge above the radiator.

Callahan did not wait for the great presses to stop vibrating and the edition to roll off. He wanted to break the news himself to Dante.

He stood on windswept Park Row looking for a cab. It was too early in the morning. He decided to walk. He headed north toward Bleecker Street, whistling into the pristine morning as he walked up Centre Street, passing granite court and civic buildings carved with pieties about justice and good government mostly ignored by the men who presided over them. Why was his heart melting like the cakes of ice in the peddler's wagon in front of the old post office?

Hey, he was riding the white charger again, slaying the fire-breathers. The mumbo-jumbo of his Catholic boyhood seemed to be working again. Maybe there was something to it.

He passed Frank Lava's gun shop near police headquarters, where the squawk box first told Joe Cyriax and the others of the murder on the merry-go-round. The go-rounds since had not been so merry, Callahan reflected. Maybe now that would change.

At Houston Street he slowed down and lit a stogie. No hurry, he thought. Dante probably would still be asleep.

Back on Park Row Hamilton Terry sank his teeth into a juicy apple. Wasn't that Mr. Callahan he had noticed hightailing it across the street? What was he doing up so early this Tuesday morning? he wondered. Don't ask him how he knew it had been Callahan's metal-tapped heels. Trade secret.

Waiting for the first editions to arrive, Ham's rabbit ears registered the sounds of an awakening city. He caught the morning mood of grumpy silence, heard snatches of conversation uncensored by the Hays Office.

Female voice: "I couldn't believe it. Gin bucks were ninety-five cents a throw."

High-pitched male voice: "You said a mouthful, kiddo."

Another female: "I hadn't oughter, but I guess I will."

"His name is Bela Lugosi and he's the creepiest dago I ever laid eyes on."

"Did you hear Lowell Thomas last night?"

"She's got the best-looking gams and cutest behind this side of Hackensack."

"I still think the colored should worship in their own churches."

Ham finished the apple and wiped his chin with a polka-dot handkerchief. He sold copies of *Ballyhoo, True Detective, Modern Screen* and an occasional copy of *Variety,* bearing the headline: WALL STREET LAYS AN EGG. Making change he smiled at customers. The sign over the Optimo cigar box containing the coins read: "If you're mean enough to steal from the blind, help yourself." Janet Gaynor stared out from the cover of *Photoplay.*

Ham was happy, business had been pretty good lately. He might make enough this week to catch "the world's greatest moaner," Clara Smith at the Lafayette. Ah, music hath charms, as the blind man knew so well.

Black Tuesday. Ham didn't know that posterity would call it that, but he knew in his bones that hard times were coming. Breadlines and shantytowns were on the horizon. As a hard-luck member of a race that had been harnessed to suffering since they were shanghaied from the shores of Lion's Ridge, Ham had the gift of foresight. Sure as night followed day, bust followed boom. The nation of the noble experiment faced a collective hangover.

But men waited in the wings brandishing brooms, the blind seer knew. He didn't know their names—Seabury, LaGuardia, Dewey, Roosevelt—but he felt their presence. He sold more newspapers and more coins jangled in the cigar box.

Callahan turned west where Bleecker Street intersected Broadway. He huffed and puffed, not used to working through the night and taking long walks. He ought to take walks more often, he told himself. He passed a traveling tin shop, a pushcart loaded with pots and pans, and smelled nearby the odor of freshly baked bread. He couldn't wait to see Dante's expression when he told him. He hoped it would restore some of his artless faith. It might even be worth the threat of Jimmy the Judge taking a pound of retribution out of his hide. He thought about what would happen to Nick. Maybe he'd skip the country. Maybe he'd do time. Callahan didn't want to dwell on the subject.

Callahan felt he had learned something important, something others had phrased better than he could. All he knew for sure was the feeling he now had of rightness, wholeness, the morning sun warming his stooped back as he walked west on Bleecker Street toward his friend's apartment building to tell him the good news. Yes, for once the newsman was bearing good news.

A block away in the building on the corner of Bleecker and Sullivan streets, in the third-floor apartment of a promising young tabloid journalist, a housefly lay dead behind the cold radiator.

Chapter

30

THIRTY

CALLAHAN wrote the obituary.

As the aftershocks of the stock market collapse reverberated, the obit, of course, was buried on a back page near the lingerie ads. Anyway, how did one write "thirty" to a man's life? Language was a fourth-rate flail.

Callahan searched the dim nooks of memory for the time when he still believed that a journalist was a professional truthteller. The conscientious reporter did the best he could, arranging the facts in descending order of importance according to the inverted-pyramid formula. But formulas and facts didn't convey truth. And journalism had trouble with gray areas, the mezzotints of reality.

Well, until he discovered a better way, Callahan would continue to wrap the fish with so-called facts.

The facts were these:

Speculators, rose-colored glasses crushed underfoot on a ticker tape-strewn floor, dumped sixteen million shares.

Bankers ran for the hills.

The panic became an octopus, spreading its tentacles all over the world.

Apple sellers surfaced on every corner.

A cop found a parrot on Maiden Lane squawking, "More margin! More margin!"

The roar of the twenties turned into a whimper.

Meanwhile the city room buzzed; news hawks loved carrion. The dayside assistant city editor got on the phone to every speak and whorehouse in town, recruiting pressmen, printers and writers to get out the big story.

The events caused the *Courier* edition containing the story slugged "Graft" to be replated after one press run, softening the blow for the crooks it exposed. Some were too busy to notice anyway as they jumped off window ledges in the financial district. Later the hard copy mysteriously vanished from the wait-order room. Callahan would lay odds that the culprit was Stinky Roth, who, he always suspected, was on the payroll of the squashed-nose crowd.

Speaking of crooks, Callahan was gratified to read of another fact:

Not long after the decade was dead, Guy Pellegrino stopped to have his shoes shined before a performance of *La Traviata.* The bootblack, Tony Coco, who had saved his nickels and dimes to purchase a gun, avenged his handsome Sicilian father by reaching into the shoeshine box, ostensibly for a brush, and produced a .38. He plugged the suave mobster in the crotch and gut. Final curtain for Gaetano Pellegrino. An irony worthy of the tabs that the target of gunsels from New York to Frisco was done in by a shoeshine boy. How was *that* for grand opera?

As for Callahan, he went back to dodging bill collectors and worrying about when the Judge would pound the gavel on him. Whenever he thought about this he would shrug. He had a long way to go to get his soul out of hock. But he had to start somewhere. He smiled at the idea of a slop barge like him back in the state of sanctifying grace.

On Saturdays, as usual, Callahan hopped a bus for Greenwood Cemetery in Brooklyn. He had had to twist the pastor's arm to make sure the kid was buried in sanctified ground. Of course a princely donation to the building-fund drive greased the wheels. Parish priests were on the pad too. How did Callahan scrape up the dough? He sold the emerald stickpin.

He also used some of these ill-gotten gains for a headstone and plot. Engraved in the granite—mica bits now sparkling in the winter sunlight—were the words:

DANTE VIOLA
NEWSPAPER MAN
AUGUST 11, 1907–OCTOBER 29, 1929."

Callahan knelt down in the slush before the hunk of stone. He brushed his cheek with the back of his hand, surprised to learn that the tear ducts still functioned. Callahan wheezed and shivered in his threadbare overcoat. His back felt like a bull's-eye on a firing range. When would Fitzgerald's triggermen materialize? Hardly a moment passed when he didn't expect a pair of lead visitors between the shoulder blades. The price of nobility. Ha!

He shifted his weight from one knee to the other. The ghost of Beethoven had vanished. Now it was Dante's ghost. The failed priest invented a prayer: "Dante, you guinea bastard, you are my son. Amen." The ghost would cling to Callahan's body until it was food for worms. He placed in a metal cone before the headstone a bouquet of bruised yellow gardenias. Nothing more graceless than a sobbing fat man.

Callahan forced himself to stop shaking. He felt the need to draw some kind of lesson from all this, but hatching wisdom was not exactly his forté. He felt even more confused than ever about the Mysteries. But at least he finally had tasted the rue of love, even if it was too late.

And what about his gazetteering trade? Well, he'd just have to keep stringing together a rosary of fact and hope for the best.